Necessity in International Law

Necessity in International Law

Jens David Ohlin
and
Larry May

OXFORD
UNIVERSITY PRESS

OXFORD
UNIVERSITY PRESS

Oxford University Press is a department of the University of Oxford. It furthers the University's objective of excellence in research, scholarship, and education by publishing worldwide. Oxford is a registered trademark of Oxford University Press in the UK and certain other countries.

Published in the United States of America by Oxford University Press
198 Madison Avenue, New York, NY 10016, United States of America.

First Edition published in 2016

Library of Congress Cataloging-in-Publication Data

Names: Ohlin, Jens David, author. | May, Larry, author.
Title: Necessity in international law / Jens David Ohlin and Larry May.
Description: First edition. | New York : Oxford University Press, 2016. |
Includes bibliographical references and index.
Identifiers: LCCN 2016010312 | ISBN 9780190622930 (hardback : alk. paper)
Subjects: LCSH: War (International law) | Necessity (International law) |
Military necessity.
Classification: LCC KZ6385 .O35 2016 | DDC 341.6—dc23 LC record available at
http://lccn.loc.gov/2016010312

1 3 5 7 9 8 6 4 2

Printed by Edwards Brothers Malloy, United States of America

For Nancy
—JDO

For Marilyn
—LM

CONTENTS

ACKNOWLEDGMENTS

Part of this book originally appeared in a different form in Larry May, *Necessity and the Lives of Soldiers*, which won the Frank Chapman Sharp prize of the American Philosophical Association for the best unpublished work on the philosophy of war and peace for 2012–2014.

Portions of the book manuscript were also drawn from Jens David Ohlin, *The Duty to Capture*, 97 MINN. L. REV. 1268 (2013).

Introduction

Necessity is quite possibly the most powerful concept in the law. It has the almost mystical power to transform what would otherwise be illegal or immoral into a justified or excused act, all because the action was "necessary." Herein lays its utter dangerousness. Whether the inquiry is individual self-defense in domestic criminal law, national self-defense under international law, or killing during armed conflict, the concept of necessity is often the key element that drives the outcome of the analysis. If the action is necessary, then it is often permitted; if the action is not necessary, it is often forbidden. But what does "necessary" really mean in these debates? And does it mean the same thing in each context, or does its meaning and function depend on the nature of the inquiry at hand? Is necessity a universal moral and legal concept, or is its meaning fundamentally context-dependent?

The following book is a taxonomical and normative study of the principle of necessity across multiple domains in international law. We aim to study necessity in each of its flavors across international law and Just War theory in order to answer these pressing questions. In law and morality one of the most challenging questions posed concerning the justifiability of war or armed conflict is that of necessity. War can only be *initiated* if it is necessary, and *tactics* can only be employed if they are necessary. These requirements are uncontroversial. What remains controversial is how properly to characterize the "necessity" condition for a just or legal war, and how to apply the concept in concrete cases. The idea that one should only use lethal force when it is necessary is one of the most important concepts in the humanitarian restrictions of action during war or armed conflict. Consequently, our book offers an analysis of the principle of necessity that is at once abstract and concrete; we start with general principles and articulate how necessity works in *jus ad bellum* and *jus in bello*, but then apply these general lessons to specific controversies regarding the appropriate rules for the conduct of hostilities in contemporary armed conflicts, including those conducted against nonstate actors and terrorists.

Because the concept of necessity is paramount in Just War theory, public international law, and international humanitarian law (IHL), we believe that a proper investigation into its appropriate usage must—out of interpretive necessity—involve both legal and philosophical elements. Prior contributions in both law and philosophy have studied the concept of necessity, but it is rare for the scholarly literature to consider both at the same time. Historical Just War philosophers, and the more contemporary philosophers known as Revisionist Just War theorists, make use of the concept of necessity in their philosophical arguments regarding both the resort to and the conduct of war. International lawyers working in the fields of international humanitarian law, human rights, the use of force, and even investor-state arbitration deploy the concept of necessity to make their arguments. We consider all of these domains relevant for our cross-disciplinary investigation into the nature of necessity.

Our ultimate goal is to understand how the concept of necessity is used today and how it ought to be properly used when brought to bear on questions of killing in war. This requires mastery of necessity's philosophical and legal manifestations and the rich interplay between them. Indeed, the two domains can never be separate, since the modern era of international regulations of *jus ad bellum* and *jus in bello* is, in a sense, a legalistic outgrowth of a prior philosophical exercise: the constraint on national conduct during warfare. Historically, that project was popularized by the nineteenth century natural law theorists, who brought to bear moral and normative thought on questions of legal regulation. Although those domains (law and philosophy) have suffered a profound normative estrangement since then, it is important to remember their historical and conceptual linkage. As such, the only way to understand necessity's role in contemporary discussions regarding resort to force and conduct during hostilities is carefully to trace its emergence from prior philosophical and legal material.

I. THREE KINDS OF NECESSITY: EXCEPTION, LICENSE, AND CONSTRAINT

Let us begin by pointing out that the concept of necessity has several distinct uses depending on the context. In this sense necessity is a cluster concept.

First, necessity can be an exception to an otherwise binding obligation in the sense that if it is necessary for one to act, say so as to avoid one's own death, one is entitled to use means, such as stealing food from someone else, that would normally not be permissible. Second, necessity can mean that one has a license to act in certain ways once one can show that the action is part of a role, and to satisfy this role it is necessary for one to act in this way. Third, necessity can be a constraint that blocks a form of activity due to the lack of necessity that activity be engaged in.

Sometimes the three kinds of necessity overlap with one another. For example, consider Lincoln's invocation of necessity to justify his issuance of the Emancipation Proclamation, which ended slavery by executive fiat.[1] Lincoln's decision was controversial because it was unclear if the President had the unilateral authority under the Constitution to issue the Proclamation. However, Lincoln argued that the action was necessary as part of the war effort and in that sense fell under his constitutional authority.[2] This invocation of necessity contains elements of both necessity-as-license and necessity-as-exception. Lincoln claimed that military necessity provided him with a license to act. But viewed in another way, Lincoln's argument also sounded in exception, because he was arguing that the usual constraints on unilateral executive action did not apply under the circumstances.

Another example of the same overlapping phenomenon might be the internment of Japanese-Americans during World War II. President Roosevelt justified the action by appealing to the concept of military necessity, and the Supreme Court upheld the President's order, and the actions of his subordinates implementing that plan, on that basis.[3] The concept of necessity was used as a license, but it was also used as an exception to basic principles of constitutional law. Even though the Constitution protects unlawful searches and seizures and the right to due process, something about the concept of necessity negated those protections. In 1983, the federal government apologized for the injustice of the internment and concluded that the action was not justified by military necessity.[4] This in

1. The Emancipation Proclamation, January 1, 1863.

2. *See* JOHN FABIAN WITT, LINCOLN'S CODE 219 (2012) ("As a war measure based on military necessity, the Emancipation Proclamation condensed a millennium of moral and legal reasoning into its short text.").

3. *See* Executive Order 9066 (1942); *Korematsu v. United States*, 323 U.S. 214 (1944).

4. *See Personal Justice Denied*, Report of the Commission on Wartime Relocation and Internment of Civilians, Part 2: Recommendations 5 (1983) ("In sum, Executive Order 9066 was not justified by military necessity, and the decisions that followed from it—exclusion, detention, the ending of detention and the ending of exclusion—were

itself shows the dangers that lurk in the notion of necessity as an exception to generally applicable rules. If the internment *had* been factually required by military necessity, then the government's 1983 statement implicitly suggests that necessity would have abrogated the usual constitutional protections. This only reaffirms the great danger of the concept of necessity to sweep aside existing normative constraints when circumstances make it "necessary."

Furthermore, once one understands necessity at a much deeper level of abstraction, it is clear that all forms of necessity have the same structure. However, at the more specific level of moral or legal arguments, necessity works in different ways depending on the context. Unfortunately, these contexts are sometimes blurred or confused, and the omnipresent language of necessity is often a barrier to clear thinking on these issues. One single word—"necessity"—hides a litany of deep and sometimes contested intuitions about the appropriateness of killing.

So practically, in terms of the way that international law works, it matters quite a lot which form the concept of necessity takes in the argument. It is therefore imperative to systematically map and catalog the various uses of the term "necessity" in the law and ethics of killing, with the hope of identifying the truly distinct role that the concept of necessity plays in these debates. Then, and only then, can we move to the normative exercise of determining when necessity—in one of its senses—justifies killing another human being in either the moral or legal sense of that phrase.

In IHL, the three different (and occasionally overlapping) notions of necessity take special form when discussions turn more specifically to what lawyers once called "military necessity," though that term has fallen out of fashion and in many ways is more confusing than illuminating. The first is necessity as an exception to generally applicable rules (military necessity in the *High Command* formulation, or necessity in criminal law), which is the most dangerous application of the concept. Francis Lieber is sometimes interpreted in this way although we think this is a simplistic and probably a mistaken reading of him. The danger of military necessity qua exception has long been recognized. For example, Westlake warned that "[t]he plea of necessity, even when justified, has a dangerous tendency to corrupt and

not founded upon military considerations. The broad historical causes that shaped these decisions were race prejudice, war hysteria and a failure of political leadership. Widespread ignorance about Americans of Japanese descent contributed to a policy conceived in haste and executed in an atmosphere of fear and anger at Japan. A grave personal injustice was done to the American citizens and resident aliens of Japanese ancestry who, without individual review or any probative evidence against them, were excluded, removed and detained by the United States during World War II.").

degrade those who urge it; and when it has sapped the foundations of one fence, no other fence into the construction of which it has been introduced can be greatly relied on."[5] Consequently, the law can and should find ways to restrain it. In that regard, we will argue in Chapter 6 that there are various ways that both international and domestic criminal law seeks to cabin or constrain the application of this "exception" version of necessity, precisely because it is so dangerous in allowing lethal violence.[6] The second is necessity as a license ("military necessity" in Lieber's sense, though he is not always consistent). The third is necessity as a constraint, in the way that human rights lawyers use the term—as in "the government is not allowed to engage in this action because it was not truly necessary."

Human rights necessity represents necessity at its most constraining. Here is the basic structure of the concept: government *x* is prohibited from infringing interest *y* unless it is necessary to achieve legitimate aim *z*. This is far different from necessity in international criminal law, whose basic structure is: individual *x* is excused from a generally applicable criminal norm *y* if required by a state of necessity. This is the opposite of constraining—it produces a state of exception that allows the individual to ignore the law. Finally, as we will show, the notion of military necessity as a license in international humanitarian law requires only a *connection*, but not a terribly tight one, between the killing of the enemy combatant and the war aim, though perhaps there are moral reasons to tighten this relatively loose notion of necessity. The important point, however, is that these versions of necessity all function differently.

At a very deep level of abstraction, the three flavors of necessity (constraint, exception, and license) might share the same conceptual structure. One could describe it in the following way: action *x* is appropriate if and only if it is necessary to achieve *y*. With this abstract formula, one could describe necessity in almost any domain, including human rights, IHL, and criminal law. However, although this deep level of abstraction reveals a structural unity in the concept of necessity across philosophical and legal domains, its stripping of all other contexts obscures the different ways that the concept functions. In criminal law, the prohibitions are already fixed and determinate, so that necessity functions as a way of exempting an agent from the

5. *See* JOHN WESTLAKE, CHAPTERS ON THE PRINCIPLES OF INTERNATIONAL LAW 275 (1894).

6. For an example of the danger of using necessity as an exemption from generally applicable rules, consider the use of necessity in arguments attempting to justify torture. For a good discussion of the legal system's attempt to grapple and constrain these arguments, see generally DAVID LUBAN, TORTURE, POWER, AND LAW (2014).

demands of the law. In contrast, necessity in human rights law functions as a way of determining the content of the rules themselves (by determining the appropriate scope of governmental conduct when its actions infringe a personal interest). Finally, necessity in IHL acts as license, not in an ad hoc or exceptional way, but rather as a justification for an entire class of behavior (killing enemy combatants as a function of belligerency).

Although necessity in each of these domains involves, in some weak sense, a limiting constraint on action, in a more relevant sense necessity functions differently because in each domain the background conditions for action are entirely different. In criminal law (whether domestic or international), the assumption is that all members of the public follow its general prohibitions. In human rights law, the default assumption is that individual rights will almost always conflict and the law needs a decision procedure to determine which infringements are permissive and which are not. In IHL, the assumption is that killing enemy soldiers is part of the basic architecture of armed conflict. Against these diverse legal and moral frameworks, the same concept of necessity operates to different effect in each domain. Tracing the conceptual unity and diversity of these approaches is critical to avoiding misunderstanding.

II. A ROADMAP

Having offered a brief introduction into the complex web of ideas embedded in the term "necessity," as well as a glimpse into some of our normative intuitions, we now offer a roadmap for the book's argument. Part A asks, and answers, the question of what is necessity in *jus ad bellum* by exploring its philosophical and legal origins. Chapter 1 begins with a historical analysis of how necessity figured in the *jus ad bellum* arguments of Gentili and Grotius, and in particular examines how the concept of necessity is used in Just War theory as a principle of last resort—a criterion that must be satisfied before the recourse to force can be justified. Chapter 2 engages in the companion exercise of evaluating this structural argument in the legal sphere, that is, showing how necessity works as a central element of *jus ad bellum* legal arguments. In particular, Chapter 2 notes that the concept of necessity works slightly differently depending on whether it is asserted as an independent excuse in international relations or whether it is one component of a self-defense analysis. In the former case it is invoked as an exception to general rules of conduct, while in the latter necessity functions as a constraint on the application of a general justification. Although both examples share structural similarities, the former is more dangerous, and for that reason international lawyers have generally placed external constraints on the application of the necessity doctrine.

In Part B, we turn our attention to necessity in *jus in bello*. Chapter 3 examines the interplay between the concept of necessity and the principle of distinction in Just War theory, in part to understand the temptation that often arises to use necessity as an excuse for departures from the demands of distinction (i.e., the normative requirement to limit one's attacks to military objectives), or the demands of proportionality (i.e., the normative requirement that civilian collateral damage must not be disproportionate to the military advantage secured by destroying the military target).

We also trace the evolution of necessity from a concept in natural law to its exposition in the Lieber Code, which in many ways is built around the concept of necessity. That being said, necessity is often misunderstood in natural law discussions, just as it is often misunderstood in discussions of Lieber. Because Lieber used the term so many times, often in seemingly contradictory ways, one can find evidence for almost any interpretation of military necessity in Lieber's writing. However, we argue that Lieber mostly understood necessity as a license (as opposed to an exception). In Chapter 4, we offer a normative and philosophical reconstruction of Lieber's view of necessity as a broad license, while at the same time rejecting any suggestion that necessity can and should be used as an exception to generally applicable prohibitions in *jus in bello*.

Chapter 5 contrasts necessity in IHL with necessity as the concept is used in human rights discourse. The task here is to explain what is distinctive about necessity in IHL and to explain why conceptions of necessity that reign in other areas of international law cannot be automatically grafted onto the laws of war without reflection and deliberation. Indeed, any attempt to transplant a more restrictive version of necessity will result in a substantial alteration of the legal architecture of *jus in bello*. Although this is not necessarily a bad thing, it can only be accomplished if one offers a separate normative defense for that alteration. It cannot be presumed. Chapter 6 examines the use of necessity as an excuse in international criminal law and notes that in this context necessity functions as a general exception to pre-established rules; in this area necessity is potentially at its most dangerous. Consequently, we examine the various constraints—both ad hoc constraints and principled constraints—that international criminal law deploys to restrict the application of the necessity defense so as to mitigate its over-permissiveness.

Finally, Part B concludes with Chapter 7, which discusses how necessity in *jus in bello* (now properly distinguished from human rights necessity) can and should be balanced against the principle of humanity. In many ways, the principle of humanity covers much of the same ground as human rights principles, except in this case the principle is already *internal* to *jus in bello*. So in this investigation, we hope to explain how some human rights principles—under the guise of the principle of humanity—have a proper role to play in checking the inherent permissiveness of *jus in bello* necessity. To accomplish this task, we examine how the principle of humanity and necessity work in both legal and philosophical arguments about just conduct during warfare.

The final section of the book, Part C, is an exercise in applied theory. The task is now to understand the concept of necessity and how it ought to apply in contemporary military conflicts that, in important ways, differ from the military contests fought during the time of the natural law theorists. Chapter 8 examines the dividing line between combatants and civilians during contemporary asymmetric conflicts against nonstate actors, the preeminent type of military conflict in this age of global terrorism. Although the dividing line between combatant and civilian is well explored in both the legal and philosophical literatures, we examine the subject explicitly through the lens of necessity. We conclude that the fundamental element of status (civilian versus combatant), which is the foundation for status-based targeting and status-based detention, is starting to break down in contemporary asymmetric conflicts. This implies a subtle shift toward conduct and behavior as morally and legally relevant conditions that can and should supersede more elementary considerations of status. Although this transformation has some normative appeal, the current law of war framework is built around status-based determinations. We are starting to articulate a new way of fighting wars but we do not yet have the legal architecture with which to properly regulate it.

Chapter 9 asks whether the principle of necessity should require disabling rather than killing in warfare. We conclude that whatever the merits of this ethical conundrum, the current state of the law does not codify this obligation. However, we express substantial unease with the current state of the law, and its permissive use of overwhelming and often brutal force against soldiers.

Furthermore, Chapter 10 asks a similar set of questions regarding necessity and the duty to capture, that is, whether necessity requires an attacking force to attempt capture prior to initiating a lethal strike. Again, we find no such duty codified in existing legal obligations, at least not where *jus in bello* is concerned. However, we do believe that restrictions on the use of overwhelming force might be found in a reinvigorated *jus ad bellum* obligation on the part of attacking forces to cease an attack when the necessity giving rise to the armed conflict has evaporated because the enemy nation has been so decimated that it is incapable of constituting a national threat anymore. Finally, we also ask whether it would be morally advisable to amend the codified rules of *jus in bello* to require non-lethal attacks in very limited and carefully circumscribed contexts.

Chapter 11 addresses force protection and the degree to which necessity permits attacking forces to prioritize the lives of their own soldiers over the lives of enemy civilians. This is a difficult problem of application; although everyone agrees that the lives of enemy civilians must be safeguarded, the question is how much must be risked in order to safeguard them. We conclude this chapter by articulating a standard of reasonable force protection that is neither too restrictive nor too permissive.

III. NORMATIVE PRESCRIPTIONS

With having identified and clarified the multiple strands of necessity, our book turns to normative assessments regarding the appropriate role for the concept of necessity in regulating the use of force. In the end, we find the concept of necessity to be a central tool for constraining potentially devastating violence during armed conflict, but at the same time we are sensitive that there are dangers associated with using necessity as a broad brushstroke to reflexively condemn all that happens on the battlefield. Just as it is clear that necessity has a morally dangerous element (the attempt to justify exceptions from legitimate principles of morality), so too necessity has a mirror image: a siren-song temptation to radically remake warfare into a glorified police action. This impulse ought to be resisted. Reality, like so many things, is in the middle.

For centuries necessity has been understood in the rules and laws of war in terms of "*military* necessity." For many theorists and practitioners, the concept of military necessity has little to do with the common-sense understanding of necessity. Rather, military necessity in the initiation of war means only that lethal violence is needed to prevent the loss of something important, and military necessity in the conduct of war means simply that there is some goal that a commander is pursuing, and that goal has some clear connection to the winning of a particular battle and the overall winning of the war. Military necessity so conceived does not appear to be especially humane, since it does not seem to limit lethal violence much at all.

Immanuel Kant characterized one of the versions of the categorical imperative as the "formula of the end in itself" or "the principle of humanity." In Kant's view, there is a practical imperative for all people, namely: "Act in such a way that you treat humanity, whether in your own person or in the person of another, always at the same time as an end and never simply as a means."[7] This principle is deeply connected to Kant's notion of the dignity of a human person. To respect the dignity in each person, we must treat each person as an end in itself, not simply as a means to our own ends.

In situations of war or armed conflict, it is hard to understand how the various participants, especially the soldiers shooting at enemy soldiers, could still treat the enemy soldiers as ends in themselves. Indeed, the idea of military necessity in its traditional formulation saw the soldier's role to be one of killing as many enemy soldiers as possible, as long as this was important for winning the war. This military goal was related to the further goal of bringing the war to an end as soon as is possible so as to have the least number of casualties in the long run. But there is no denying that the traditional principle of military necessity was aimed at using enemy soldiers as a means to ending the war as quickly as possible, and did not see enemy soldiers as ends in themselves.

It is also part of the more modern understandings of necessity that this principle is to be balanced against what international lawyers call the principle of humanity. Yet, the question to consider is whether these principles can indeed be balanced if the principle of military necessity contains such a strong presumption in favor of the right of soldiers to kill as many enemy soldiers as possible. How though can soldiers be treated humanely if they can be killed at will? Indeed, this seems to be especially difficult unless the principle of humanity calls for protection of combatants and not merely noncombatants.

To combat the leniency of the traditional understanding of military necessity, some authors have recently argued for a more expansive principle, namely, the least harmful means principle.[8] This principle would sweep across all decisions by commanders during war and would require that commanders only order that use of force that is the least harmful of all options. We will propose a more moderate thesis that merely calls for less than lethal force when it is not necessary to use lethal force. Our proposal will not affect non-lethal use of force and is hence not nearly as restrictive as the least harmful means principle. Also, our proposal sounds in moral theory and is not a description of the state of the law today.

In any event, the question is how to reconcile the principle of humanity, which since Kant's time has meant that all people are to be treated with

7. *See* Immanuel Kant, Grounding for the Metaphysics of Morals 36 (James W. Ellington trans., Hackett Publishing Co. 1981) (1785).

8. *See* Gabriella Blum, *The Dispensable Lives of Soldiers*, 2 J. Legal Analysis 69 (2010).

dignity and respect, with the principle of necessity. It is our view that this reconciliation can only occur when the restrictions that come from the necessity principle are extended to all who are affected by war, soldiers and civilians alike. The principles of humanity and of necessity should not be irreconcilable, and we will develop in more detail later a way to reconcile these important principles in the morality and legality of war, while at the same time recognizing the realities of modern warfare and the inherent risk that all soldiers are ultimately subject to.

PART A

Necessity & *Jus ad Bellum*

CHAPTER 1

Necessity and the Principle of Last Resort in the Just War Tradition

Thomas Aquinas, writing at the height of the Middle Ages, talks of it being unlawful if a man initiates violence, even in self-defense, and "uses more than necessary violence."[1] Here necessity and last resort are linked conceptually. But even if *jus ad bellum* necessity, or last resort, can be satisfied, Aquinas tells us, it is never justified to kill an *innocent* person. As early as the seventeenth century, theorists such as Alberico Gentili challenged this idea, by saying that "a legitimate cause of fear" even without any real danger, is sufficient to justify the initiation of the use of lethal force.[2] In this chapter we will look at these important historical debates concerning necessity and last resort, especially in connection with a principle not much discussed in the literature: the first strike or priority principle.

In the legal and moral debates about the justifiability of initiating war, two powerful ideas are dominant: The State that uses violence and strikes first is normally thought to initiate an aggressive war, and the State that uses violence as a last resort to stop the assault is normally thought to initiate a defensive war. These temporal signs are only prima facie indicators of justifiability of initiating war, but they are omnipresent in the literature of at least the last 500 years, if not for the past four millennia.

1. Thomas Aquinas, Summa Theologica Pt. II-II, Qu. LXIV, art. 6, at 1464 (Fathers of the Dominican Province trans., Benzinger Bros. 1948).
2. Alberico Gentili, De Jure Belli (On the Law of War) Bk. I, ch. 14, at 62–63 (trans. John C. Rolfe, Clarendon Press 1933) (1598).

The intuition behind the first strike or priority principle is based on the analogy between war and the two-person altercation. To identify, in a preliminary way, the aggressor in a barroom brawl, one typically asks: "Who threw the first punch?" Similarly, when investigations are launched into police shootings, one also asks: "Did the police shoot first or were they attacked first?" And if the barroom brawler or the police officer did eventually strike, one would next ask: "Was there any other reasonable alternative to stop the assault?" If there was a reasonable alternative, then the shootings were not a last resort, and hence not defensive.

One of the most difficult questions posed by these simple intuitive approaches to the justifiability of initiating war concerns the State that strikes first but also had no reasonable alternatives to prevent an assault. This case is often labeled "anticipatory self-defense" or "preemptive strike." We will also explain why the idea of last resort may not do the work that it was once thought to do, at least in the case of anticipatory self-defense.

In this chapter we wish to reassess the doctrine of anticipatory self-defense, and the larger question of the justifiability of preemptive and preventive war, from the Just War perspective. In the second and third sections, we will rehearse an important debate between Alberico Gentili and Hugo Grotius of 400 years ago on our topics. Then we will spend the remaining sections looking first at "first strikes" and then at "last resorts" to see what, if anything, is to be said for these as markers of aggressive or defensive war. In those sections, we will address directly the justifiability of preemptive war with reference to the principle of necessity in *jus ad bellum* debates in Just War theory.

I. DEFINING AGGRESSION IN THE JUST WAR TRADITION

Traditional Just War theory argues that some wars can be justified, even required, out of respect for the protection of innocent life. Self-defense and defense of others are the key bases for the justification of war. This position was historically articulated in opposition to strict pacifism, although it ended up calling only for a kind of limitation on certain versions of pacifism. If pacifism is itself grounded in respect for life, especially innocent life, then it appears that some wars may be justified, from the standpoint of certain versions of pacifism, if those wars will prevent massive loss of innocent life without risking a corresponding loss of life that occurs as a result of the waging of the war itself.[3] Indeed, the early Church Fathers saw

3. *See generally* LARRY MAY, CONTINGENT PACIFISM (2015).

themselves as sympathetic to pacifism and yet also thought that some wars could be justified on just the grounds we have been discussing, namely, concern or respect for the lives of fellow humans. Of course, we may want to question whether the early Church Fathers really were pacifists, but the point is only that war can sometimes be justified on the same grounds on which certain forms of pacifism are themselves grounded.

Strict pacifists will not support any war since war involves the intentional taking of human life. But few people would follow these strict pacifists in saying that one should not use violent force to defend an innocent person's or one's own life from mortal attack. As an analogy think of the abortion debates. Strict adherents to a pro-life position will argue that all abortions are unjustified. But they do not gain many adherents to their position when the focus is on those cases of abortion that are necessary to save the life of the pregnant woman. And the reason regarding abortion is similar to the case of war. It seems odd to think that abortion or war should be condemned in all cases on grounds of protecting life and yet not recognize the conflicting intuitions that many people have about the cases in which abortion or war is *necessary* to protect innocent life as well. Except in the most extreme view of it, the principle of respect for life does not seem clearly to require that all wars or all abortions be prohibited.

To say that war is justified is to say that the moral or legal reasons in support of waging war in a given context outweigh the moral or legal reasons against waging war in that context. To say that waging war might be justified is to say that even though the balance of reasons weigh against waging war, special considerations might warrant that waging war in this case not be blamed or punished. Think of the example of murder. One can say that a person is guilty of murder even though he or she had some reason to engage in this act. But one can also say that a person has performed a killing and yet his act can be justified as in the case of killing in self-defense, or excused as in the case of insanity. One can kill someone and yet still be excused from punishment.

One strong strain of the Just War tradition has taken off from the above position, namely that some wars can be allowed or at least excused even if one is generally sympathetic to pacifism. This is the position of Augustine and of Thomas More, as well as some of the followers of Thomas Aquinas, who specifically discuss abortion as well as war in just these terms, namely that some wars may be justified out of respect for life. The extreme pacifist early Church Fathers began to lose adherents throughout the late Roman era, and it seems likely that the Just War doctrine came into being as a way to save much of the sentiment behind the pacifist position, especially the strong support for life, by admitting that some, but only very few, wars could be justified or excused. Contrary to what is often thought today, we read the Just War tradition as continuing a tradition of generally condemning war. And in this respect, Just War theory and contemporary international legal theory are quite similar to each other, in the sense that both *gesture* toward a *jus contra bellum* but do not entirely embrace it without reservation. Indeed, there are very similar debates today in legal circles about how to regard recourse to force, and whether and when war can be justified or at least excused if it seems necessary to use even lethal force to restore or maintain the peace.[4]

Thomas More, in his book *Utopia*, explained when State use of force is justified as follows: "Utopians go to war only for good reasons: [1] to protect their own land, [2] to drive invading armies from the territories of their friends, or [3] to liberate an oppressed people in the name of humanity, from tyranny and servitude."[5] Aggression then, is State use of force that is not an instance of self-defense, defense of others, or taken contrary to tyranny. Augustine has a similar view, writing at the beginning of the Just War tradition; for him, self-defense and defense of others were the only proper just causes.[6] Following in the tradition of over a thousand years, from Augustine to More, there is a fair amount of agreement. Aggression is the unjustified use of force, and the main forms of unjustified use of force are those that are not taken in self-defense or defense of others, but instead, for instance, merely to increase one's territory.

Two centuries after Thomas More, Emer de Vattel, an eighteenth century theorist, articulates the general idea of self-defense and the corresponding idea of aggression in his book, *The Laws of Nature or the Principles of Natural Law*:

> A Nation has the right to resist the injury another seeks to inflict upon it, and to use force and every just means of resistance against an aggressor. It may even anticipate the other's design, being careful, however, not to act upon vague and doubtful suspicions, lest it should run the risk of becoming itself the aggressor.[7]

4. *See* THOMAS FRANCK, RECOURSE TO FORCE (2002), especially ch. 2.

5. THOMAS MORE, UTOPIA 89–90 (George M. Logan & Robert M. Adams eds., Cambridge University Press 1989) (1516).

6. *See* AUGUSTINE, THE CITY OF GOD, Book 19, *reprinted in* THE MORALITY OF WAR 19 (Larry May, Eric Rovie & Steve Viner eds., 2006).

7. EMER DE VATTEL, LE DROIT DES GENS, OU PRINCIPES DE LA LOI NATURELLE (THE LAW OF NATIONS OR THE PRINCIPLES OF NATURAL LAW) 130 (Charles G. Fenwick trans., Carnegie Institution 1916) (1758).

Here are the classic elements of aggression: one State unjustifiably inflicts, or threatens to inflict, injury on another State by the use of force. Preemption is here countenanced, but only under strict constraints, since preemptive assault can turn into aggression itself.

II. GENTILI AND THE JUSTIFICATION OF OFFENSIVE WAR

We first examine the writings of a figure in the history of international legal thought, Alberici Gentili, who best epitomizes the long tradition of understanding necessity, before then turning to the challenges to that view in later times starting with the writings of Grotius. And we will eventually offer a few additional challenges as this first chapter proceeds. But our main focus is simply to provide an account of several of the most prominent historical ways of understanding necessity.

In 1594, Gentili, who was Regius Professor of Civil Law at the University of Oxford, provided a good place for us to begin concerning how to regard the necessity requirement for initiating *defensive* war:

> We call defense now necessary, now expedient, now honorable; yet in every case we should regard it as necessary. "He who defends himself is said to act through compulsion." So says Baldus, who refuses to distinguish whether one is defending oneself, one's possessions, or one's subjects; or whether what is defended is near or at a distance. . . . Thus in speaking of necessity we are not speaking with absolute accuracy, but we mean that which is not uncommon in human relations, and which is ordinarily called necessary; it may however not be true and absolute necessity.[8]

Gentili here forthrightly admits that what has been called necessity is not really about necessity properly understood when we are considering defensive war.

Indeed, Gentili goes on to argue that absolute necessity has nothing to do with justice: "For to kill in self-defense is just, even though the one who kills may flee without danger and so save himself."[9] And he gives an example that is bizarre from the standpoint of anything that would commonly be called necessity today. Gentili says that "the cause of Romulus

8. Alberici Gentili, De Jure Belli Libri Tres (On the Law of War in Three Books) 58 (John C. Rolfe trans., Oxford University Press 1924) (1594).
9. *Id.* at 58–59.

will rightly be called just, when he defended himself with arms against the invasion of the Sabines, although he had himself given cause for anger and war by carrying off the Sabine women."[10] Here, as in all cases of self-defense for Gentili, necessity is satisfied whenever a State is defending itself from an invading army. And he concludes this discussion by saying "extreme necessity forms an exception to every war." This is the dangerous sense of necessity as an exception to other normative standards we discussed earlier. Even in cases of nonextreme necessity, as where Romulus could have avoided the invasion by giving back the Sabine women his army had kidnapped, Gentili says that he still had the "right to defend himself from enemies who were presently going to attack him."[11]

Concerning *offensive* war, Gentili also employs a weakened notion of necessity: "Necessity, we understand in the sense that we cannot maintain our existence without making war." As an example Gentili again turns to the Roman case of Romulus carrying off the Sabine women because the Romans could not maintain their new city without wives imported from outside Rome.[12] Later in *De Jure Belli Libri Tres*, Gentili advances what has been the historical position often taken on necessity among legal theorists: "A just and unavoidable necessity makes anything lawful."[13] But even Gentili says that we may still only provide grounds for tolerance of certain conduct, not that necessity makes initiating or conducting war fully just.[14] And this caveat, as we will see, is not well recognized in the history of the treatment of necessity.

As we will see, another obvious way to understand necessity is that there is no other way to achieve what one has a right to achieve. This view, often associated with Grotius, was propounded just a few short years after Gentili wrote his treatise. The "no other way" understanding of necessity stands in sharp relief against the position of Gentili that any defensive action should be seen as satisfying necessity.

Gentili's views can best be seen as embodying a kind of common sense approach that clearly resonated with his students and readers. He was not the theoretician or historian that Grotius was, but his views have held up surprisingly well over the centuries and have a distinctly contemporary ring. As will become clear in subsequent chapters, Gentili anticipated

10. *Id.* at 59.
11. *Id.* at 60.
12. *Id.* at 79.
13. *Id.* at 351.
14. *Id.* at 352.

the underlying ideas about necessity of the Lieber Code. In *the jus ad bellum* domain Gentili is also close to the status quo position today in international law.

In Gentili's view, even "an offensive war may be waged justly . . . there is always a defensive aspect, if they are just."[15] Gentili supports this claim by the following argument:

> we have discoursed at length of the law pertaining to every kind of defense. . . . As a matter of fact, offensive warfare has the same motives, arising from necessity, expediency, or honor. Necessity, however, we understand in the sense that we cannot maintain our existence without making war. . . . A second variety of this necessary warfare will be found in the case of those who, because they have been driven from their own country or are compelled to leave it through some emergency and to seek another home, from necessity make war upon others. . . . the destruction of their cities has driven them into the lands of others[16]

As we will see, Gentili goes on to argue that many forms of offensive war, not just that waged by exiles trying to support their own livelihood, can be justified. If offensive wars can be waged for necessity, then there is a sense in which offensive wars can be waged as a last resort and can be justified.

Concerning the case of exiles who must fight a war to preserve themselves from destruction, Gentili says:

> Or do we think it right for men to have no pity for their kind, and allow nothing but death for these exiles, who have been driven from their fatherland? Yet care must be taken lest those wanderers grow discontented with the humble means which of course they can acquire for themselves without war.[17]

Underlying Gentili's general position here is the idea that people should not be forced to do what is opposed to their sense of honor and dignity. In a very curious passage, Gentili says: "Suppose that some one desires to issue a scurrilous book against you, and that there are no available magistrates to whom you may appeal. I maintain that it is your right to protect yourself from insult by force of arms."[18] Apparently, Gentili thinks that generally you should not have to flee rather than use violent force to defend what is valuable to you.

15. Gentili, De Jure Belli, *supra* note 2, at 30.
16. *Id.* at 79.
17. *Id.* at 80.
18. *Id.* at 84.

By taking the position that he does, Gentili disputes the age-old idea that those who strike first are prima facie in the wrong, even as he supports the idea that last resort is of key—although not of completely overriding—importance for determining when offensive war might be justified. Gentili maintains that "to kill in self-defense is just, even though the one who kills may flee without danger to himself"[19] for "every method of securing safety is honorable"[20] and that it is almost always dishonorable to be forced to flee rather than to stay and defend one's rights.[21] Indeed, Gentili defends the idea that wars can be fought in anticipation of "dangers already meditated and prepared" but not yet launched.[22]

Regarding this latter doctrine, Gentili is justly famous for providing two key analogies to explain why first strike as anticipatory defense is justifiable. First, he argues that "we ought not to wait for violence to be offered us, if it is safer to meet it half way . . . one may at once strike at the root of the growing plant and check the attempts of the adversary who is meditating evil."[23] And employing another metaphor he says: "That is an excellent saying of Philo's, that we kill a snake as soon as we see one, even though it has not injured us and will perhaps not harm us. For thus we protect ourselves before it attacks us."[24]

These two powerful images, of stopping the growing plant before it is a major problem for us to weed out, and killing a snake that has not yet shown any signs of harming us but might eventually do so, play into deep-seated intuitions of many people. Indeed, Gentili says: "No one ought to expose himself to danger. No one ought to wait to be struck unless he is a fool."[25] It is not clear whether these last remarks are meant to be based in prudence or morality.

For Gentili it is reasonable that precautions of various types be taken, "even though there is no great and clear cause for fear, and even if there really is no danger, but only a legitimate cause for fear."[26] Gentili adds further support by saying that it is also reasonable that "while your enemy is weak, slay him."[27] And he then concludes this discussion by saying that "a defense is just which anticipates dangers that are already meditated and prepared, and also those which are not meditated, but are probable and

19. *Id.* at 58–59.
20. *Id.* at 59.
21. *Id.* at 83.
22. *Id.* at 66.
23. *Id.* at 61.
24. *Id.*
25. *Id.* at 62.
26. *Id.* at 62–63.
27. *Id.* at 65.

possible." Here we have an articulation of a common nineteenth and twentieth century view that any action that is aimed at self-defense satisfies the necessity requirement.

Today, several theoretical positions, such as that espoused by Margalit and Raz,[28] capture the flavor of Gentili's position:

> The value of national self-governance is the value of entrusting the general political power over a group and its members to the group . . . the right of self-determination . . . is grounded in the wider value of national self-government, which is itself only instrumentally justified . . . the right to recover a territory by force is a possessory right. It does not depend on the ultimate soundness of one's title.[29]

For Margalit and Raz, the right of self-defense of a State is grounded in the right of its people to self-determination, and this right is grounded in the importance of group identity and culture. A people has a right to defend itself as it sees fit, as long as the people does not cause undo harm to other peoples. In this sense, Margalit and Raz argue for a right of self-defense that recognizes few restraints in terms of necessity. We next turn to Grotius and Grotians today who dispute the loose idea of *ad bellum* necessity, especially concerning how to understand last resort.

III. GROTIUS ON FEAR OF ATTACK

With Gentili's arguments clearly in mind, Hugo Grotius argues that it is very difficult to justify offensive wars, even in anticipation, or fear, of attack. Grotius maintains that "those who accept fear of any sort as justifying anticipatory slaying are themselves greatly deceived."[30] For, as he says, "there are certain causes which present a false appearance of justice," and that "such a cause is the fear of something uncertain." Grotius develops an example here that is also quite telling:

> Wherefore we can in no wise approve the view of those who declare that it is a just cause of war when a neighbor who is restrained by no agreement builds a

28. Avishai Margalit & Joseph Raz, *National Self-Determination*, 87 J. PHIL. 439–61 (1990), *reprinted in* THE GLOBAL JUSTICE READER (Thom Brooks ed., 2008) [subsequent page references to this edition].

29. *Id.* at 78–79.

30. HUGO GROTIUS, DE JURE BELLI AC PACIS (ON THE LAW OF WAR AND PEACE) 173 (1625) (Francis W. Kelsey trans., 1925).

> fortress on his own soil, or some other fortification which may some day cause us harm. Against the fears which arise from such actions we must resort to counter fortifications on our own land and other similar remedies, but not to force of arms.[31]

This example, perhaps not as powerful as those of Gentili, clearly seeks to counter the intuitive support that Gentili's own examples had received. For Grotius, fear may be a just motivation for some actions, but certainly not war when less lethal means are available.

Grotius takes from Gellius, a second century Roman author, another example that is directed specifically at first strikes:

> When a gladiator is equipped for fighting, the alternatives offered by combat are these, either to kill, if he shall have made the first decisive stroke, or to fall, if he shall have failed. But the life of men generally is not hedged about by a necessity so unfair and so relentless that you are obliged to strike the first blow, and may suffer if you shall have failed to be first to strike.[32]

Grotius then adds this gloss on our theme: "while it is permissible to kill him who is making ready to kill, yet the man is more worthy of praise who prefers to be killed rather than to kill."[33]

At another point in his seminal work on the laws of war and peace, Grotius argues:

> that the possibility of being attacked confers the right to attack is abhorrent to every principle of equity. Human life exists under such conditions that complete security is never guaranteed to us. For protection against uncertain fears we must rely on Divine Providence, and on a wariness free from reproach, not on force.[34]

Equity here is that gap-filler that gives us a fair and reasonable way to act when there do not seem to be rules that prevent violent conduct. Grotius then puts his position in stark contrast to that of Gentili when, as we saw earlier, he says: "I maintain that he cannot lawfully be killed either if the danger can in any other way be avoided, or if it is not altogether certain

31. *Id.* at 549.
32. *Id.* at 174.
33. *Id.* at 176. This passage should remind us that Grotius seems to adopt a non-standard form of pacifism best described as contingent pacifism.
34. *Id.* at 184.

that the danger cannot be otherwise avoided."[35] And Grotius provides us with the simple formula that is still the *jus ad bellum* doctrine in international law today: "The danger, again, must be immediate and imminent in point of time."[36] To establish this condition, evidence of planning that is virtually completed needs to be shown.

One of the main reasons Grotius argues against the position that Gentili had defended is that Grotius believes that it is too easy to speak of fear as a mere "pretext" for clearly unacceptable grounds for going to war.[37] Pretexts are the publicly declared reasons for going to war, but behind them lurk other reasons that are hidden and would be considered unjustifiable grounds for going to war if exposed to the public light of reason. Grotius argues that it is important not to confuse "the terms 'cause' and 'pretext,'" for example, "the 'pretext' of the Second Punic War was the dispute over Saguntum, but the cause was the anger of the Carthaginians at the agreements that the Romans had extorted from them in times of adversity."[38] The difficulty of distinguishing mere "pretext" from just "cause" makes Grotius much more cautious than Gentili, especially in respect to anticipatory attacks.

For example, some have said that the Iraq War of 2003 was started on a pretext, namely the fear of attack by Saddam Hussein's use of weapons of mass destruction, but that the hidden cause was merely to gain control over Iraq's extensive oil reserves by the United States, or some other ulterior motive.[39] We should here recall the words of Ian Brownlie, namely that the having, or apparently having, of long-range missiles allows almost any State to say that another State presents a threat to it, thereby undercutting any restraint on what would count as a just cause for anticipatory attack.[40] Weapons of mass destruction (WMDs) ratchet up Brownlie's concern about long-range missiles, since WMDs are, as the name implies, meant to be even scarier than regular weapons launched from one State against another unsuspecting State. Even more than long-range missiles, every state has reason to fear WMDs. Once fear becomes generalizable and omnipresent, it ceases to become a reliable indicator for the justness of military force.

35. *Id.* at 175.
36. *Id.* at 173.
37. *Id.* at 169.
38. *Id.* at 546.
39. Seymour Hersch, among many others, has defended this view. See his series of articles in THE NEW YORKER, as well as his book, CHAIN OF COMMAND (2004).
40. *See* IAN BROWNLIE, INTERNATIONAL LAW AND THE USE OF FORCE BY STATES 366–68 (1963).

IV. THE GROTIAN PRINCIPLES OF LAST RESORT AND *AD BELLUM* NECESSITY

To review, imminence along with immediacy, have been employed for centuries in the Just War literature to make sense out of the principle of necessity in *jus ad bellum* considerations. After Grotius writes that "[t]he danger again must be immediate and imminent,"[41] he follows this up by saying: "I maintain that he cannot lawfully be killed, either if the danger can in any other way be avoided, or if it is not altogether certain that the danger cannot be otherwise avoided."[42] There are three standards of necessity articulated here. The first is the "imminence" standard just discussed. The second is "immediacy," a spatial or temporal concept that is arguably stricter than even imminence. And the third is the standard that there cannot be "any other way [the killing can] be avoided." This multilayered standard throws into sharp relief the differences between the Grotian and Gentilian views of necessity. Grotius says that "We take this Course [war] as the only Means left to preserve ourselves."[43] And he follows this comment with the following explanation: "But here 'tis necessary that the Danger be *present* [immediate], and as it were contained in a *Point* [imminent]."[44] Several pages later, he follows up with an even a clearer articulation of the position: "I maintain that we cannot lawfully kill him, if either such a danger can be possibly avoided any other way."[45]

Grotius offers yet a stronger and clearer statement of what he thinks *ad bellum* necessity requires:

> therefore the Dread . . . of our Neighbour's encreasing Strength, is not a warrantable Ground for making War upon him. To justify taking up Arms in our own Defense, there ought to be a Necessity for doing so, which there is not, unless we are sure, with a moral Certainty, that he has not only Forces sufficient, but a full Intention to injure us.[46]

Grotius is here responding to Gentili's claim that we should not have to wait for the danger to be at our doorstep, but the sheer beginning to build

41. Grotius, De Jure Belli ac Pacis, *supra* note 30(On the Law of War and Peace) 173 (1625) (Frances W. Kelsey trans., 1925).
42. *Id.* at 175.
43. Grotius, De Jure Belli ac Pacis, *supra* note 30, at 398.
44. *Id.*
45. *Id.* at 401.
46. *Id.* at 1102.

a castle should suffice. The requirement that we have "moral certainty" that what we are doing is necessary adds yet another level of restriction on the use of the military necessity in defense of initiating war. Necessity, as we saw in the case of Gentili, could be claimed if there was any kind of threat posed by another State. Grotius's introduction of the idea of moral certainty takes us out of the realm of purely prudential political considerations. Indeed, Grotius is well known for his distinction between reasons to go to war and motive for going to war.

In *De Jure Belli ac Pacis*, Grotius worries, as we said, about the use of pretexts as if they were good reasons to initiate war. Merely seeing an advantage in going to war does not "give us as good a Right as a Necessity for one."[47] Grotius also argues that the pursuit of "glory, empire, or riches" is not sufficient to warrant a just war as there is nothing necessary about attaining such things. On the other hand, reasons such as vengeance may be justifying reasons, but only if war is the only way that vengeance can be meted out.[48] Indeed, Grotius argues strongly that past injury is not a just cause to go to war; only the mitigation of truly threatening injury can satisfy the necessity condition.

Consider again the case of the Sabine women. According to the myth, Romulus, the founder of Rome, discovered that there were not enough women in Rome to guarantee that Rome would survive to the next generation. He asked the residents of Sabine, an area contiguous to Rome, to allow Roman men to marry Sabine women. The Sabine rulers refused. Romulus then sent his troops to kidnap Sabine women, who were then raped by Roman men. As a result, the Sabine rulers declared war on Rome and prepared to send an army to punish Rome for its transgressions. Romulus mounted his own attack on Sabine forces, claiming that Rome was about to be invaded, and it was necessary to attack so as to prevent the invasion.

Gentili and most authors before him argued that Romulus was justified in initiating war so as to defend Rome, even though war was not needed if the Sabine women had been returned to their country. Grotius is not terribly clear on what he thinks of this case.[49] But from many things that Grotius says, one could argue that Grotius should be against Gentili's analysis here. Indeed, Grotius would caution against war in nearly all cases. As Grotius says: "It results that war is not undertaken, unless of necessity.

47. *Id.* at 1103.
48. *Id.* at 1097.
49. *Id.* at 204.

Therefore a cause for engaging in war which either may not be passed over, or ought not to be, is exceptional."[50]

The Grotian approach is to recognize that there is a right of self-defense for States, but to see such a right as severely limited by certain temporal and spatial considerations that are embodied in a last resort or *ad bellum* necessity condition. Following Grotius's injunction that "the danger, again, must be immediate and imminent in point of time,"[51] Yoram Dinstein talks of the "immediacy condition" that he finds articulated in the International Court of Justice's *Nicaragua* case:

> Immediacy signifies that there must not be an undue time-lag between the armed attack and the exercise of self-defense. However this condition is construed "broadly." Lapse of time is almost unavoidable when—in a desire to fulfill letter and spirit the condition of necessity—a tedious process of diplomatic negotiations evolves, with a view to resolving the matter amicably.[52]

Immediacy has to do with how close in time an attack *has occurred* in order for the State attacked to claim that it can engage in a reprisal war as a means of self-defense.

Imminence involves responding to an attack that is seemingly about to occur. There is a lively debate in international legal circles about whether the doctrine of imminence countenances anticipatory self-defensive acts. Dinstein, like Brownlie, argues that threats of attack, even if imminent, only allow counter-threats, not anticipatory attacks. But Dinstein does allow for a category he calls *interceptive* self-defense.

> Interceptive, unlike anticipatory, self-defense takes place after the other side has committed itself to an armed attack in an ostensibly irrevocable way. Whereas a preventive strike anticipates an armed attack that is merely "foreseeable" (or even just "conceivable"), an interceptive strike counters an armed attack which is "imminent" and practically "unavoidable." It is the opinion of the present writer that interceptive, as distinct from anticipatory, self-defense is legitimate even under Article 51 of the Charter [of the United Nations].[53]

50. *Id.* at 575.

51. GROTIUS, DE JURE BELLI AC PACIS, *supra* note 30 (ON THE LAW OF WAR AND PEACE) 173 (1625) (Frances W. Kelsey trans., 1925).

52. YORAM DINSTEIN, WAR, AGGRESSION, AND SELF-DEFENSE 184 (3d ed. 2001).

53. *Id.* at 172. The first part of Article 51 of the United Nations Charter says: "Nothing in the present Charter shall impair the inherent right of individual or collective self-defense if an armed attack occurs against a Member of the United Nations until the Security Council has taken measures necessary to maintain international peace and security."

Dinstein joins the majority of contemporary international law scholars in thinking that imminence must be read very narrowly. The example that he gives is telling: if the United States had miraculously figured out that the Japanese carrier striking force was on its way to Pearl Harbor, and the U.S. Navy destroyed it while still on route, this would be justified as a form of interceptive rather than anticipatory self-defense. Notice that the United States would have to know that the Japanese had irrevocably begun their attack.

Another excellent example, written about by both Dinstein and Michael Walzer, is Israel's Six Days War in 1967. Dinstein agrees that the first strike by Israel was justified as interception of Egypt's forces massing on the border, even as Dinstein recognizes that this case is somewhat different from the Pearl Harbor one.

> True, no single Egyptian step, evaluated alone, may have qualified as an armed attack. But when all of the measures taken by Egypt (especially the peremptory ejection of the United Nations Emergency Force from the Gaza Strip and the Sinai Peninsula; the closure of the Straits of Tiran; the unprecedented build-up of Egyptian forces along Israel's borders; and constant saber-rattling statements about the impending fighting) were assessed in the aggregate it seemed to be crystal clear that Egypt was bent on an armed attack, and the sole question was not whether war would materialize but when.[54]

By contrast, in the hypothetical Pearl Harbor case, there was no question of when the attack would occur. Similarly, Walzer uses Israel's Six Days War to illustrate what he calls "just fear" because the massing of Egypt's forces at Israel's border "served no other more limited goal" than initiating war.[55]

Walzer differs from Dinstein, though, in recognizing that his conclusion about the justifiability of Israel's Six Days War requires a "major revision" of the Just War doctrine, as it is understood today.

> For it means that aggression can be made out not only in the absence of a military attack but in the (probable) absence of immediate intention to launch such an attack or invasion. The general formula must be something like this: states may use military force in the face of threats of war, whenever the failure to do so would seriously risk their territorial integrity or political independence.[56]

54. *Id.* at 173.
55. Michael Walzer, Just and Unjust Wars 84 (Basic Books ed. 2000).
56. *Id.* at 85.

Walzer is clearly not working solely within the Grotian tradition. He moves closer to Gentili, although he still keeps to the spirit of Grotius's concerns about limiting self-defense.

More recent authors in the Just War tradition have argued that States have a right to use whatever they think is needed to defend themselves.[57] Indeed, one set of authors has described what they call "the political defensive privilege,"[58] a philosophical position that allows States to use defensive force to protect their political arrangements. On the other hand, philosophers such as David Rodin are highly critical of this expansive right of States to defend themselves, and have articulated a much more limited set of situations when defensive force is justified.[59] Indeed, Rodin goes so far as to suggest that defensive force is not justified when a country is faced with military aggression from another State that will result in political domination of the local government. In this way, the debate between followers of Gentili and followers of Grotius continues to play itself out among very recent writings by Just War theorists.

V. LAST RESORT AS THE ULTIMATE RESTRAINT

The Grotian strain of the Just War tradition sees war as justified only as a last resort, not as a part of normal policy. War can only be justified, on the Grotian view, when diplomatic efforts have been extensively tried and come up wanting. Let us begin to understand last resort within the contemporary Just War tradition with one attempt to define the principle of last resort. Douglas Lackey says that it involves this consideration: "If the just cause might be achieved by other means that have not been attempted, then war for that just cause is not just war."[60] Yet, this is highly problematical, for in some sense, as Walzer admits, "there are always other means, more or less dangerous, more or less effective."[61]

The idea of last resort is initially quite baffling. If the doctrine says that there must be no other means of defending oneself before one can be justified in using armed attacks to secure one's State, then the principle appears to set an unlimited restraint since there are always other means available.

57. Margalit & Raz, *National Self-Determination, supra* note 28.
58. Patrick Emerton & Toby Handfield, *Understanding the Political Defensive Privilege, in* THE MORALITY OF DEFENSIVE WAR 40–65 (Cecile Fabre & Seth Lazar eds., 2014).
59. *See* David Rodin, *The Myth of National Self-Defense*, in Fabre & Lazar, *supra* note 58, at 69–89.
60. DOUGLAS P. LACKEY, THE ETHICS OF WAR AND PEACE 40 (1989).
61. WALZER, JUST AND UNJUST WARS, *supra* note 55, at 213.

But the principle is not utterly without limits, for as Paul Christopher has argued:

> The "last resort" condition is meant to restrain nations that are considering initiating hostilities—it is not relevant to nations that have already been attacked! . . . The condition of last resort was met [in the first Iraq War] as soon as Iraqi soldiers invaded Kuwait.[62]

Even when so limited, the principle of last resort, on almost every interpretation, seems to place very severe limitations on self-defense. And in any event we might wonder why minor attacks by one state against another should not also have to pass the test of diplomatic alternatives. In this section we will explore whether this understanding of the principle of last resort is plausible.

On one level, last resort seems quite intuitively plausible. If you are in a barroom brawl and wonder whether you can throw the first punch, it is not enough to think that doing so will attain security for yourself. In addition, there must be no other reasonable steps you can take that would attain your security. In this sense, last resort is quite similar to necessity; indeed it is often treated as an *ad bellum* necessity principle. One way to show that striking first was a last resort is to show that it was necessary for one's self-defense. For if it is strictly necessary to throw the first punch for self-defense, then there are no other alternatives that could have achieved this result. If there is an alternative that truly could attain the same result of self-defense, then the alternative that involves the least suffering and typically the least violence is the one that should be chosen on a doctrine of last resort.

The latter part of the doctrine, that one should choose the least violent means that can achieve a given permissible end, needs some additional support. For Gentili's comments make one wonder about seeing a snake, perhaps near the open front door of one's house. Even if one could avoid the snake's bite by leaving the room by the back door, rather than confronting and killing the snake at the front door, doesn't it make more sense to take the more violent action and kill the snake, thereby eliminating any future threat? One could ask in general whether retreating should always be attempted first before confronting a hostile threat. If one sees a very large menacing person at one's front door, and one can leave by the back

62. Paul Christopher, The Ethics of War and Peace: An Introduction to Legal and Moral Issues 88 (3d ed. 2004).

door without risking injury to self or the menacing person, must one take that option rather than to confront the menacing person? Again doesn't it make sense to try to eliminate any future threat, especially since it is one's own home?

An analogy to domestic criminal law would be helpful. In almost every jurisdiction, the target of an offensive attack is not justified in using defensive force if he or she can safely retreat. If safe retreat is possible, then the use of defensive force to repel the attack is not truly necessary. However, U.S. law has traditionally granted an exception to the duty of retreat in cases arising inside the target's home. This exception is known as the Castle Doctrine. Its practical consequence is that a homeowner may use deadly force to stop an invader even if the homeowner could escape the house without killing the attacker. In recent years, several American jurisdictions have broadened the Castle Doctrine and applied it to public spaces as well. These statutes, known commonly as "Stand Your Ground" provisions, controversially permit the target of a deadly attack to launch a lethal counterstrike to repel the attack even if escape was a viable alternative. The only constraint on the doctrine is that the defender must be located in a place that he or she has a lawful right to occupy at the moment in time when the attack occurs.

One way to respond to these questions in the realm of national self-defense is to insist that the alternatives that should be pursued as a last resort must be likely to accomplish the same self-defensive goals. Going out the back door, or retreating generally, often does not gain one self-defense except in the very short-term. Self-defense often requires long-term planning. Think again of the Six Days War between Israel and Egypt. It certainly was possible for Israel to mass its own troops at the border where Egypt was massing its troops, or to build up armaments at the point where these troops were massing. But such a strategy is only likely to have rendered Israel temporarily secure. Since Israel's forces were much smaller than Egypt's, attacking first with the element of surprise seemed best for Israel's long-term security. If last resort cannot accommodate such thinking then perhaps it is shortsighted.

Last resort is only opposed to acting on long-term security interests if there are options, either short- or long-term, that have not been seriously contemplated, and that do not involve lethal violence. So, considerations of last resort are not going to block nearly as many actions as one might at first suppose. One of the chief things that last resort forces a State to contemplate is diplomacy, something that it is sometimes hard to contemplate in the midst of bellicose talk on both sides. But that is just the point. In the barroom brawl example, it is indeed difficult to take a breath and try to reason with the person who is acting in a menacing manner. But it is indeed a very good thing to take a breath, to stop and think, before acting violently in most situations. Of course, the problem is that in some other situations stopping to think may not be reasonable since the moment of surprise may be fleeting. So part of the calculation has to be not only whether there are less violent alternatives that might achieve the same short-term goal, but also there must be long-term calculations as well as calculations about whether the element of surprise is so crucial that even such calculating might be too dangerous.

Last resort is mainly a restraint on calculations about initiating war for self-defense and defense of others. Initially it merely says that in most cases alternatives that are not lethal need to be seriously considered. If it is a true emergency, then last resort calculation is probably off the table. But in all other cases, last resort calls for serious consideration of non-lethal alternatives that might be able to accomplish the same objectives as the lethal means. In part what this means is that one is caused to stop and think, where thinking more often results in coming up with alternatives to what first appears to be the only reasonable strategy. For self-defense and defense of others, it is not sufficient to show that a given strategy will indeed secure one's defense. And it is this part of the doctrine of last resort that has brought forth the most criticism.

These ideas have a very long history extending back at least until 500 B.C.E. in China. There we find Mozi, who probably lived in the next generation after Confucius. Mozi provides powerful arguments against aggressive wars, but he also opposed most defensive wars as well. Yet Mozi is not a pacifist in the normal sense of that term. Instead, he argues that in most cases attention to defensive structures and strategies can successfully replace lethal use of defensive force. Mozi was known as an accomplished engineer. Indeed, his defensive alternatives were seen as so plausible that various kings were persuaded to implement them rather than to engage in defensive war. Today, several theorists are beginning to pursue the idea that non-lethal strategies could come to replace lethal use of defensive force. Mozi's writings could be a source for such theorists as well as for other theorists who are exploring the increased use of military police actions instead of defensive war. And such an argument affected how the legality of the use of defensive force came to be understood.[63]

And as we saw, Gentili makes the obvious point that if it is in our self-defense, then we should be permitted to do whatever will secure it. But

63. *See* MOZI: BASIC WRITINGS 53–60 (Burton Watson trans., 2003).

even in the case of the snake, there is a lingering doubt that we should be permitted to kill merely for our own peace of mind if there are non-lethal means easily at hand. For the snake, like our opponent in the barroom brawl, has interests just as we do, including the interest not to be harmed by disproportionate or unnecessary levels of force. Last resort begins to make sense by urging that whenever violent means are contemplated, because of the effects of such means, we need to make sure that there is not some way of resolving the problem by non-lethal means. But as with the case of the snake at the door, we need not risk long-term security in order to protect our potential attacker. What last resort calls for is a serious consideration of alternatives. Last resort does not dictate that we must always choose the least violent means, but only the non-lethal *and* equally efficacious means, time permitting. In this sense, last resort is like first strike, a kind of rule of thumb that guides us initially in thinking about what is a just cause to initiate or wage war. We will now look at the idea of "equally efficacious" options in the final section of this chapter.

VI. EQUALLY EFFICACIOUS MEANS

There are two things that are meant by saying that last resort or *ad bellum* necessity requires that there be no other equally efficacious means available. First, there must be other ways to accomplish a needed military objective in initiating war. And second, there must be other ways that do not require unreasonable risk to the troops that are sent to accomplish the military objective. In both cases the principle of last resort or *ad bellum* necessity might be significantly restricted in scope. We end this chapter by considering the scope of the principle of last resort.

The "no other way" requirement is best not understood literally. In part this is because of temporal considerations—there may be some other way to accomplish the goal, but it may be not sufficiently clear that the other way could be accomplished in enough time. Of course, if the goal turns out not to be accomplished in this way then it is not a case of there being "any other way." We must also realize that in many cases, such as where an invasion is occurring or is imminent, what is at stake is such that it would be unreasonable to demand much consideration be given to possible alternatives to initiating a defensive war. As the stakes go up what counts as a reasonable alternative, in terms of the probabilities in question, is greatly limited.

Each alternative to initiating war has a probability of success, as does initiating war itself. According to some in the Just War tradition, what matters is whether it is just to act defensively. As noted earlier, Gentili says that

"Every method of securing safety is honorable."[64] He then goes on to agree with Plato that if the defense is just then it is not merely permissible but required, in the sense that not to defend is subject to punishment.[65] Again, for Gentili, "in speaking of necessity we are not speaking with absolute accuracy, but we mean that which is not uncommon in human relations, and which is ordinarily called necessity; it may however not be true and absolute necessity."[66] In this view, one need not show that there was no other way but only that one had a right so to act, and it is not uncommon so to act. At least in part this is because Gentili focuses on acting honorably rather than on making sure that all alternatives have been exhausted. And acting in defense of self or others is nearly always honorable.

The question of how remotely likely it is that some alternative to initiating war could also succeed is itself difficult to answer. Gentili says that we must make such determinations by considering it "from the standpoint of human conditions."[67] We understand Gentili to be saying that we should not expect a person to try to think of all possible alternatives, but to be especially guided by what is going on around him or her. Yet, how much one should consider alternatives is not answered with any precision by this means, and Gentili forthrightly admits as much. In this way we can see how necessity can be understood not to require that there be "no other way," at least if that is understood literally.

Another set of concerns is that of how much risk to one's own citizens one must countenance in pursuing alternatives to initiating war. In this respect some recent work by theorists of the Just War tradition is especially telling. We need to take seriously the risks to one's own population when one pursues alternative means to that of initiating a war of self-defense, for instance.[68] But the problem is that leaders of States will often exaggerate how risky it is to the citizenry if war is not immediately launched in response to threats from belligerents. A test of sincerity is seemingly needed in such cases to make sure that war is not merely being pursued as a first rather than a last resort.

Perhaps we could adopt something that Michael Walzer says about *jus in bello* necessity to the case of *jus ad bellum* necessity and last resort. In a case of deciding whether or not a soldier is acting out of necessity when clearing out a cellar of insurgents, the question was if the soldier could simply

64. Gentili, De Jure Belli, *supra* note 2, at 59.
65. *Id.* at 68.
66. *Id.* at 58.
67. *Id.* at 60.
68. *See, e.g.*, Gabriella Blum & David Luban, *Unsatisfying Wars: Degrees of Risk and the* Jus ex Bello, 125 Ethics 751–80 (2015).

throw a grenade into the cellar. Walzer famously proposes that the soldier should have to yell first into the cellar that anyone in the house should come out. This would expose the soldier to some peril, but it is minimal compared to what will happen to the unsuspecting innocent civilians when the grenade is simply lobbed into the cellar.

It is an old principle in the Just War tradition that before war is initiated there must be first a public announcement of the intention to initiate war. Such an announcement requirement was supposed to give the other side the opportunity to sue for peace or to stop engaging in threatening behavior. Of course, if the other side did indeed sue for peace, initiating war in such a situation would not be considered to be just. Like shouting into the cellar, making a public announcement of one's intentions to initiate war was supposed to be a good faith effort to see if there were other ways to secure what is needed without recourse to war.

Self-protection is to be prized, but for *jus ad bellum* necessity to be satisfied there must not only be alternatives to war that are considered but there must be some risk taken by the party that is about to initiate war to see if there is not an obvious alternative to war that could be pursued instead. Yet, even here necessity must be constrained by what it is reasonable to risk. And such reasonableness must be construed so that it does not swamp necessity, as sometimes seems to be true of thinkers such as Gentili, who approvingly quotes the unqualified remark that "The law allows one to take up arms against those who are in arms."[69]

Certainly after Grotius, necessity is seen as more restrictive than the way that Gentili understood necessity. But the precise limit that necessity sets on *jus ad bellum* is not easy to trace. There is disagreement in the Just War tradition about how strict or absolute the *jus ad bellum* necessity condition should be, and especially about how much latitude should be allowed for cases where there has already been either an invasion or the serious threat of such an invasion.

VII. CONCLUSION

In this chapter we have canvassed the major *jus ad bellum* arguments that have emerged from the Just War tradition. By exploring the classic debate between Gentili and Grotius, we have shown that the contemporary

69. Alberico Gentili, De Armis Romanis (The Wars of the Romans) 112, 147 (David Lupher trans., 2011) (1599).

debates in Just War philosophy are really echoes of a much earlier one. This is not to suggest that the philosophical literature has not advanced or that the latest debates are simply rehashing or recycling the arguments made by Gentili and Grotius. Rather, we are simply clarifying that the center of the debate over the use of force is how to understand the principle of last resort. Our own contribution to this debate is to insist that any account of "last resort" requires, by definition, an exposition of the alternatives that should have been pursued rather than lethal military force. And that exposition requires reference to whether the hypothetical alternative was *reasonable* for the State to bear. Indeed, it would be wrong to suggest that the State had a moral duty to forgo military force because it was unnecessary, when the "alternative" strategy that was posited required the State to bear unreasonable risks or burdens.

The following chapter moves from the philosophical domain to positive international law. We will explore the role that necessity plays in contemporary international legal doctrine regarding the use of force. This will be the next step in determining whether our philosophical position regarding "reasonable alternatives" can be translated into legal doctrine.

CHAPTER 2

Necessity and the Use of Force in International Law

The concept of necessity allows a nation to escape liability under the law of state responsibility for its actions that would normally constitute a violation of the law of nations.[1] In this context, one is usually most concerned about violations of sovereignty and other more extreme violations of *jus ad bellum* such as unlawful military incursions. However, the defense of necessity under international law is far broader, and we must first examine the contours of necessity under basic principles of public international law before applying it to more extreme situations.[2] Consequently, Section I of this chapter examines the evolution of the defense as applied to both customary and treaty-based norms. The general trend is that the defense, which was once considered marginal, is now coming to the forefront of public international law, suggesting that more and more states will argue necessity in the future to escape responsibility for their actions. Section II briefly examines the use of the necessity doctrine in investor-state disputes, where claims of necessity dominate—to varying degrees of

1. *See* ANTONIO CASSESE, INTERNATIONAL LAW 255 (2d ed. 2005) ("What is now in danger, however, is not the life of a State official and the persons who may have been entrusted to him, but the *whole State or its population* (or part of the population)."). *But see* IAN BROWNLIE, PRINCIPLES OF PUBLIC INTERNATIONAL LAW 466 (7th ed. 2008) ("However, necessity as an omnibus category probably does not exist, and its availability as a defence is circumscribed by fairly strict conditions.").

2. For a discussion, see M. Agius, *The Invocation of Necessity in International Law*, 56 NETHERLANDS INT'L L. REV. 95 (2009).

success—the legal arguments of states that have allegedly violated their legal duties to private investors. Finally, Section III considers the most serious type of necessity arguments: as a defense to violations of sovereignty and other *jus ad bellum* obligations. Inevitably, this will lead to a consideration of the possibility of using necessity as a justification for humanitarian intervention—a rhetorical strategy with conceptual promise, but that runs afoul of the technical requirements of the necessity doctrine.

This chapter concludes in Section IV with a consideration of necessity as one component—arguably the most important—of the doctrine of self-defense. Indeed, other components of self-defense, including imminence and proportionality, can be viewed as conceptually linked and even subordinated to the principle of necessity. The overall picture presented in this chapter suggests lingering confusion and uncertainty over two interlinked issues: (1) whether a successful necessity claim requires an overall balancing judgment that the harm avoided exceeded the harm imposed; and (2) more fundamentally, whether necessity should operate as a justification or an excuse under international law. The two issues are interrelated because the need to satisfy a balancing requirement is traditionally the purview of a utilitarian-based justification—at least in the criminal law. However the issue remains largely undecided, and even unexplored, because the language of "excuse" is generally foreign to the contemporary discourse of public international law.

I. NECESSITY UNDER CUSTOMARY AND TREATY LAW

The customary principle of necessity is codified in Article 25 of the ILC Draft Articles on State Responsibility, which states that necessity may negate state responsibility if the act "(a) is the only way for the State to safeguard an essential interest against a grave and imminent peril; and (b) does not seriously impair an essential interest of the State or States towards which the obligation exists, or of the international community as a whole."[3] Necessity is unavailable as a defense if "(a) the international obligation in question excludes the possibility of invoking necessity; or (b) the State has contributed to the situation of necessity."[4] The latter condition—fault in

3. Draft Articles on the Responsibility of States for Internationally Wrongful Acts, in Report of the International Law Commission on the Work of Its Fifty-third Session art. 25, U.N. GAOR, 56th Sess., Supp. No. 10, at 43, U.N. Doc. A/56/10 (2001), annexed to G.A. Res. 56/83 (Dec. 12, 2001) [hereinafter ILC Draft Articles].
4. *Id.*

the creation of the state of necessity—mirrors a similar constraint on the defense's application in the criminal context, where the principle is best thought of as a more specific example of the clean hands doctrine, or even the principle of *actio libera in causa*.[5] The clean hands doctrine is an equitable principle that prevents a party from making particular arguments in court when that party has engaged in wrongdoing.[6] The *actio libera in causa* principle entails that defendants cannot set the conditions for their own defense.[7] This principle exemplifies our moral intuition that it would be wrong for an individual to engineer a particular situation that then provides the factual foundation for an exculpatory defense.

All of this requires a deeper discussion of the conceptual foundation for the defense of necessity, which involves a normative assessment that a party "without a choice" because of the exigency of the situation cannot be held morally responsible for that party's actions. However, if the party was free in the *creation* of the situation, even if not free in his response to the state of necessity, the law can rightly hold the party responsible for that earlier free action.[8] The doctrinal codification of this moral intuition is to simply deny the application of the necessity defense to situations where the party was responsible in some way for the creation of the state of necessity. However, one should be careful to distinguish contributions to the state of necessity that are purposeful from those that are merely reckless. The former clearly triggers the *actio libera in causa* principle whereas the latter is more complex and involves holding the party responsible for her own recklessness. One reason these conceptual foundations are under-analyzed in public international law is that the doctrine usually does not ascribe complex mental states (e.g., purpose or recklessness) to nation-states. If public international law were to do so, the exact contours of the necessity defense might be better conceptualized.

As mentioned above, the necessity defense can be applied to circumvent a treaty or customary obligation.[9] One famous example of the former is the *Gabčikovo-Nagymaros* dispute between Hungary and Czechoslovakia.[10]

5. For a discussion, see Joachim Herrmann, *Causing the Conditions of One's Own Defense: The Multifaceted Approach of German Law*, BYU L. REV. 747 (1986).

6. *See, e.g.*, Ori J. Herstein, *A Normative Theory of the Clean Hands Defense*, 17 LEGAL THEORY (2011).

7. *See* Susan Dimock, Actio Libera in Causa, 7 CRIM. LAW & PHIL. 549, 550 (2013).

8. The ICL Draft Articles state that the necessity defense does not apply if the State is responsible for the creation of the state of necessity, although it does not explicitly explain why.

9. *See* Malgosia Fitzmaurice, *Exceptional Circumstances and Treaty Commitments*, *in* THE OXFORD GUIDE TO TREATISES 605, 628 (Duncan Hollis ed., 2012).

10. *See* R. Lefeber, *The Gabčikovo-Nagymaros Project and the Law of State Responsibility,* 11 LEIDEN J. INT'L L. 612 (1998).

In that case, Hungary terminated a 1977 treaty originally signed with Czechoslovakia that contemplated the joint creation of a series of dams in the region. Hungary sought to vitiate its commitment because the completion of the dams would cause environmental and economic harm to its state interests; consequently it argued before the International Court of Justice (ICJ) that it was necessary to terminate the treaty. Specifically, Hungary claimed that the relevant conditions for the defense were met: the asserted state interests were vital (economic and ecological), the damage posed to them by the dam was grave, and so termination was unavoidable. Slovakia (as continuer of Czechoslovakia) questioned the very concept of an ecological state of necessity; it also seemed that the original treaty had contemplated and resolved the very burdens and possible negative outcomes that Hungary was now asserting as a state of necessity to avoid fulfilling its bilateral obligations under the treaty. The ICJ concluded that necessity could be applied—in theory—to the environmental context, though the court questioned whether the standard of a "grave and imminent" peril was met in this case because the potential negative outcomes were mere future risks and not imminent in nature.[11] Furthermore, termination of the treaty was not unavoidable; Hungary had other means at its disposal for mitigating the potential risks.

Although this dispute is modern, the ILC Commentaries refer to several historical examples in order to justify its codification of the necessity defense. For example, Portugal argued in 1832 that its expropriation of property from British subjects, in violation of treaty law, was justified by a state of necessity.[12] At the time the property was needed to provide for the "subsistence" of troops who were deployed to quell an internal disturbance. Since the illegal disturbance threatened the "safety" and even the "existence" of the Portuguese state, the infringement of British interests was allegedly necessary under the circumstances. The ILC Commentaries also cite the 1893 Russian Fur Seals controversy.[13] When Russia banned sealing in international waters in order to protect the seal population from total destruction, it argued that the action was immediately necessary given the timing of the upcoming hunting season. Neither case was litigated by an international tribunal, though the bare *assertion* of necessity as an exculpating factor for violations of international obligations arguably provides data for the existence of the doctrine under customary international law (through state practice and *opinio juris*).

11. *The Gabčikovo-Nagymaros Project (Hungary v. Slovakia)*, 1997 ICJ Rep. 7.
12. ILC Draft Articles at 81.
13. *Id.*

No one seriously doubts that the necessity defense is real.[14] Given its power to exempt states from legal responsibility for their violations of international law, the requirements of a "grave and imminent" peril and the "unavoidability" of the state action are designed to carefully constrain the doctrine to a narrowly defined set of circumstances.[15] In theory, the notion of "unavoidability" as expressed by the Draft ILC Articles could perform the same work as the "least harmful means" test of necessity does in human rights law. Whether the standard has real regulatory bite in reality is another question, and one that we will evaluate as we consider more substantial violations of state interests in Sections III and IV of this chapter.

II. NECESSITY IN INVESTOR-STATE ARBITRATION

Necessity also plays a role in the more specific context of investor-state arbitration.[16] Perhaps picking up on the growing salience of the necessity doctrine in international law generally, states have recently argued necessity as a defense to claims that they violated their responsibilities to private investors. In these cases the necessity arguments appeal either to Article 25 of the ILC Draft Articles or to specific treaty provisions that codify necessity-like defenses.[17]

For example, the General Agreement on Tariffs and Trade (GATT) includes several provisions on necessity.[18] Article XX allows for exceptions that are "necessary to protect public morals . . . necessary to protect human, animal or plant life or health . . . (or) necessary to secure compliance with laws or regulations which are not inconsistent with the provisions of this Agreement."[19] Furthermore, Article XXI more explicitly deals

14. *But see* Robert D. Sloane, *On the Use and Abuse of Necessity in the Law of State Responsibility*, 106 AM. J. INT'L L. 447 (2012), who accepts the notion of necessity but concludes that Article 25 does not codify the customary law version of the doctrine. Also, Sloane criticizes the ICJ and ILC for their mutual bootstrapping because the ICJ's key judgment on necessity relied on the ILC Draft Articles, and the Draft Articles relied on the ICJ Judgment. *See id.* at 453 ("This institutional circularity is troubling.").

15. The exact phrase in the Draft Articles is that the prohibited action is "the only way for the State to safeguard an essential Interest . . . "

16. For a lengthy discussion, see Cynthia C. Galvez, *"Necessity," Investor Rights, and State Sovereignty for NAFTA Investment Arbitration*, 46 CORNELL J. INT'L L. 143 (2013).

17. *See* Sarah F. Hill, *The "Necessity Defense" and the Emerging Arbitral Conflict in Its Application to the U.S.-Argentina Bilateral Investment Treaty*, 13 LAW & BUS. REV. AMS. 547, 551 (2007).

18. General Agreement on Tariffs and Trade, Oct. 30, 1947, 61 Stat. A-11, 55 U.N.T.S. 194 [hereinafter cited as GATT].

19. GATT article XX.

with security exceptions, and states that the agreement shall not be construed "to prevent any contracting party from taking any action which it considers necessary for the protection of its essential security interests."[20] Similarly, bilateral investment treaties commonly include exclusions based on the principle of necessity.[21] The U.S.-Poland Bilateral Investment Treaty (BIT), for example, states in Article XII(3) that nothing in the agreement shall "preclude the application by either Party of measures necessary for the maintenance of public order, the fulfillment of its obligations with respect to the maintenance or restoration of international peace or security, or the protection of its own essential security interests."[22] This is typical language for a BIT and is replicated in many other agreements.

Investment disputes involving necessity are frequently litigated in international tribunals and arbitration, and the principle is likely to become even more prominent in investment disputes in the future. When Argentina's economy collapsed after its debt crisis, the government backtracked on legal obligations made to private investors, who then claimed that Argentina's actions violated their rights under bilateral investment treaties.[23] In several arbitration proceedings, Argentina argued that its actions were necessary to vindicate state interests. Indeed, Argentina's necessity arguments were buttressed by the fact that its economic collapse triggered substantial political and social unrest, so its interests were not merely economic in nature. The necessity defense was accepted in some of the arbitrations but rejected in others; some of the decisions were based on Article 25 of the ILC Draft Articles whereas others were based on necessity clauses in the relevant bilateral investment treaties.[24] The result of these decisions is that the necessity defense is increasingly being deployed in the economic context, and that at least some international arbitration panels are coming to accept that an economic situation can qualify as an imperative security situation that necessitates government action in contravention of its preexisting legal obligations.[25]

20. GATT article XXI.

21. *See* Galvez, *supra* note 16, at 147.

22. *See* U.S.-Poland Bilateral Investment Treaty.

23. José E. Alvarez & Kathryn Khamsi, *The Argentine Crisis and Foreign Investors: A Glimpse into the Heart of the Investment Regime*, *in* YEARBOOK ON INTERNATIONAL INVESTMENT LAW & POLICY, 2008–2009 (Karl P. Sauvant ed., 2009).

24. William W. Burke-White & Andreas von Staden, *Private Litigation in a Public Law Sphere: The Standard of Review in Investor-State Arbitrations*, 35 YALE J. INT'L L. 283 (2010).

25. *See, e.g.*, *LG&E Energy Corp. v. The Argentine Republic*, ICSID Case No. ARB/02/1, Decision on Liability, Oct. 3, 2006, 46 I.L.M. 40, 72 (2007).

Arbitration panels hearing necessity claims have effectively balanced the interests of the state against those of the investors, and have asked whether the state action was truly necessary to vindicate the state interest. To some scholars, this suggests a convergence between necessity claims in the investor-state arbitration context and more general proportionality analysis under human rights law.[26] As we will discuss in greater depth in Chapter 5, proportionality review under human rights law requires a determination that the state action was necessary, which is defined as the least restrictive means to achieve the legitimate result. This balancing of interests is inherently utilitarian, because it allows—in some limited circumstances—the infringement of personal liberties in situations where it represents the only legitimate avenue to achieve the social need (as represented by the governmental aim). In the investor-state arbitration context, the utilitarian balancing is even more evident: Argentina argues that the interests of individual investors must give way to a greater social need, that is, to move forward with economic reform and avoid the effects of continued economic collapse. For scholars such as Stone-Sweet, this suggests that the least-restrictive-means test of necessity has migrated from human rights law to the investor-state arbitration context.[27]

III. NECESSITY IN *JUS AD BELLUM* VIOLATIONS

We now turn to the application of the necessity defense in the most controversial arena: incursions of sovereignty and other *jus ad bellum* scenarios. We consider two very different case studies: (1) the construction of the security wall by Israel, which prompted judicial review by both the Israeli Supreme Court and the ICJ; and (2) the military intervention by NATO forces against Serbia in order to stop ethnic cleansing and other human rights violations in Kosovo. In the *Wall* case, the ICJ considered and rejected the necessity defense although the parties did not raise it. In the Kosovo situation, the exact opposite happened: the ICJ heard extensive arguments on necessity, but ultimately rejected the case on jurisdictional grounds and never reached the merits. However, a consideration of these cases provides a roadmap for future claims based on necessity in *jus ad bellum* situations—a disturbing possibility that potentially opens up a third legal category for justifying the use of force, in addition to the classic

26. *See* Alec Stone Sweet, *Investor-State Arbitration: Proportionality's New Frontier*, 4 LAW & ETHICS HUM. RTS. 47 (2010).
27. *Id.*

categories of self-defense under Article 51 of the U.N. Charter and Security Council authorizations for the use of force pursuant to its Chapter VII authority. The question is whether the doctrinal constraints on the necessity doctrine are sufficiently robust that they can prevent the doctrine from overwhelming the general prohibition against the use of force.

The Israeli cabinet authorized construction of a security wall in 2002 in order to stop security threats emanating from the West Bank. Whether the wall achieved its security objectives is a matter of dispute; what is not in dispute is that the wall imposed certain burdens on the individuals and communities whose movements were now restricted by the wall. The case was first heard by the Israeli Supreme Court after litigants argued that military necessity did not justify the construction of the wall along its planned route and that the underlying purpose of the wall was to effectuate an illegal annexation of portions of the occupied territories (the settlements) to make them de facto pieces of Israel.

The Israel Supreme Court concluded that construction of the wall in general could be justified on the basis of "military necessity," though it asserted that the wall's exact route also required justification, and that the needs of the local population should be taken into account.[28] Consequently, the version of the necessity doctrine applied by the Court looked awfully similar to the doctrine of necessity that reigns in human rights law, that is, the least-restrictive-means test, even though the Court by its own terms was a bit unclear whether it was applying international human rights law, the international law of occupation, principles of *jus in bello*, Israeli administrative law, or some motley amalgamation of all four. Indeed, the Court seemed to be suggesting that the result would be the same under all four bodies of law as each requires some assessment of proportionality analysis.[29] Consequently, the Court concluded that the Israeli government could have constructed the wall in a different manner such that it fulfilled its legitimate security objectives while at the same time reducing its burden on the affected communities.

This is a paradigmatic example of the "least-restrictive-means" test and an overall assessment of proportionality analysis as that term is used in human

28. *Beit Sourik Village Council v. The Government of Israel and Commander of the IDF Forces in the West Bank*, The Supreme Court Sitting as the High Court of Justice, HCJ 2056/04 (June 30, 2004).

29. *Id.* at para. 39 ("Indeed, both international law and the fundamental principles of Israeli administrative law recognize proportionality as a standard for balancing between the authority of the military commander in the area and the needs of the local population. Indeed, the principle of proportionality as a standard restricting the power of the military commander is a common thread running through our case law.").

rights law.[30] Consequently, the Court concluded that the "injuries are not proportionate. They can be substantially decreased by an alternate route, either the route presented by the experts of the Council for Peace and Security, or another route set out by the military commander. Such an alternate route exists. It is not a figment of the imagination. It was presented before us."[31]

In evaluating the legality of the wall, the ICJ reached the same conclusion—that the route of the wall was unjustified by the concept of necessity—but through a different doctrinal route.[32] The ICJ first considered and rejected the argument that the security wall was justified under human rights law as a restriction "necessary to protect national security, public order, public health or morals or the rights and freedoms of others" as stated by Article 12 of the International Covenant on Civil and Political Rights (ICCPR). It then considered the defense of necessity as articulated in customary international law and Article 25 of the draft ILC Articles on State Responsibility, even though the litigants in the case had not pressed the court to decide that question in its advisory opinion.

In applying the defense of necessity under customary law, the ICJ noted that it only applied in exceptional circumstances (or "strictly defined conditions") that were substantially constrained by the doctrine.[33] The Court applied the basic standard that it had previously applied in the Hungary-Slovakia dispute over the Gabčikovo-Nagymaros Project, and referenced the ILC Draft Articles standard that the state measure must be the "only way for the state to safeguard an essential interest against a grave and imminent peril."[34] The Court concluded that this standard was not met since the wall's route was not the *only* way for Israel to safeguard its legitimate interests, and a different, presumably less injurious route, could have been used.

The Court was clear that there was a legitimate security interest here; the crux of the dispute was the necessity of the planned response and whether reasonable alternatives might have existed.[35] Like the criminal law standard

30. For the present analysis, we use the terms "least-restrictive-means" and "least-harmful-means" interchangeably, although they suggest subtle differences. Both expressions share a common intuition: that the government should be required to select the course of action that advances its legitimate interests while causing the fewest infringements on third party rights and interests.

31. *Id.* para. 61.

32. *See Legal Consequences of the Construction of a Wall in the Occupied Palestinian Territory*, ICJ Advisory Opinion (July 9, 2004).

33. *Id.* para. 140.

34. *Id.*

35. *Id.* para. 141 ("The fact remains that Israel has to face numerous indiscriminate and deadly acts of violence against its civilian population. It has the right, and indeed the duty, to respond in order to protect the life of its citizens. The measures taken are bound nonetheless to remain in conformity with applicable international law.")

of "unavoidability" that we will discuss in Chapter 6, the word "only" in the ILC Draft Articles standard is designed to constrain the application of the necessity defense to situations where no other legitimate choice presents itself to the State. Just as Argentina could not claim (according to some arbitrators) that its economic reforms were the *only* means of dealing with its economic crisis, so too Israel could not argue that it had no other choice but to erect the security barrier along the path that it had chosen.

The striking aspect of the Israeli and ICJ opinions is the similarity of their conclusions given that they were evaluating necessity under different bodies of law. Whereas the Israeli Court was engaged in proportionality review under international or Israeli law (or both), the ICJ in the sections we just analyzed was applying necessity as a general defense to violations of public international law. The two doctrines are arguably different, although they share the same conceptual constraints to limit their application: the requirement that the State have no other alternative at its disposal to pursue its legitimate state aim. In both cases, the arguments of the Israeli government were doomed because the courts remained unconvinced that the route of the wall was the only alternative. However, this leaves open the possibility that the wall—constructed, sited, and managed in a different manner—could be permissible under international law if it effectively mitigated the consequences to the local population.

There is, though, profound uncertainty over whether these analyses require that the state action be justified on utilitarian grounds. From the perspective of the proportionality analysis conducted by the Israeli Supreme Court, it seems clear that the doctrine requires a utilitarian balancing, because the individual interests of the affected individuals must be outweighed by the legitimate needs of the greater community (as represented by the legitimate government aim). Is the same true of the necessity defense under Article 25 of the ILC Draft Articles as applied by the ICJ? This is not clear at all, since in this case the necessity defense is not balancing the needs of the community against the needs of the *individuals* whose rights are being violated. In the context of Article 25, the doctrine is considering the interests of one State under international law (Israel) as against other States whose interests will be impacted by the violations of international prohibition performed by the State in question. This is not a question of balancing away the needs of the individual in service of the needs of the community. Rather, it is a question of exempting one State under international law from fulfilling its obligations toward other nation-states. Does this require a balancing of interests? And if so, how would that balancing be performed or conceptualized? This demonstrates the difficulty of taking the notion of necessity from one legal context and applying it in another.

We will now consider the possibility of using the necessity defense as a legal justification for military force in so-called humanitarian interventions. After the NATO intervention in Kosovo, the government of Serbia commenced a proceeding at the ICJ against Belgium for its role in the NATO-led coalition.[36] Belgium was in a difficult spot, legally speaking, since the intervention was neither a classic case of self-defense nor authorized by a Security Council resolution. In the absence of a traditional justification for the use of force under *jus ad bellum*, some viewed the intervention as illegal full stop, while others (including Cassese) concluded that the attacks were illegal but legitimate.[37] In subsequent years, scholars and activists have argued that a Responsibility to Protect (RTP) provided a legal or moral justification for the intervention, though at the time of the ICJ proceedings the RTP movement was undeveloped and not the fully fledged doctrine that it is today.[38]

Consequently, the Belgian legal representative argued that Belgium's actions, which would otherwise constitute a violation of *jus ad bellum*, were justified by the doctrine of necessity. Specifically, the Belgian government proposed a balancing test to evaluate the appropriateness of the action under the doctrine of necessity: the violation of Serbian sovereignty (and the prohibition against the use of force contained in Article 2(4) of the U.N. Charter) was necessary because it was the only way of avoiding an even greater evil: the systematic human rights abuses of the innocent civilians who were being killed on the ground by the ethnic cleansing.[39] This argument involved a balancing of interests but not a strict balancing of particular outcomes. In other words, the argument was not a bare balancing of lives in the sense that the bombing would save more lives than would be killed during the military campaign. Rather, the balancing was far more abstract because it involved the balancing of two particular norms under international law: the protection of sovereignty and the protection of human

36. *See Legality of Use of Force (Yugoslavia. v. Belgium)*, Request for the Indication of Provisional Measures, 1999 I.C.J. 124.

37. *See* Antonio Cassese, Ex iniuria ius oritor, *Are We Moving Towards International Legitimation of Forcible Humanitarian Countermeasures in the World Community?*, 10 EUR. J. INT'L L. 23 (1999) ("this particular instance of breach of international law may gradually lead to the crystallization of a general rule of international law authorizing armed countermeasures for the exclusive purpose of putting an end to large-scale atrocities amounting to crimes against humanity and constituting a threat to the peace"). *Cf.* Thomas Franck, *Lessons of Kosovo*, 93 AM. J. INT'L L. 857–60 (1999).

38. *See* INTERNATIONAL COMMISSION ON INTERVENTION AND STATE SOVEREIGNTY, THE RESPONSIBILITY TO PROTECT (2001).

39. *See* Oral Pleadings of Rusen Ergec in *Yugoslavia v. Belgium, available at* http://www.icj-cij.org/docket/files/105/4515.pdf.

rights.[40] Belgium was arguing that when the only way to stop a massive violation of human rights is to infringe upon the sovereignty of the territorial State, then the infringement would be justified by the doctrine of necessity.[41] It is hard to interpret whether this argument is broadly utilitarian or deontological. In one sense it is utilitarian because it suggests that the overall outcome is the lesser of two evils,[42] but in another sense the argument is deontological because the reason that human rights are given moral priority in the argument is presumably because of some underlying account of human dignity. How these two elements mix together is uncertain and under-theorized in the legal arguments.

The ICJ never resolved the arguments on the merits because the proceedings were dismissed on jurisdictional grounds. However, if the ICJ had considered the merits and applied the same analysis as it did in the *Wall Opinion* and the *Gabčikovo-Nagymaros* dispute between Hungary and Slovakia, the Belgium necessity argument would have faced substantial legal obstacles. First, the classic description of the doctrine in Article 25 of the Draft Articles requires that the State act to secure an essential security interest of the State. That is what justifies an economic regulation (with regard to Argentina), an ecological decision (with regard to Hungary), or a security barrier (with regard to Israel). Each action could be—in theory—necessary to preserve the interests of the State. In the case of Belgium, however, it was intervening along with NATO to secure a vital interest of an outside group of people, that is, the ethnic Albanians in Kosovo who were subject to attack by pro-Serbian forces. If the Belgium government was intervening on self-interested grounds to protect Belgian nationals, that would have easily constituted a vital state interest, but in this case Belgium was intervening altruistically in support of someone else's interests. Ironically the necessity defense as formulated by the ILC Draft Articles does not provide any exculpation for such lofty intentions. That seems backward, but that is how the provision is written.

Could one stretch the inquiry in order to locate an essential interest in Belgium's participation in the NATO intervention? This is difficult to do

40. *Id.* ("A state of necessity is the cause which justifies the violation of a binding rule in order to safeguard, in face of grave and imminent peril, values which are higher than those protected by the rule which has been breached.").

41. *Id.* ("What are the higher values which this intervention attempts to safeguard? They are rights of *jus cogens*.").

42. *Id.* ("And the final element of a state of necessity, I almost forgot, is that the acts must be proportionate; the intervention must be proportional to the threat. The intervention is wholly in proportion to the gravity of the peril; it is limited to aerial bombardments directed solely and exclusively against the war machine of the aggressor and against its military-industrial complex.").

because the whole point of humanitarian intervention is to intervene for *humanitarian* reasons. However, there are plausible legal arguments that can be made here. In the Kosovo intervention, lawyers working in the Clinton administration faced a similar problem, albeit one stemming from U.S. domestic law. Under standard interpretations of Article II of the U.S. Constitution, it is generally assumed that as commander in chief of the military the president has the responsibility and authority to direct military forces to protect essential U.S. interests. Of course, this requires locating a particular national interest in every military intervention authorized unilaterally by the president's Article II authority (as opposed to authorized concurrently with congressional approval). In the case of Kosovo, the Office of Legal Counsel (OLC) produced a memo concluding that the Kosovo operation implicated U.S. national security interests because it was necessary for regional security and taken pursuant to a regional security arrangement—NATO—that is essential to U.S. national security.[43] In other words, participation in NATO led operations is part and parcel with the *protection* offered by the NATO arrangement, such that every aspect of NATO operations (even ones performed for the benefit of other nations) are by logical implication actions in furtherance (albeit in some remote way) of U.S. national security interests.

Furthermore, one could also argue that the military intervention was necessary to effectuate relevant Security Council resolutions regarding the Balkans. This too arguably implicates U.S. national security interests; not the underlying human rights violations per se but the legitimacy and effectiveness of the Security Council resolutions taken in *response* to those human rights violations are an issue of national interest for the United States. If the Security Council and its enforcement regime were undermined, this would harm U.S. national security interests. This national security interest is remote, hypothetical, and speculative, but it is true that a strong and effective Security Council is in the national interest of its members.

A similar dilemma arose for the Obama administration during the Libya operation. Congress did not authorize that action, and the Obama administration relied on his Article II commander-in-chief authority. Once again,

43. *See Authorization for Continuing Hostilities in Kosovo*, Memorandum Opinion for the Attorney General, 24 Op. O.L.C. 327 (2000) ("the President ordered a series of air strikes in the Federal Republic of Yugoslavia 'to demonstrate the seriousness of NATO's purpose so that the Serbian leaders understand the imperative of reversing course; to deter an even bloodier offensive against innocent civilians in Kosovo; and, if necessary, to seriously damage the Serbian military's capacity to harm the people of Kosovo.'") (internal citations omitted).

the OLC produced an opinion that heavily emphasized the U.S. interest in vindicating Security Council resolutions.[44] However, the argument for a national security interest in Libya was arguably stronger than it was in Kosovo, since the Security Council authorized the Libya intervention in accordance with the Council's Chapter VII authority to restore international peace and security, whereas the relevant resolutions regarding Kosovo fell far short of authorizing military action. But even in the case of Libya, the argument for a U.S. national interest required leveraging the legitimacy of the U.N. security arrangement as a basis for legitimizing presidential action. A similar argument could be made in an international context in order to squeeze a humanitarian intervention into the doctrine of necessity, though it is unclear how the ICJ would react to this argument if it ever reached the merits of a dispute. It would require asserting that Belgium, or some other intervening State, is facing a grave or imminent peril to its national interest if Security Council authorizations or NATO arrangements are ignored or rendered impotent. Although these are clearly grave *interests* in the broadest sense, it is unclear if they are *imminent* in nature.

There is, however, a much more ambitious conceptual argument that requires changing the focus of the discussion from the individual state that claims necessity to the international community as a whole that has collectively performed the intervention. If one asks why the international community has engaged in the intervention, then the previous argument becomes much more stable. The international community *as a whole* has a legitimate interest in securing the safety and security of all human beings, which is precisely why the international community has jurisdiction to prosecute crimes against humanity. Since all human beings enjoy inalienable rights that are protected and ensured by international law, their protection falls naturally to the international community that has an inherent interest in seeing the vindication of those rights.[45] It is humanity writ large working to protect humanity writ large.

Although the structure of this argument is conceptually sound and plausible from the perspective of moral theory, it is difficult to frame the argument in terms that are cognizable under current public international

44. *See Authority to Use Military Force in Libya*, Memorandum for the Attorney General (Apr. 1, 2011) ("The President explained in his March 21, 2011 report to Congress that the use of military force in Libya serves important U.S. interests in preventing instability in the Middle East and preserving the credibility and effectiveness of the United Nations Security Council.").

45. There are echoes of this argument in Belgium's oral pleadings to the ICJ when it stated: "Where is the imminent peril, the grave and imminent peril? There it was—no doubt about it—at the time of the armed intervention; there it is still, the humanitarian catastrophe recorded in the resolutions of the Security Council—an impending

law. Broadly speaking, the international law regulation of *jus ad bellum* asks whether a particular State—not the international community at large—has a legitimate reason for launching a military attack. And the necessity doctrine allows the State to exempt itself from these rules on occasions where the State needs to protect an essential state interest. But the interests of humanity writ large fall outside of the Westphalian conception of state interests that dominates the current structure of international law. The one situation when public international law is comfortable with speaking vaguely about the international community is when the Security Council authorizes military force, and individual States enforce those resolutions; in that situation it is clear that the State is acting not to enforce its own interests but rather to enforce the dictates of the international community as represented by the Security Council. But the necessity doctrine falls well outside of this narrow exception to the Westphalian conception of States as the primary unit of analysis. So appealing to the "essential interests" of the international community will not work unless the very foundations of the necessity doctrine are reformulated in substantial ways.

The last issue is whether the necessity doctrine should be conceptualized as a justification or excuse. Based on its application in previous situations, the answer is unclear.[46] Most scholars are inclined to think and talk of necessity as a justification, although this is not necessarily the only way of conceptualizing it. One reason for the assumption is that States are usually justified or not in their putative breaches of international law, and to speak of States being excused for their behavior sounds awkward. An excuse would entail that the act is wrongful but the State is not *culpable* for the violation, but what does culpability mean when the actor is a nation-state (as opposed to an individual)? Westphalian international law has no conception of a State's culpability, so the language of justification usually prevails.[47]

However, recently some scholars have asked whether the language of excuse would be helpful for international lawyers.[48] The doctrine could

peril." The Belgium representative was deliberately vague regarding the legitimate state interest prong of the standard.

46. *See* Sloane, *supra* note 14, at 455 ("Whether these publicists understood necessity as a justification or an excuse is unclear, in all likelihood because this distinction, though routinely drawn today, is a comparatively modern legal development.").

47. *See* Gabriella Blum, *The Crime and Punishment of States*, 38 Yale J. Int'l L. 57 (2013).

48. *See* George P. Fletcher & Jens David Ohlin, Defending Humanity: When Force Is Justified and Why (2008); Vaughan Lowe, *Precluding Wrongfulness or Responsibility: A Plea for Excuses*, 10 Eur. J. Int'l L. 405 (1999).

allow a State to escape the consequences of its violation (such as liability at the ICJ or reparations) but still retain the conclusion that the State's actions were, in some way, wrongful. This would be helpful, for example, in evaluating cases of reasonable mistakes regarding self-defense (so-called imperfect self-defense) that should be excused but not justified.[49] There are other scenarios where the language of excuse might provide a third category in-between "justified" and "not justified" when evaluating State behavior.

Second, there is disagreement in the criminal law literature over whether necessity is a justification or an excuse.[50] It is a justification if it requires a balancing of evils, but what of situations where the defendant is faced with an exigent threat from the environment, but he does not select the lesser of two evils? If the threat emanates from a third party, the situation is classified as one of duress and an excuse is conferred. Why not allow a similar excuse in necessity-type situations? Some jurisdictions, following this logic, have instituted two separate necessity defenses in their criminal law, one a justification and the other an excuse.[51] Justified necessity requires that the defendant selected the lesser of two evils, whereas excused necessity does not.[52] The same distinction could, in theory, be imported into public international law so that States could be justified or excused when they act in response to a state of necessity, depending on whether the action meets the balancing-of-evils requirement. The concept of excused necessity would give public international law a category for States who could not be expected to have acted otherwise, but whose behavior did not meet the requirements of the utilitarian balancing test. This result might be better than the current uncertainty over whether necessity (as codified by the ILC Draft Articles) requires a balancing test or not.

49. *See* Francisco Munoz Conde, *Putative Self-Defense: A Borderline Case between Justification and Excuse*, 11 New Crim. L. Rev. 590 (2008).

50. *See* Youngjae Lee, *The Defense of Necessity and Powers of the Government*, 3 Crim. L. & Phil. 133 (2008).

51. Strafgesetzbuch [StGB] [Penal Code] May 15, 1871, Reichsgesetzblatt [RGBl] 583, §§ 34–35 (F.R.G.) translated in 1 Gerold Harfst & Otoo A. Schmidt, German Criminal Law (1989).

52. For example, the German Penal Code provision on justified necessity states: "A person who, faced with an imminent danger to life, limb, freedom, honour, property or another legal interest which cannot otherwise be averted, commits an act to avert the danger from himself or another, does not act unlawfully, if, upon weighing the conflicting interests, in particular the affected legal interests and the degree of the danger facing them, the protected interest substantially outweighs the one interfered with. This shall apply only if and to the extent that the act committed is an adequate means to avert the danger" (Michael Bohlander trans.).

IV. NECESSITY AS A COMPONENT OF SELF-DEFENSE

In this final section, we consider necessity as one component of national self-defense. Originally self-defense and necessity were not separate defenses under international law. The nineteenth-century treatise writers often spoke of self-defense, using terms such as "self-preservation" and the "necessity of self-preservation."[53] Furthermore, one of the most famous descriptions of the doctrine of self-defense uses the language of necessity to explain why a State should be allowed to use military force that infringes upon the sovereignty of another State. In the *Caroline* Affair, U.S. secretary of state Daniel Webster explained the U.S. view of the doctrine of self-defense in the following terms: the threat had to be "instant, overwhelming, leaving no choice of means, and no moment of deliberation." This formulation focused on the necessity of using force as a means of neutralizing the threat against the State's security. Although necessity is not the only criterion for self-defense, even under the Webster standard, it certainly takes center stage in his formulation that requires an instant and overwhelming threat.

It is no surprise that the Webster formulation focuses on necessity since, as indicated above, the right of self-defense under national law was often referred to using the language of necessity. The connection between necessity and self-defense—and the centrality of necessity as one essential component of self-defense—becomes even clearer in domestic legal systems. Germany, for example, uses the phrase "*Notwehr*" in its penal code to denote self-defense, which literally translates into the phrase "necessary defense."[54] If physical force is not truly necessary as a means of averting the threat, then the defender's exercise of defensive force can never be justified under either criminal or international law. That is the key element of the Webster formulation—that the situation leaves "no choice of means." If the responding state has nonmilitary means at its disposal to avert the threat, then defensive force is not justified.

Part of the problem with understanding necessity as an element of self-defense is that it is closely linked to other major requirements of self-defense: imminence and proportionality. Although separating necessity,

53. *See, e.g.*, HENRY WHEATON, ELEMENTS OF INTERNATIONAL LAW 90 (5th ed. 1916) (1836).

54. *See* Penal Code Section 32 ("(1) Wer eine Tat begeht, die durch Notwehr geboten ist, handelt nicht rechtswidrig. (2) Notwehr ist die Verteidigung, die erforderlich ist, um einen gegenwärtigen rechtswidrigen Angriff von sich oder einem anderen abzuwenden.").

imminence, and proportionality is hard to do, it is possible after sustained reflection.[55] The dividing line between necessity and imminence is complicated because the imminence requirement demands that the threat be imminent—which seems to be the time pressure that Webster is referring to. So is imminence simply *part* of the necessity requirement? Well, not exactly. There are two separate temporal windows that are relevant, and they should not be conflated. The first window is the time between the moment of decision and the future attack that will cause harm to the State's interest. That is the nature of imminence. The second is the time between the moment of decision and when action must be taken in order to deflect the threat. Usually these two moments coincide. For example, if the tanks and planes are rushing toward the border right now, the defending state must act now to repel the attack and perhaps even destroy the troops that stay on the invader's side of the border. However, in theory it is possible to conceive of a situation where the two elements slip apart. Imagine one where the attack is coming in the future, but the last chance for the defending State to stop the attack is right now. The imminence requirement measures the time until the attack is consummated; the necessity requirement measures the time between the moment of action and the last chance to stop the threat. This possibility has given rise to the controversial doctrine of preemptive (or even preventive) war, or the idea that action is required now to stop a future threat.[56]

Of course, both preemptive force and preventive force are controversial doctrines. In order to determine whether they are applicable under current rules of *jus ad bellum*, one would need to understand the interplay between the necessity and imminence requirements. If imminence is an additional constraint on defensive force over and above the necessity requirement, then preventive war is illegal, because it would satisfy the necessity requirement but not the imminence requirement. The only way to get around this conclusion is to subordinate the imminence requirement to the necessity requirement and conclude that the former element does not need to be met if the latter element is satisfied.

55. *See, e.g.*, David Kretzmer, *The Inherent Right to Self Defence and Proportionality in* Jus ad Bellum, 24 Euro. J. Int'l L. 235, 273 (2013) ("Necessity in this context implies that the victim state has unsuccessfully tried non-forcible measures to persuade the host state to stop the activities directed against it by the non-state actors acting in that state's territory, and that, given the pattern of attacks, it is left with no other effective way to defend itself.").

56. *See, e.g.*, Robert J. Delahunty & John Yoo, *The Bush Doctrine: Can Preventive War Be Justified?*, 21 Harv. J.L. & Pub. Pol'y 843, 851 (2009) ("Demanding a standard for lawful anticipatory self-defense that is all but impossible to meet makes little sense now, at least in cases when preventive action may be necessary to forestall a foreseeable, albeit not imminent, threat from a state or group that is openly committed to the mass killing of civilians.").

In a way, that is precisely what proponents of preventive war argue for. They are suggesting that the imminence requirement should give way to the necessity requirement. The best way of understanding this argument is that imminence should be entirely replaced with a new standard of "immediate necessity."[57] That would entail that force is legitimate if it is immediately necessary to use force at the moment in time when force is deployed, regardless of whether the triggering threat is manifest, imminent, or distant. According to this view, the relevant time period is the one measured by the concept of necessity, not that measured by imminence, so the best result is to reform or abandon the imminence requirement in favor of a new requirement of immediate necessity.

Sometimes lawyers appeal to immediate necessity without actually using these words. For example, U.S. Attorney General Eric Holder described the Obama administration's view of self-defense in a major speech at Northwestern University that focused on the administration's policy regarding targeted killings.[58] The speech focused on the determinations that the administration makes regarding when it is appropriate to use lethal force against a terrorist threat, including if the threat is an American citizen. The killing of U.S. citizen Anwar al-Awlaki had prompted the administration to more explicitly outline its legal views and policy standards as to how it selects targets and conducts strikes against them.

Holder noted that the United States launches military strikes against terrorist targets, including U.S. citizens abroad, that represent an imminent threat to the United States. However, Holder then went on to argue that in some circumstances, the United States will be unable to wait until the last possible moment to deploy force against the target—doing something might be too late in order to alleviate the threat.[59] In those situations, the use of defensive force must be deployed earlier because the earlier moment in time represents the last, best chance that the U.S. military has to stop the threat.[60] Speaking hypothetically, one could very well imagine

57. The phrase "immediately necessary" appears in the U.S. Model Penal Code provision on self-defense, § 3.04(1).

58. Eric Holder, Attorney General, Address at Northwestern Law School (Mar. 5, 2012), *available at* http://www.justice.gov/opa/speech/attorney-general-eric-holder-speaks-northwestern-university-school-law.

59. *See id.* ("The evaluation of whether an individual presents an 'imminent threat' incorporates considerations of the relevant window of opportunity to act, the possible harm that missing the window would cause to civilians, and the likelihood of heading off future disastrous attacks against the United States.").

60. *Id.* ("Given these facts, the Constitution does not require the President to delay action until some theoretical end-stage of planning—when the precise time, place, and manner of an attack become clear. Such a requirement would create an unacceptably high risk that our efforts would fail, and that Americans would be killed.").

a terrorist who is plotting a future attack, but the terrorist is only visible for a brief moment before he goes into hiding again.[61] Although the attack might be a month or more away, it may nonetheless be the case that the defensive force must be deployed now or never. The emergence of the terrorist provides the one moment when defensive force can effectively stop the attack; waiting until the attack is closer to fruition will mean giving up the most reasonable chance to stop it. Holder was making the point that the United States does not wait until the attack is on the horizon; if defensive force is necessary *now*, the United States acts.[62]

We take no position right now regarding the merits of this position under current principles of self-defense and *jus ad bellum*. The more important point is a conceptual conclusion regarding the relationship between imminence and necessity. In the prior definition of imminence, Holder did not simply offer a new definition of imminence—he jettisoned imminence entirely in favor of a new concept of immediate necessity. What he described was not a new definition at all but rather a *replacement* for imminence. Why the intellectual dishonesty? As a matter of legal advocacy, one can understand the impulse behind Holder's description. Imminence remains, and is likely to remain, a central component of the legal doctrine of self-defense. Although there have been proposals to eliminate imminence, they have not garnered enough support in the international community to constitute the *opinio juris* for a diverging norm of customary law.[63] Consequently, participants in the international system are stuck with imminence whether they like it or not. For advocates, the only viable solution is to "redefine" imminence in a more self-serving way rather than argue—against all realistic hope—that imminence should be dropped in favor of immediate necessity.

We now turn to the concept of proportionality, in which the relationship between that concept and necessity is similarly vexed. Proportionality in *jus ad bellum* requires that the war aim of the defending party be proportional to the nature of the threat that the party needs to advert or respond to. So, for example, the relatively uncontroversial case of the

61. *Id.* ("As we learned on 9/11, al Qaeda has demonstrated the ability to strike with little or no notice—and to cause devastating casualties. Its leaders are continually planning attacks against the United States, and they do not behave like a traditional military—wearing uniforms, carrying arms openly, or massing forces in preparation for an attack.").

62. *Id.*

63. For a discussion, see CHRISTINE D. GRAY, INTERNATIONAL LAW AND THE USE OF FORCE 212 (2008) ("The opposition by many states to Operation Iraqi Freedom (which started in March 2003) made it clear that they were not willing to accept pre-emptive self-defence as a legal basis for that particular action.").

Falkland Islands is often used to examine the issue. The Argentinian government (under the direction of the ruling generals) took control over the Falkland Islands and asserted Argentinian sovereignty over them. Britain responded by dispatching the Royal Navy and engaging in a naval battle with Argentina over the islands. Now, if we assume for the sake of argument that Britain's claim to the islands was legitimate under international law, it was clearly proportionate to engage in a naval campaign to defeat the Argentinian forces that were stationed at the Falkland Islands.[64] Doing so allowed British forces to retake the islands and station troops there for the future protection of the Falkland Islands citizens. However, had Britain then launched a ground assault against the Argentinian homeland in order to completely destroy its military capabilities and oust the ruling generals from their control over its government, this would have been a far different matter. Arguably, the defensive force in that instance would not have been proportional to the nature of the threat faced by Britain. The threat to British sovereignty imposed by the illegal annexation of the Falkland Islands triggered a proportionate response against the islands themselves and the military force surrounding them, but a broader campaign against Argentina proper would have constituted a disproportionate response.

The difficulty here is that one can express the same intuition using the language of necessity. Would it really be *necessary* for Britain to launch a ground invasion against Argentina's homeland? Presumably it was not necessary to do so. It was gratuitous. It went too far.[65] This intuition has led some to suggest that proportionality and necessity are not really distinct elements of *jus ad bellum* at all, but rather proportionality is one subset of necessity. According to this view, if one understood the role that necessity plays in *jus ad bellum*, one could dispense with the troubling and vague talk of proportionality altogether and limit the analysis to necessity. This would have added benefits since these discussions always risk confusing *jus ad bellum* proportionality with *jus in bello* proportionality. If we could eliminate *jus ad bellum* proportionality and replace it with a rich notion of necessity, there would be one less version of proportionality around to confuse us.

If this is the case, why do proportionality and necessity persist as distinct elements of the doctrine of *jus ad bellum*, given their close conceptual

64. *See* Jeff McMahan, *What Rights May Be Defended by Means of War?*, *in* The Morality of Defensive War 115, 136 (Cecile Fabre & Seth Lazar eds., 2014) (killing 650 Argentine combatants was proportionate, but killing 100,000 would not have been).

65. *Cf.* Antonio Cassese, International Law 355 (2d ed., 2005).

connection? There is a point to separating them and keeping them as distinct elements of the doctrine, because it helps structure the analysis in a clear way. One *could* conflate them under the rubric of necessity, but it might be confusing to do so. Instead, necessity as the term is deployed in *jus ad bellum* asks a simpler, flatter question: Was it necessary to use defensive force *at all* or was a nonmilitary recourse possible as a solution to the conflict?[66] Once that question is answered in the affirmative, the analysis proceeds to the proportionality question, that is, whether the nature of the military aim was proportional to the threat faced by the defending state. These are two logically distinct inquiries.

Of course, this notion of necessity is very limited. It is necessity in the recourse to force only. If we adopt a broader and richer notion of necessity, we could subsume both imminence and proportionality under the rubric of necessity and produce a one-stop-shopping test for resolving claims regarding *jus ad bellum*. But this would not necessarily be preferable. Part of the goal of legal inquiry is to separate out a standard into its component parts so that each one can be identified and then applied in an orderly way. This allows for more transparent decision-making; multiple layers in the analysis facilitate discussions regarding each of the steps. If everything is conflated into a single, one-step notion of necessity, it is hard to have a meaningful debate about what is truly necessary when a State engages in defensive force.

As it stands, the current doctrine proceeds in a number of steps. First, the doctrine asks whether the State faces an unlawful attack or similar infringement of its sovereignty. Next, it asks whether the attack is imminent. Then, it asks whether defensive force in general is necessary to stop the threat. Finally, the test asks whether the specific goal of the defender's military operations is proportional to the threat faced by the victim of the aggressor. By proceeding along these steps, the doctrine allows each to be considered in isolation and allows for an independent assessment of whether the facts meet the standard. Subsuming all of these questions under a wider notion of necessity would be conceptually coherent but not necessarily conducive to better legal reasoning. In this respect, the current legal doctrine does a relatively good job of structuring the analysis in a way that promotes transparent analysis.

However, there is still one area of the positive law that remains underexplored in the doctrine, and that is the issue that was highlighted in the previous chapter: the degree of risk that the attacking force must accept

66. *See* Kretzmer, *supra* note 55, at 239 (necessity in the resort to force).

when determining whether military intervention is truly necessary. As we explained in the previous chapter, this determination of necessity requires canvassing the range of possible actions and determining whether there exists an alternative plan of action, other than the contemplated use of force, that will achieve the State's legitimate goal of protecting itself. For example, if the State could defend itself through a non-lethal cyber-operation rather than a kinetic military campaign, then the military force would not be, all things considered, necessary.[67] In evaluating these alternatives, we must consider the risks inherent in the other approaches. What if, for example, the State could forgo the contemplated military action, but doing so might be incredibly risky, and could result in the state's destruction if the nonmilitary option fails. This seems like an inappropriate burden to place on the attacking force, especially if there is only time to pursue one course of action (rather than going down the list and trying each one). On the other hand, it is almost always less risky for the State to launch a military assault rather than selecting nonmilitary options, and if we allow a de minimis risk to negate the legal requirement to pursue nonmilitary options, then the necessity requirement effectively collapses and loses all normative bite. This suggests that the law must require (in order to stay relevant) that States accept some level of intermediate or *reasonable* risk when fulfilling their obligation to exhaust nonmilitary options first before resorting to defensive force. Unfortunately, the positive legal doctrine does not offer much guidance on what constitutes a reasonable risk in this context, in part because international tribunals rarely litigate use-of-force disputes and *jus ad bellum* issues.

Recently, the U.S. government has asserted—and exercised—the right to use defensive force extraterritorially against a non-state actor located on foreign soil.[68] Recent examples might include the Navy Seals raid against Osama Bin Laden's compound in Pakistan, or the use of force by multiple countries against ISIS targets located on the sovereign territory of Syria. In these situations, the U.S. and French governments have asserted that the right of self-defense justifies the military action because the host state is either unwilling or unable to resolve the threat itself.[69] In contrast, several

67. For a similar argument, see Duncan B. Hollis, *Re-thinking the Boundaries of Law in Cyberspace: A Duty to Hack?*, *in* CYBER WAR: LAW & ETHICS FOR VIRTUAL CONFLICTS 129 (J. Ohlin, C. Finkelstein & K. Govern eds., 2015).

68. See Brian Egan, U.S. State Department Legal Advisor, *International Law, Legal Diplomacy, and the Counter-ISIL Campaign*, Address at the American Society of International Law Annual Meeting (April 1, 2016).

69. *Id.* ("Upon commencing air strikes against ISIL in Syria in September 2014, the United States submitted a letter to the U.N. Security Council explaining the international legal basis for our use of force in Syria in accordance with Article 51 of the U.N.

scholars have asserted that defensive force under these circumstances would be illegal because it violates Article 2(4) of the U.N. Charter and would not be justified by national self-defense under Article 51.[70]

The legal discussions surrounding the "unwilling and unable" test are often mangled. The important thing to understand is that the test is not a new doctrine at all. Rather, it is simply an application of the necessity requirement for the use of self-defense.[71] In these circumstances, the proponents of the use of force are conceding that force is not permitted if the host state is willing or able to resolve the threat; in that case, external intervention would be unnecessary and therefore illegal. If, on the contrary, the host state is unwilling or unable, the foreign state may claim that the necessity requirement is fulfilled. This is a straightforward application of necessity as a constraint, though some legal scholars might be confused into thinking that the argument involves necessity as a license. The confusion stems from the fact that the state claiming the right to use defensive force is making a controversial claim that is highly contested under international law. But the fact that the claim is contested does not turn this into an example of necessity as an exception from basic principles of *jus ad bellum*. It is still necessity operating as a constraint on the exercise of defensive force.

The real dispute here is less about the necessity requirement and more about the attribution requirement. Under one conception of self-defense, the right to use self-defense is only triggered if the threatened attack can be attributed to the state whose sovereignty will be violated by the defensive force. In the case of using defensive force against ISIS targets in Syria, the ISIS attacks cannot be attributed to Syria because Syria has no control over ISIS. Consequently, the right to use defensive force against ISIS provides no justification for violating the sovereignty of Syria. Under a competing

Charter. As the letter explained, Iraq had made clear it was facing a serious threat of continuing attacks from ISIL coming out of safe havens in Syria and had requested that the United States lead international efforts to strike ISIL in Syria. Consistent with the inherent right of individual and collective self-defense, the United States initiated necessary and proportionate actions in Syria against ISIL. The letter also articulated the United States' position that Syria was unable or unwilling to effectively confront the threat that ISIL posed to Iraq, the United States, and our partners and allies.").

70. *See* Mary Ellen O'Connell, *Dangerous Departures*, 107 AM. J. INT'L L. 380, 383 (2013). *See also* Tom Ruys, 'ARMED ATTACK' AND ARTICLE 51 OF THE UN CHARTER 454-55 (2010) (discussing possibility of recent state practice and opinio juris constituting a "new departure for the interpretation of Article 51"); Kevin Jon Heller, *The Absence of Practice Supporting the "Unwilling or Unable" Test*, OPINIO JURIS (Feb. 17, 2015).

71. For more discussion of this point, see Marty Lederman, *ASIL Speech by State Legal Adviser Egan on international law and the use of force against ISIL*, JUST SECURITY (April 4, 2016).

conception of self-defense, this attribution requirement is not necessary. One argument in favor of abolishing the attribution requirement is that the text of Article 51 of the U.N. Charter says that the right of self-defense applies when an "armed attack occurs" without specifying *who* is responsible for the original attack. But there are competing considerations, including a purely conceptual argument that there must be a one-to-one correspondence between the source of the threat and the sovereignty violation that is justified by self-defense. The dispute over the "unwilling or unable" doctrine really boils down to a dispute over collateral consequences under *jus ad bellum*. Does the justification for using defensive force against a non-state actor provide a justification for the collateral consequence of also violating the sovereignty of the host state on whose territory the non-state actor is located? In this chapter we will not resolve this *jus ad bellum* controversy, which would also require us to determine whether crossing the border of a state to militarily engage a non-state actor, without directly engaging military assets of the host state, constitutes a sovereignty violation that requires justification under the doctrine of self-defense. For the purpose of this chapter, the more important conclusion is that the entire "unwilling and unable" doctrine—if it exists under international law—is a constraint on the use of defensive force because it acts as an application of the necessity requirement in self-defense cases.

V. CONCLUSION

In this chapter we have defended a conception of necessity in *jus ad bellum* that shows the different uses the doctrine takes in different contexts. The power of the necessity defense is undeniable in the law of state responsibility: it creates a state of exception that allows a State to escape the consequences of violating a rule of international law. The greatest difficulty for the doctrine stems from the *nature* of the exculpation—a question that is generally ignored by mainstream public international law. Does the state of necessity justify the State's behavior, or simply excuse it? In the context of self-defense, the State's behavior is clearly justified, but in that case necessity is only playing a small role in the overall structure of the exculpation. In the context of necessity, as the term is used in the ILC Draft Articles on State Responsibility, the question is not so clear.

The concept of necessity could be understood as a justification based on utilitarian balancing, or it could be an excuse due to an autonomy-reducing exigent circumstance that places the State in an impossible situation for which the law cannot reasonably demand compliance. On a conceptual level both are coherent possibilities, though the language of current public international law is so weighted toward justifications that it would seem that the doctrine should require that the harm imposed be less than the harm avoided. In any event, no such requirement is codified in the ILC Draft Articles. As a final point, we have demonstrated that although the necessity defense is overwhelmingly powerful as an exception to generally applicable norms of international law, its power is not limitless. The requirement of a bona fide state interest prevents the doctrine—in its current form—from being used to justify interventions that vindicate the interests of humanity or the global community writ large, as opposed to the interests of one particular State. Whatever the merits of humanitarian intervention, the necessity doctrine as it currently exists in public international law is a poor fit for its legal foundation.

PART B

Necessity & *Jus in Bello*

CHAPTER 3

Necessity and Discrimination in Just War Theory

In this chapter we switch gears from *jus ad bellum* to *jus in bello*, with a particular goal in mind. The previous chapter examined the many different forms that necessity arguments take in public international law. In contrast, in this chapter we want to trace the influence of philosophical principles from Just War theory on concrete questions regarding the conduct of war. Specifically, we will discuss the *jus in bello* principle of necessity, what was in previous eras thought to be a cornerstone of Just War theory. We will be especially interested in how necessity is linked to the principle of discrimination. In general, the idea is that civilians should not be directly targeted, because targeting civilians for attack cannot be seen as necessary to advance a legitimate aim of war. Of course, attacking soldiers is crucial for many legitimate aims of war, if wars are to be legitimate at all, but attacking civilians is rarely needed. Hence, the principle of discrimination, which provides that civilians not be directly targeted during war, is linked to the principle of necessity in that only those acts of war that are directed at a legitimate aim of war can be justified.

The principle of *jus in bello* necessity is seemingly simple indeed. In situations where the only way to achieve military victory in a just war requires the employment of a certain tactic, say the bombing of a city, then that tactic is justified regardless of other normative considerations. Yet, necessity is often confusingly presented. It is often associated with a need that something be done lest a war be lost. In this sense there is a necessity that *something* be done. But sometimes there is more than one thing that can be done. So, there may be a necessity, and yet it may not be that a particular tactic is necessary for winning a war. Here proportionality matters since among those things that could avoid defeat, the common view is that the one that involves less harm should be employed. (In many ways, the structure of this analysis replicates the relationship between necessity and proportionality in *jus ad bellum*.) Necessity also sometimes means that *one particular tactic* must be employed lest the war be lost. In this sense, not employing that tactic means defeat. Proportionality seems not to intrude here, and yet it may because the winning of a war may itself not be morally significant, in which case it would matter how costly it is to win that war. Finally, even when it is believed that one particular tactic is necessary to win a war, this is often not certain, and because of this uncertainty proportionality again enters the picture.

In the first section we will briefly look at how *in bello* necessity was understood in the work of the sixteenth- and seventeenth-century philosophers, and we will explain how necessity is related to the principle of discrimination in the Just War tradition. In the second section we show how a revised understanding of necessity fits into the kind of considerations that are involved in the principle of humanitarian treatment. Based on that analysis, we argue that the principle of necessity creates a very small class of cases that may be treated in an exceptional way. In the third section we discuss the problem that occurs when it is realized that considerations of *jus in bello* necessity seem to involve the irrelevant factor of luck. In the fourth section, we relate necessity to the philosophical concept of practical necessity. In the final section, we attempt to spell out how the principles of necessity and proportionality relate to each other. Here we argue that proportionality puts a restraint on the principle of necessity, and that the two must be understood in tandem. This replicates, and is consistent with, the relationship between necessity and proportionality in *jus ad bellum* that we articulated above. It should come as little surprise that we extend this analysis now to the domain of *jus in bello*, since the relationship between necessity and proportionality is a conceptual one whose basic structure is mirrored on both sides of the *jus in bello—jus ad bellum* divide.

In short, we wish to raise the question of what we are to think of the principle of *in bello* necessity. Does it indeed so disrupt things that it eliminates absolute prohibitions on certain types of weapons during war? Or is the principle of necessity so restricted in its application that it rarely if ever comes into effect—a form of throat clearing where one says something like "well of course, there is always the theoretical possibility of exceptions to any rule"? Our tentative conclusion is that the answer to these questions is unclear and depends on which version of the principle of necessity one is referring to. If one is thinking of necessity as a state of exception to legitimate rules of warfare, we have reason to think that the principle of necessity, disconnected from the principles of discrimination and humanity, is not best seen as a cornerstone of international humanitarian law. But to understand the relationship between necessity and discrimination, we must first examine the introduction of necessity as a key component of early modern Just War theory.

I. NECESSITY AND DISCRIMINATION IN EARLY MODERN JUST WAR THEORY

Samuel Pufendorf helpfully urges us to distinguish between necessity as a right and necessity as a privilege:

> The power of necessity is a phrase upon the lips of all men, because it lacks the restraint of law, and is understood to form an exception in all the rules of men . . . And although honorable conduct takes precedence over safety, yet now and then the latter can be preferred to the former if, in consulting for our safety, what for the present has been detracted from honorable conduct, may at some time be restored by virtue and justice.[1]

If a person's safety requires that he or she do something that would otherwise be illegal or immoral, that act may be justified nonetheless. But often, considerations other than necessity restore honor and justice to how a war is fought.

Necessity as a right might allow for the killing even of those who are innocent. Pufendorf says that he is considering cases of what he calls "extreme necessity."[2] Necessity as a right follows from a perfect obligation, and in most cases this is the obligation to defend oneself from imminent death. But even in the case of imperfect obligations, to aid others when they are in distress, necessity may create not a right but a privilege, which can be overridden in certain cases.[3]

Theorists in the Just War tradition strongly condemned the killing of the innocent during war. Francisco Suarez states the general view that "no one may be deprived of his life save for reason of his own guilt."[4] Suarez

1. SAMUEL PUFENDORF, DE JURE NATURAE ET GENTIUM (THE LAW OF NATURE AND OF NATIONS) 295 (C.H. Oldfather & W.A. Oldfather trans., 1934) (1688).
2. *Id.* at 297.
3. *Id.* at 302.
4. FRANCISCO SUAREZ, DISPUTATIONE TRIPLICI VIRTUE THEOLOGICA: CHARITATE (SELECTIONS FROM THREE WORKS, DISPUTATION ON CHARITY) VII.14, at 845 (Gladys L. Williams, Ammi Brown & John Waldron trans., 1944) (1610).

extended this category of people who are innocent to include those who carry weapons as long as "they have not shared in the crime nor in the unjust war."[5] Hugo Grotius also articulated a very strong and encompassing principle: "No action should be attempted whereby innocent persons may be threatened with destruction."[6]

The key discrimination consideration, then as well as now, concerns who should count as innocent. Often this group is referred to as civilians, but there is a long history of worrying about whether all civilians during war are indeed innocent and therefore entitled to protection from the effects of conflict insofar as possible. There has been considerable debate about whether the targeting only includes intentional acts, and whether collateral damage to civilians counts as violating the principle of discrimination. If collateral damage cannot be justified under any moral or legal analysis, then most wars, and indeed almost all uses of military power, are unjust.

The principle of discrimination requires that those who are directly participating in the war be distinguished from those who are not, and only the former category can be directly attacked. Here is where necessity and discrimination are connected. Only if a civilian is directly participating in war can that civilian's death be necessary for a legitimate war aim. Only where the death of the civilian is necessary can the principle of discrimination and civilian immunity be overridden. And as we will see, each of these principles is grounded in, and limited by, the principle of humanity.

Prior to modern discussions, in war the guilty were those who were either members of a society that committed harms, or members of a subgroup that did so. This is why Averroes said that all able-bodied men could be slain, since he was speaking of members of an infidel society. As infidels, they were already guilty, and then since the men were all able to fight they could also be slain. It is interesting that Averroes does not think that all infidels, even children, women, and old men could also legitimately be slain in a jihad. It was assumed that even in a society of infidels, only those who could take up arms to defend their society could be legitimately attacked. Muslims could attack able-bodied infidel men, regardless of whether they had taken up arms, because of the guiltiness of their beliefs accompanied by the fact that they could take up arms, and hence that they could defend themselves. Generally in the Middle Ages, there was not such a fine line between soldiers and civilians, with people passing out of one group into another quite rapidly, and without putting on uniforms. The point here is

5. *Id.* at 846.
6. HUGO GROTIUS, DE JURE BELLI AC PACIS (ON THE LAW OF WAR AND PEACE) Bk. III, ch. 11, sec. VIII, at 734 (Francis W. Kelsey trans., 1925) (1625).

that Averroes tried to establish a firm line between those who can legitimately be killed and those who have immunity from attack, and made this distinction on the basis of guilt.

Francisco Suarez, reacting against a long tradition to the contrary, tried to demarcate the truly innocent and separate them from those who are "guilty" in war. Theorists such as Averroes had said that it is justifiable to kill any males who might take up arms.[7] Suarez instead held to the general principle that "no one may be deprived of his life save for reason of his own guilt." The innocent include "those who are able to bear arms, if it is evident that in other respects they have not shared in the crime nor in the unjust war."[8] Suarez says that the innocent in war "neither consented to the war nor gave any assistance in it, but who on the contrary, urged the acceptance of peace."[9] This is an important point since if we allow, as Averroes did, that anyone who could take up arms is counted as guilty or even non-innocent, then counterintuitively wars can be waged "indiscriminately," says Suarez.

We should also consider Grotius's views of who can count as innocent, views that could have led him to a kind of contingent pacifism.[10] In *On the Law of War and Peace*,[11] Grotius begins by articulating a very strong version of the principle of discrimination: "No action should be attempted whereby innocent persons may be threatened with destruction." He is led to support the view that the guilty can be released if it is "for the sake of the innocent."[12] Grotius defends this principle by reference to mercy and also to justice, for from the standpoint of justice the innocent surely do not deserve to be killed, and mercy dictates that in any event "from humanitarian instincts" the innocent must be protected.

Grotius says that children, women, and old men are normally to be afforded the status of innocents, since they are generally "untrained and inexperienced in war."[13] For similar reasons, those whose occupation concerns

7. Averroes, *Jihad, (from Al-Bidaya), in* JIHAD IN CLASSICAL AND MODERN ISLAM 33 (Rudolph Peters trans., 1996) (c. 1167).

8. Francisco Suarez, *On War (Disputation XIII, De Triplici Virtute Theologica: Charitate), in* SELECTIONS FROM THREE WORKS 845–46 (Gladys L. Williams, Ammi Brown & John Waldron trans., 1944) (1610).

9. *Id.* at 847.

10. *See* Larry May, *Grotius and Contingent Pacifism, in* GROTIUS AND LAW 357–77 (Larry May & Emily McGill, eds., 2014).

11. GROTIUS, *supra* note 6, at 733–44.

12. *Id.* at 734.

13. HUGO GROTIUS, ON THE LAW OF WAR AND PEACE 735. On the general topic of whether women should be treated different from men in combat situations, see JEAN-MARIE HENCKAERTS & LOUISE DOSWALD-BECK, CUSTOMARY INTERNATIONAL HUMANITARIAN LAW 475–79 (2005); and on the special respect owed to children, see *id.* at 479–82.

religious matters or letters are not to be considered guilty,[14] as is also true of farmers and merchants.[15] Furthermore, those who have surrendered or who are prisoners of war are innocent rather than guilty.[16] For our purposes, it is especially interesting that Grotius says that "it is not sufficient that by a sort of fiction the enemy may be conceived as forming a single body," indeed even "a quite obstinate devotion to one's own party, provided only that the cause is not altogether dishonorable, does not" mean that one should be grouped with the guilty.[17] This claim suggests that even when one is in a military unit, it cannot be assumed that one is guilty and can legitimately be killed. Rather, fine distinctions need to be made to see why one is serving in the military, for if one is merely serving out of patriotism, he is not to be grouped with the guilty. For these reasons, in Grotius's account, very few if any soldiers may be legitimately killed. And in any event, Grotius's arguments make it illegitimate to discriminate on the basis of large class categories at all. This is the complete opposite of total war; it is *limited* warfare in the most restrictive sense.

The rights of soldiers are often described in international law as humanitarian rights. By this is meant, in part, rights to be treated humanely. For example, a soldier is not supposed to be subjected to unnecessary or overly severe treatment, even as it is generally acknowledged that in many situations soldiers can be killed without violating their rights. And in this sense, it is odd that humanitarian rights of soldiers are often defended on grounds of dignity, since there are at least two major dignity considerations that would seem to apply to armed conflict. The first is how a soldier is treated in terms of his or her suffering, and the rules or laws of war have addressed this directly with what we consider to be proper restraints on tactics and weapons used during war. But the second aspect of the dignity of soldiers concerns how the right to life is regarded. For human beings generally, the right to life is normally thought to be the most significant of the human rights, rather than the right not to suffer, although certainly these two rights are very close to the top of any rights hierarchy. But traditionally a soldier in armed conflict is thought to have a much more heightened right not to suffer than a right to life. And Gentili is an especially good representative of that tradition of allowing, or at least tolerating in war as exceptions, wholesale killing on weak necessity grounds.

14. Grotius, *supra* note 13, at 736.
15. *Id.* at 737.
16. *Id.* at 739.
17. *Id.* at 741.

Grotius also discusses the idea of necessity in the conduct of war. In chapter 1 of Book III of *De Jure Belli ac Pacis*, Grotius recognizes that "[i]n war things which are necessary to attain the end in view are permissible."[18] Yet, Grotius also argues that what is permitted is not always the morally best response: "But as we have admonished upon many occasions previously, what accords with a strict interpretation of right is not always, or in all respects, permitted. Often, in fact, love for our neighbor prevents us from pressing our right to the utmost limit."[19] This analysis sees necessity as a regulating constraint. Necessity severely restricts the kind of conduct during war that is permissible just as necessity severely restricts the kind of cause that can justify initiating war. In both cases necessity means that there must be no other non-lethal way to accomplish the justified goal.

There is a serious question of whether those who are currently taking up arms can morally be distinguished from those who would do so if given the chance, and also from those who perform other militarily necessary functions, but do not take up arms. It is hard to see that merely carrying arms, especially if one has no intention of using them except in self-defense, is enough to make one morally guilty. And it is harder still to see that those who do choose to take up arms can be seen as guilty, and yet those who choose to work in munitions factories cannot. There has been quite a lot of good argumentation by other theorists on this count, so we will not belabor this point here.[20] The point is only to indicate that guiltiness (or culpability) will be a poor basis for providing a bright line between those who are subject to attack and those who are immune from it.

Guiltiness is not only a poor basis for giving us a bright-line basis for conceptually identifying social groups and making particular judgments about their members. But there are also serious questions about its general moral relevance in a discussion of war. Since at least the time of Augustine, it has been debated whether wars could justifiably be waged as a means of punishing the guilty, instead of being only justified on grounds of self-defense or protection of the innocent. It is somewhat controversial that one State could seek to punish another State, and it is highly controversial that one State could seek to punish social groups within another State by means of war. The reason for this second point is that one wonders why battlefields rather than courtrooms are the appropriate place for punishments to be

18. *Id.* at 599.
19. *Id.* at 601.
20. The best recent essay on this topic is Christopher Kutz, *The Difference Uniforms Make: Collective Violence in Criminal Law and War*, 33 PHIL. & PUBLIC AFFAIRS 148–80 (2005).

meted out.[21] Even if we can distinguish those who are complicit in a war of aggression, and separate them out from those who are mere bystanders, a question remains: Why should this be the kind of morally relevant distinction that would justify the use of lethal violence against the complicit without any attempt to ascertain whether all of the members of a group are indeed guilty enough to make them liable to be punished by a State's armies?

The guiltiness of individual persons normally is judged in degrees, as is the innocence of individual persons. When we make moral judgments on the basis of rough-grained markers, such as large social group membership, we necessarily must eliminate or diminish morally relevant differences among members of a group. Individual combatants or soldiers are not all guilty to the same extent, even if the basis of their guilt is that they are representing an aggressing State.

II. NECESSITY AND HUMANE TREATMENT

It is our contention that the philosophical principles of discrimination and necessity are both grounded in the principle of humane treatment. This principle of humaneness has two parts. The first has to do with how others are to be treated that captures what both compassion and mercy would require. Compassion and mercy are at least as important, if not more so, in discussions of war crimes than is (retributive) justice. The other part of the principle of humaneness has to do with acting in ways that are true to, or respectful of, oneself, of one's honor as a decent person. Humaneness is about what is owed to others and what is owed to oneself. Even when it is unclear that anything is strictly speaking owed to another, it may display a lack of humaneness for us to act in a cruel way to that person in any event, for it would not be honorable to do so. It is in this way that the principle of humane treatment often places quite severe restraints on the type of tactics that soldiers can use during war, even if they are pursuing a just cause.

21. Indeed, the idea that punishment should be a justification for waging war was seemingly laid to rest after the ratification of the United Nations Charter, where Article 51 said that only matters of individual and collective self-defense could warrant a State in going to war. The Bush administration has nonetheless recently claimed that it was justified in waging the second Gulf War to punish Saddam Hussein for the murders and tortures of his own people. It also may be that the rationale for NATO's bombings of the former Yugoslavia in light of ethnic cleansing in Kosovo, namely to defend regional stability, signals a new interpretation of Article 51.

On the face of it, the principle of necessity seems to be at odds with the principle of humane treatment. The principle of necessity is often characterized in a simple way as holding that: "Military forces should cause no more destruction than is strictly necessary to achieve their objectives."[22] And although this looks like a limitation on what tactics can be employed, it is often understood as a kind of exception to violate the normal prohibitions of the laws of war in those cases where the use of poisons or torture, for instance, is indeed necessary to achieve a military objective. As with most principles, the principle of necessity both rules some things out as unacceptable and rules other things in as acceptable, or at least not unacceptable. The principle of necessity seems to rule some things in that the principle of humane treatment would definitely rule out, such as the use of torture.

But, despite appearances, the principles of necessity and humane treatment can be reconciled, especially if one carefully peels away the different senses of necessity. The principle of humane treatment is not an absolute one, and the principle of necessity is not a breaker of all absolute prohibitions in any event. Indeed, the principle of *jus in bello* necessity carves out a remarkably narrow set of exceptional cases to the general prohibition on inhumane treatment, where it would be odd indeed if the principle of humane treatment were not amenable to such a class of cases, and on the very grounds of what humane treatment is all about. For if there is a tactic that must be employed in order to win a war, and the winning of the war is morally very important, then it would be only the rule-fetishist who thought that, on grounds of humaneness itself, this exceptional case must be subject to absolute prohibitions.

Yet there is a legitimate difficulty that needs to be addressed. It seems to some that the principle of necessity simply destroys the possibility of there being any absolute, or near absolute prohibitions, during war, since a war may be merely a series of military necessities. Military campaigns proceed from one battle to another, seemingly endlessly. And it can be argued that employing certain tactics is necessary for winning each battle, and that winning each battle is militarily necessary in the sense that if it is not won then the war will likely be lost. On this account, the principle of necessity does not have narrow scope at all. And the gulf between acting humanely and doing what is necessary in order to wage war effectively seems very wide indeed. In this sense, humane treatment will often be trumped by military necessity.

22. Douglas Lackey, The Ethics of War and Peace 59 (1989).

But it turns out not to be true that in war situations of military necessity are rampant. Think of the use of torture to get militarily needed information. Of course it is true that in wars more and better information is always needed. But the question is whether it is needed right here and now to win a particular battle or achieve a particular objective. Here there are two considerations that diminish the likelihood that such situations occur very often in war. First, although information is always needed, it is not often obvious where the best place is to get the needed information. One first needs to identify who might have reliable information, then one needs to figure out how to capture the person who has this information, and then one needs to figure out how to extract the information that is needed. Second, there is the problem that certain tactics, for instance torture, are not very reliable methods of obtaining information. In many situations, the torture victim eventually talks, but often what is revealed is what the victim believes that the torturer wants to hear, not necessarily the truth. For these reasons, there will not be many situations where military necessity will justify the violation of the humanitarian prohibition on torturing.

To justify the use of torture, it is often said that one also needs to show that there was no other way to achieve the military objective that would involve less suffering for the victim. We will dispute this view, but at the moment we want merely to highlight the fact that it is not sufficient to show that there is a situation where it is necessary to get a certain military result. One also needs to show that using just this tactic is likely to accomplish the needed military objective, and that using this tactic is the only means to accomplish that objective, in order truly to claim the emergency exemption to the torture prohibition. Along with the points made in the previous paragraph, at the very least this shows that there will not be a huge number of cases where military necessity will trump humane treatment considerations. And indeed, it is better to see the principle of necessity as grounded in the principle of humane treatment.

For the Grotian tradition in Just War theory, the principle of humane treatment is the cornerstone of international humanitarian law, as well as the bridge to human rights law and a possible rapprochement between these fields. Humane treatment plays a significant role in our understanding of why military necessity has a strong normative pull and why military necessity needs to be tightly circumscribed. When wars are fought, it is crucial that soldiers on both sides retain their honor. If tactics are used that call for soldiers to destroy their honor, as happens in the use of torture, then often whatever military gains are achieved are offset by loss of honor. Indeed, not all objectives that are militarily necessary have a strong normative pull. Winning a war by annihilating the enemy even when this is the only way to win does not in itself have strong normative weight. For if there is no prima facie basis for thinking that one side should win a war, the principle of necessity alone does not provide the strong normative pull for using certain tactics.

As Douglas Lackey has put it, "the principle [of necessity] does not say that whatever is necessary is permissible, but that everything permissible must be necessary."[23] Two more things must be shown. First, the military objective itself must be normatively compelling in light of the objectives of the war in question, as well as in light of how humans should treat one another. It is here that humanitarian considerations can supply moral weight to the principle of necessity. Second, there must be no other less lethal tactics available that would achieve the same objective. This second consideration moves us directly into discussions of the principle of proportionality, a principle that is designed to limit the principle of necessity, and to do so by reference to humanitarian considerations. We take up the relation between *jus in bello* necessity and proportionality in the last section of this chapter.

III. LUCK AND NECESSITY

In arguing for his revisionist view of Just War theory, Jeff McMahan has said that necessity has an important role to play in a theory that focuses on liability rather than deservingness.

Because people can be liable to harm only in relation to a goal of this sort, the assignment of liability is governed by a requirement of necessity. If harming a person is unnecessary for the achievement of a relevant type of goal, that person cannot be liable to be harmed. The infliction of deserved harm, is by contrast, not governed by a requirement of necessity, since the value of a person's getting what he deserves is not instrumental and hence is not necessary for anything beyond itself.[24]

McMahan then makes it seemingly very clear that necessity plays a very prominent role in his revisionist theory of the Just War:

> A person cannot be liable to attack when attacking him would be wrong because it would be unnecessary or disproportionate. Rather, if attacking him is unnecessary for the prevention or correction of a wrong for which he is responsible . . . then he is simply not liable to attack.[25]

23. *Id.*
24. Jeff McMahan, Killing in War, Oxford, 2009, p. 9.
25. *Id*

Of course, what counts as necessity in this account is still not yet clear, and something that will be the main focus of our book.

In recent Just War theory, necessity has not often received much sustained attention. But one exception here is an essay by Joanna Mary Firth and Jonathan Quong that raises an especially important question about the role of luck in necessity calculations.[26] They begin their essay with a formulation of the necessity condition that we find also to be a good nuanced statement of a common understanding of necessity in contemporary Just War theory:

> It is necessary to impose defensive harm on an attacker *only* if doing so has a reasonable prospect of successfully averting an unjust threat posed by the attacker, and *only* if there is no alternative way of averting the threat that is suitably low-cost (relevant costs include the harms suffered by attackers, victims, and third parties). The presence of alternatives that are too costly—those that would involve heroic acts or significant rights transgressions to third parties—are not sufficient to render the imposition of defensive harm unnecessary.[27]

We prefer this way of initially characterizing *jus in bello* necessity since it is not as strong as the alternative that demands that the chosen action be the least costly.

The point that we wish to take up concerns the claim that the principle of necessity is too influenced by luck to be a fair or just principle. Firth and Quong continue:

> There is something deeply troubling about the proposal that an innocent person under threat has no liberty whatsoever to *defend* herself. Even if a person's attempt to defend herself is predetermined to fail there is, we think, a nonconsequentialist sense in which a prohibition on futile defensive action denies the victim an important moral liberty: there is something problematic about the view that morality can render an innocent person defenseless.[28]

26. Joanna May Firth & Jonathan Quong, *Necessity, Moral Liability, and Defensive Harm*, 31 Law & Phil. 673–701 (2012). Other exceptions to the paucity of discussion of necessity today are Seth Lazar, *Necessity in Self-Defense*, 40 Phil. & Public Affairs 3–44 (2012); Daniel Statman, *Can Wars Be Fought Justly? The Necessity Condition Put to the Test*, 8 J. Moral Phil. 435–51 (2011); Thomas Hurka, *Proportionality and Necessity*, *in* War: Essays in Political Philosophy 127–44 (Larry May & Emily Crookston trans., 2008).

27. *Id.* at 678.

28. *Id.* at 690.

Here Firth and Quong express a very serious objection to one of the standard ways that consequentialists understand necessity. If necessity means that there must be a reasonable hope of success in responding to a lethal attack, then the person who is too weak, too small, or too lightly armed will be rendered defenseless because he or she is not justified in using force against an aggressor since such force will not likely stop the attack. This seems absurd. Indeed, in the context of individual self-defense in the domestic realm, it seems wrong (and offensive) to suggest that a rape victim cannot fight back if the violation to her bodily integrity is inevitable because the perpetrator's strength is so disproportionate to the victim's capacity to resist the attack.

The solution that Firth and Quong offer is, for us, quite reasonable: necessity is not the only important consideration in determining whether a person is justified in trying to counter an aggressive attack. In our view, the principle of humanity, which ultimately works to support the principle of necessity, can supply independent grounds for attempting to counter an attack in the cases where the counter is not likely to succeed. The victim's humanity, especially her dignity, can be appealed to in order to defend a counterattack. This Kantian account would suggest that individuals have the moral right to resist unlawful or unjust aggressions, and that this right is independent of the particular consequence of successfully repelling the assault. But such considerations do not undermine the principle of necessity unless one sees necessity considerations as an end-all to the discussion about the use of lethal counterforce.

However, there is a crucial difference between futile self-defense in the domestic context and futile self-defense in the context of armed conflict. In the case of the inevitable assault described above, the defensive force will usually involve injuring but not killing the assailant, so the question is whether the victim of the assault has the right to injure the aggressor even if the injury will not prevent the attacker from completing the assault. As stated above, we believe that the victim has this Kantian right to resist, and we agree with Firth and Quong that the victim should not be rendered defenseless by such considerations. In contrast, the use of lethal force in an armed conflict situation is slightly more complicated, because those situations involve the killing of the enemy, and perhaps might even involve the killing of a large number of individuals in furtherance of the resistance.

In the context of international armed conflict, if one cannot stop an attack, then any means one employs seems to fail the necessity test. Perhaps the stringent necessity condition should remain in place if the action to be taken is the lethal use of force by the potential victim, and the defensive killing will do nothing to improve the situation of the potential victim. Killing an attacker when such action will not in fact stop the attack, in the rare cases where this might occur, is a case that should continue to give us pause. It is difficult to determine the correct balance between the principles of necessity and humanity in cases of lethal force. On one view, justified lethal force should require that the lethal action stand some reasonable chance of success. Perhaps in these cases, necessity requires that unnecessary killing should not occur. Otherwise the humanity of the *attacker* will not be afforded proper weight. This suggests a conflict between the humanity of the attacker and the humanity of the victim—a troubling tension. But in the vast array of cases, it seems uncontroversial to conclude that a victim can defend himself or herself in any manner short of lethal use of force even if there is little hope of success.

Helen Frowe has weighed into this debate and has criticized the view of Firth and Quong that we have been discussing, and to a certain extent defending. Frowe helpfully points out that "necessity is a luck-based element" in the sense that what is necessary to avert a lethal attack is not up to the victim or the attacker.[29] And she also points out that killing someone may not be necessary to save one's life but may be necessary for some other important good, such as averting an assault on one's honor. And in general, it is useful to see how the arguments about necessity are influenced by whether or not one is an internalist. Frowe defines internalism as holding "that one can be liable to harm on grounds of defense only if the infliction of that harm is the least harmful means of averting a threat."[30]

Yet, there is a difference between the types of alternatives that must first be pursued before a claim of necessity can be made out: a distinction between lethal force that is the "least harmful means," and lethal force that is an alternative and suitably low-cost. One does not have to select the alternative that is the least harmful means in order to satisfy the necessity requirement. In cases of lethal use of violence, one can choose means that are low-cost but that are not the lowest cost. Necessity is a very strong requirement but it is not as strong as Frowe seems to think in the passage we cited above.

McMahan is on the right track in our view when he says that necessity directly affects liability to be killed. If it is unnecessary to kill Jones to achieve a goal because there are alternatives to achieving the goal that are low-cost, then Jones has not lost his general immunity not to be killed and hence is not liable to be killed. And although it is true that the range

29. Helen Frowe, Defensive Killing 95 (2014).
30. *Id.* at 91.

of alternatives open at any given time is largely a matter of luck, nonetheless luck does affect who can rightly be killed in the two-person cases that McMahan and Frowe are both concerned with.

When we then turn to the situations of war and armed conflict, the range of alternatives for any *jus in bello* tactical decision typically increases compared to the two-person case. The decision would be very difficult to make if the decider had to consider every alternative to find the least harmful one. This is one reason we favor the less strict standard of merely making sure that there is no alternative that is low-cost. Figuring out if there are such low-cost alternatives, when presented with many alternatives, is not nearly as difficult, and indeed can be seen as a plausible standard of necessity. But the key consideration here is that unnecessary killings are unjust, and those who engage in unnecessary killings, even if for otherwise legitimate military objectives, might be acting wrongfully. Unnecessary killing, where there were low-cost non-lethal alternatives, is a much more serious restraint during war or armed conflict than is normally recognized.

An operational example is in order. Let us contrast three different examples that trigger different intuitive responses. The first is a target of a sexual offense during peacetime who fights back but whose resistance is ultimately futile. The second is a small country that is facing invasion from a much larger and more powerful neighbor; resistance is futile because the small country simply does not have the military strength to successfully repel the larger nation's military campaign. The third scenario is somewhere in between: a platoon of soldiers is advancing on a hill guarded by two lonely sentries who are tasked with holding their ground and keeping control of their installation, though their defeat is inevitable because they simply cannot stop the platoon of soldiers from winning the engagement.

Our intuition is that the victim in the first aggression is entitled to fight back and injure the aggressor, even if the defensive force is ultimately futile; this resistance is an expression of the victim's autonomy as a center of moral worth. She has a moral dignity that both allows and perhaps even demands resistance. The resistance vindicates her humanity without unduly infringing upon the humanity of the attacker. As for the second example, *jus ad bellum* should not require that the weaker State simply give up and permit the stronger state to take over the weaker's country; the State is permitted to defend itself against the unjust intrusion, even if defeat is inevitable. The hard case is the example of the platoon whose victory is inevitable. Can the lonely sentries fire their weapons or must they surrender? Under one view, their fighting back will only kill additional soldiers of the platoon without improving their own situation—ultimately they will be defeated. If the principle of necessity requires success, then their killing of the enemy is ultimately unnecessary because it is ineffectual.

It seems absurd to us to suggest that the lonely sentries cannot use deadly force in the confrontation simply because doing so would be ineffectual—it seems to place them in the uncomfortable position of having no options simply because they are weaker, while giving the stronger adversary the right to use many more options, including deadly force, simply because they are stronger. Again, that seems to get things backward. The key difference here is that success should be understood in more complex terms than is usually the case in these thought experiments. Success ought to be understood in Bayesian terms. When the lonely sentries must decide whether to fight back, their decision to use lethal force should be based on whether using lethal force—and killing the enemy—will reasonably increase their likelihood of success. If the addition of lethal force will not increase their likelihood of success, then indeed a robust understanding of the principle of necessity might preclude the deployment of lethal force. However, in almost all situations of operational relevance, the use of deadly force may very much increase the defenders' likelihood of success, even if (in the end), success is not achieved. In those situations, the increase of likelihood of success, even if success is not achieved, makes the deployment of lethal force necessary, because it improves the defenders' chance of success. In particular, even if the two sentries are likely to be killed, their infliction of casualties on the stronger force increases their platoon's likelihood of success in the overall military campaign, since the attacking force will now have fewer soldiers with which to launch an attack on the second hill down the road. These are all relevant moral considerations.

The philosophical debate we have just rehearsed, including the role of luck in these debates, does not deny the importance of the restraint of necessity. The revisionist Just War theorists, no less than the traditional Just War ones, regard necessity as at least as important a restraint as proportionality or discrimination. Indeed, some revisionist Just War theorists such as Frowe seemingly see necessity as a very significant restraint on justified killing, and those such as McMahan, Firth, and Quong also see necessity, despite its connection to luck, as severely restraining as well.

This debate has rather direct implications for the topic of innocent threats. Innocent threats can justly be killed if it is necessary to do so to save the life of the person who kills the innocent threat. And during war, soldiers can find themselves as innocent threats who are then targetable despite being innocent. We cannot here resolve all of the difficulties that are involved in the terribly troubling cases of innocent threats. But we believe, like most philosophers, that innocent threats can only be killed justly if killing them is indeed necessary for saving the life of the person who does the killing, or perhaps to save the life of certain others. The role of luck here makes matters even more difficult than these cases would be otherwise, yet it is still true that despite the connection between luck and necessity, unnecessary killings are not just.[31]

IV. MILITARY NECESSITY AS A FORM OF PRACTICAL NECESSITY

Let us next turn to several attempts to separate the various meanings of necessity in philosophical discourse in recent years. One fairly standard understanding of necessity is "that it could not have been otherwise." Like many understandings of necessity, here there is an attempt to indicate how to assess the current situation vis-à-vis counterfactual situations. Another conception of necessity is that some proposition or statement "*must* be true." Here necessity is contrasted with possibility, where a proposition or sentence "*might* be true." A stronger version of this conception of necessity is that a proposition or sentence is true in all possible worlds.[32]

Kit Fine urges us to understand the varieties of necessity by beginning with logical necessity: "a proposition is necessary if it *must* be true."[33] He then divides logical necessity into two further categories: narrow or broad logical necessity. In the narrow sense, a necessary proposition would be of the sort "red is red." Logically necessary propositions are necessary because they are true by application of some law, such as the law of identity, namely a thing must be identical to itself. In the broad sense, sometimes called "metaphysical necessity," we begin from the identity of things, where one thing is necessarily not another thing; a red thing is not also a green thing.

Of somewhat more relevance for discussions of military necessity is what Fine calls conceptual necessity. "Conceptually necessary truths" are those that are logically "necessary relative to or conditional upon the basic conceptual truths."[34] We are especially interested in seeing necessity as conditional, since that is clearly the way that we must understand military necessity if this term is to have any practical meaning at all. In a sense

31. For a sustained treatment of luck and necessity, see BERNARD WILLIAMS, SHAME AND NECESSITY (1993).

32. We thank Eric Ritter for help in this section, especially in the previous paragraph.

33. Kit Fine, *The Varieties of Necessity*, *in* CONCEIVABILITY AND POSSIBILITY 253, 254 (Tamar Szabo Gendler & John Hawthorne eds., 2002), *reprinted in* KIT FINE, MODALITY AND TENSE: PHILOSOPHICAL PAPERS (2005).

34. *Id.* at 255.

most forms of necessity are conditional on something—logical necessity is conditional on the laws of logic, and metaphysical necessity is conditional on the laws of nature. But conceptual necessity is somewhat different than these other two in that it can be relative to what a particular person's conceptual framework is, although this is clearly not the usage Fine has in mind. Fine is thinking about fixed, objective conceptual truths that are "perhaps given by the definitions of the concepts."[35] Yet, it seems to us, definitions framed in terms of words that stand for concepts are not utterly fixed the way that logic or nature is—indeed they can change every time a dictionary is updated. In the remainder of this section we will consider this idea, and in so doing hopefully make progress on ascertaining a plausible beginning notion of military necessity.

Of greatest relevance to our topic of military necessity is the category of "practical necessity." Bernard Williams has posed a puzzle for the way that we understand the necessity of doing something because it is our duty to do it. In his essay, "Practical Necessity," Williams is attempting to respond to a Kantian understanding of morality, where there are actions that are morally necessary for us to engage in, and where this takes on an objectivity that is independent of a person's subjective standpoint. Williams says:

> It is worth mentioning that there are important second- and third-person uses of what is in effect, this ought, in contexts of advice or of discussion of what it is reasonable for an agent to do. So used, this ought also reveals itself to be relative, in a broad sense, to the projects, motives, and so on of the agent in question.[36]

Practical necessity, for Williams, is about what must be done, but where "must" is often relative to facts about the agent as well as facts about the external world.

Williams makes two points that we believe are relevant to discussions of military necessity. First, on the question of what one must do, he says: "It is very rarely the case that there is only one thing I can do . . . Usually, the alternatives are vastly more costly, or are excluded by some moral restraint."[37] Williams then follows with this comment:

> The recognition of practical necessity must involve an understanding, at once of one's powers and incapacities, and of what the world permits, and the

35. *Id.* at 255.
36. Bernard Williams, Moral Luck 125 (1981).
37. *Id.* at 125.

> recognition of a limit which is neither simply external to the self, nor yet a product of the will, is what can lend a special authority or dignity to such decisions.[38]

Here we come to the idea of dignity. Practical necessity involves restraint of one's behavior at least partially in conformity with what is morally or legally required, but also in consideration of what a person understands of himself or herself. Practical necessity, and we want to say also military necessity, is based in both an external restraint and a subjective sense of what it is reasonable for one to do.

To turn to the specific ways of cashing out the idea of military necessity, we can make progress in two respects. The Grotian construal of military necessity that we will partially endorse involves imminence and immediacy, as well as the third standard that there cannot be any other way the killing can be avoided. Our discussion of Kit Fine is relevant here in that we do not mean that it is inconceivable in an objective sense of what is a conceptual truth, but in a somewhat subjective sense of what the commander takes to be conceivable in the circumstances. Indeed, as Bernard Williams argued, one must have a recognition of one's own powers as well as what seems to be accomplishable in the world at the moment. In addition, even among the options that are conceivable, it is fair to rule out those that are vastly more costly than what one contemplates doing. Military necessity is in this sense different from logical or metaphysical necessity.

Williams makes another point that will be important for our analysis of military necessity:

> if A wants X, and if it is true that if he wants X he must do Y, it does not follow that he must do y; that will follow only if, further, X is the thing that he must pursue. So. in the first person: if I conclude that I must do Y, then it is because I have come to see not just that it is the only means to some end I have, but that it is the only thing I can do.[39]

As we will see later, there is a double necessity in military necessity, understood in a morally plausible way. It needs to be necessary that I take this action to achieve this military objective; and it must be necessary that I achieve this military objective. These assessments are to be made from the first-person standpoint of the commander in a given situation.

38. *Id.* at 130–31.
39. *Id.* at 125.

Military necessity, as a form of practical necessity, is the employment of objective legal standards by a person who must judge at the moment from a significantly subjective standpoint. Military necessity is a mixture of these objective and subjective factors, and cannot easily be reduced to merely one or the other perspective.[40] So, the nineteenth-century German doctrine of *Kriegsraison*, which saw military necessity as a matter of what is perceived by a commander to be needed to win an important battle and that overrules all legal restraints, is wrong in that it only considered one component of the practical necessity of military necessity.[41] But the very strict standard of necessity that may be employed by some pacifists, and that takes no account of the subjective considerations of the commander at the moment, is also mistaken—at least in part because it fails to understand what is reasonably conceivable in such situations.

One more thought might be helpful as we try to get a preliminary sense of what a reasonable understanding of military necessity might entail. Kit Fine asks us to consider two claims of normative necessity concerning the claim that "every war is wrong."

For this might be meant in the sense that every war in the circumstances that actually prevail, is wrong; or it might be meant in the sense that every war, in whatever circumstances might prevail, is wrong. In the latter case, the claim is taken to be necessary—to hold unconditionally, or in all possible circumstances; while in the former, the claim is not taken to be necessary, but merely to hold conditionally upon the circumstances that actually obtain. The distinction between accidental and necessary generalizations in nature is often drawn in terms of the ability to sustain counterfactuals.[42]

This distinction is quite useful for sorting out what is a reasonable understanding of military necessity. But the counterfactuals that should be employed do not ask about all possible worlds, but only about possible worlds that very closely resemble our current one. We set out the argument for this position in later chapters.

There may be a reasonable, and very strong, moral sense of necessity that asks about all possible worlds. But military necessity, as a concept of moral or legal necessity, cannot reasonably ask of a commander in a given situation that all possible alternative counterfactual situations be examined.

40. For a similar analysis of the principle of proportionality in armed conflict, see Michael Newton & Larry May, Proportionality and International Law (2014), especially chapter 2, section 5.

41. *See* Michael N. Schmitt, *Military Necessity and Humanity in International Humanitarian Law: Preserving the Delicate Balance*, 50 Va. J. Int'l L. 795–839 (2010).

42. *See* Fine, *supra* note 33.

But it does involve asking about many possible alternatives that are within what is conceived by the commander to be realizable. In this sense, military necessity does not merely require considering one or two alternatives, just as it does not require considering all possible alternatives. And when decisions are made that take into account a fairly rich set of alternatives there is also a sense, as Bernard Williams put it, that such decisions have a certain dignity that calls out for respect, just as such decisions must take many alternatives into account before lethal force is used so that those against whom the lethal force is used are also treated as having dignity.

V. RELATING *JUS IN BELLO* PROPORTIONALITY AND NECESSITY

The principle of necessity does not apply to every battlefield decision, for it kicks in, and possibly allows for the normal laws of war to be abridged, only when a very serious matter is at stake such as where losing a battle will mean that a legitimate community is overrun or destroyed. Even wars that were not initiated for a just cause may indeed reach certain points where various otherwise inappropriate tactics seem to be needed, and might be thought to be justified by the principle of necessity. But a normatively plausible principle of *jus in bello* necessity will not automatically warrant such tactics. In this section, we briefly explore how necessity and proportionality should be related. This mirrors our discussion of *jus ad bellum* necessity and proportionality from the first two chapters.

Let us turn to the further restrictions on the principle of necessity that its connection with the principle of proportionality might engender. For if necessity is to mean anything at all, it cannot mean merely that one has to establish that some action needs to be taken to achieve an important military objective, and thereby justify any action to accomplish this necessary objective. Rather, the objective must be tightly connected to the particular tactic employed. A political leader might be right that it is imperative that something be done to stop a terrorist threat. But this does not mean that the rules of war do not apply, for they will still apply as a means to restrict the tactics that can be legitimately selected by the political leader, in terms of proportionality, even in situations where something needs to be done.

Think about one of the classic cases involving terrorism. For several decades there has been a debate about whether torture could be justified to find the location of a ticking time bomb set to explode in a crowded area of a city. Here torture seems potentially justifiable since the good to be accomplished, the saving of thousands of lives, seems clearly greater than the harm to be done, the suffering inflicted through the torture tactics against a few people thought to have information about the ticking time bomb. But for this justification to succeed there has to be no other way to get the information that is needed in time to stop the tragedy. It is not merely that it is necessary to get information and that torture is quite likely to secure that information. But now there is a weighing of tactics, unless there is only one tactic that could achieve the significant and needed result. Even if there seems to be only one way to achieve it, we often do not know how certain it is that it can be achieved in this way. And hence as we said at the beginning of this chapter, it is rare indeed that we know in advance that only one particular tactic will achieve a military objective.

Suppose there is the ticking time bomb and the possibility of securing *needed* information to avert the tragedy by means of torture. But if the threat is not imminent, we may miss the fact that other tactics can also achieve the needed result. In the attempt to get what is needed, it may be that it is not noticed that there could be several ways to get what is needed. Of course, if there are other ways to achieve the needed information, then neither one of the ways are themselves truly necessary to obtain the information. In addition it might not be noticed that there was also the possibility, indeed the likelihood that the information could be secured by bribing the same people who are about to be tortured. If necessity is confused with what is needed, then there is no particular reason to use bribery rather than torture since either tactic will secure the information needed to find the ticking time bomb. Yet this result is deeply counterintuitive.

If the very same needed information can be secured by much less costly means, should it not be required that one choose the less costly rather than the more costly tactic? What could possibly justify the intentional choosing of a tactic that will cause such suffering when there were other less costly tactics that could be used for achieving the desired result? We cannot appeal to the goal of ending the emergency if it is not imminent and there are other less costly ways to achieve this goal, and hence the principle of proportionality must be seen as continuously relevant.

Now think again of a political leader who claims that she was not getting needed information about where terrorists would strike next against innocent citizens. Could the necessity of getting this information justify breaking the provisions of the Geneva Convention, and other rules of war, that forbid the use of torture? The key consideration is whether there are any less costly tactics available that would achieve the same needed result, that is, we need to appeal to proportionality and imminence, not merely to bare necessity. Had the political leader seriously attempted to bribe, rather than torture, the people that were held in captivity? The difficulty arises if there were very many possible tactics that could have been employed, and were apparently not tried. But what if political leader were running out of time, and torture seemed likely to work, as did bribery, but that torture was thought to be slightly more likely to succeed. Would necessity alone justify using it? Again, our response is that proportionality seems to matter. If the alternative was far less costly, then it is not at all clear that the political leader was justified in using torture, unless it truly was the last resort open to the political leader.

There are thus two ways to understand the relationship between the principles of necessity and proportionality. Either the principle of proportionality is itself one of the conditions of the principle of necessity, or the principle of proportionality is an independent limitation on the principle of necessity. The principle of proportionality is clearly at least a background constraint whenever there is a normatively plausible invocation of the principle of necessity, since the very thing that is said to require the otherwise prohibited tactic may not itself be worth the cost of using the tactic. In addition, it is rare that one knows for sure that other tactics will not also achieve the needed objective.

As we have seen, it is considerably better to rest international humanitarian law not on necessity but on the principle of humane treatment, which at least has a much clearer scope of application, and will restrain soldiers on the battlefield and make war less morally problematic. So, it may be that there is no good basis for thinking that poisons should be treated differently than bombs. Military necessity neither makes one more nor less prone to be the subject of a complete ban. Indeed, military necessity seems to sweep quite even-handedly in making us aware that at least in situations of emergency, hardly any tactic should be taken completely off the table.

CHAPTER 4

The Foundations of Necessity in IHL

In this chapter, we extend the analysis of the previous chapter but shift from philosophical inquiry to legal analysis. The goal of our inquiry is to determine how much of our philosophical understanding of necessity maps onto the current legal landscape, and whether our philosophical position suggests that legal doctrines should be revised or maintained without alteration. In other words, is there a gap between *lex lata* and *de lege ferenda*? To the extent that necessity remains a salient category in today's scholarly debates about military action, the question is how it should be applied to factual scenarios that could not have been imagined by the natural law theorists or even Francis Lieber.

Section I starts by analyzing the definition of *jus in bello* necessity offered by the International Committee of the Red Cross, and we explain how contemporary explanations of necessity owe much to Lieber and his historical antecedents. We then try to provide a normative defense of Lieber's version of *jus in bello* necessity. The goal of the inquiry is to explain why Lieber's notion of necessity has had such staying power and continues to structure the contemporary legal landscape. If the Lieberian worldview still endures, there must be some reason for it. Indeed, Lieber's broad notion of necessity as a license, coupled with more specific *jus in bello* prohibitions that have real regulatory bite, provide combatants with relatively clear and precise rules that can be transparently administered on the battlefield. In other words, Lieber's notion of *jus in bello* necessity scores high marks when it comes to ease of application.

However, this does not mean that Lieber's notion of *jus in bello* necessity is beyond reproach and does not suffer from some normative deficits.

Indeed there are costs associated with Lieber's licensing version of necessity. Necessity can be viewed as a complex set of institutional decisions over where and in what manner to regulate military force. There are many principles in the philosopher's toolbox, and many rules in the lawyer's toolbox; decisions need to be made about where and how to concentrate one's regulatory efforts. In this chapter we start the process, which will only be consummated in later chapters, of questioning the foundational underpinnings of necessity in the current legal system. Although we find most of it normatively defensible, we do not consider it beyond criticism and amendment. Later chapters will explore and debate in more detail with proposals to amend the legal principle of necessity.

I. THE ICRC AND NECESSITY

The International Committee of the Red Cross (ICRC) definition of *jus in bello* necessity harkens back to the principle's earliest codification in Article 14 of the Lieber Code: "Military necessity, as understood by modern civilized nations, consists in the necessity of those measures which are indispensable for securing the ends of the war, and which are lawful according to the modern law and usages of war."[1] Although the Lieber Code does not provide a complete account of military necessity, it does explain in more detail what it does and does not allow, fleshing out the principle via family resemblance. Regarding permissions, it famously states that

> [m]ilitary necessity admits of all direct destruction of life or limb of *armed* enemies, and of other persons whose destruction is incidentally *unavoidable* in the armed contests of the war; it allows of the capturing of every armed enemy, and every enemy of importance to the hostile government, or of peculiar danger to the captor; it allows of all destruction of property, and obstruction of the ways and channels of traffic, travel, or communication, and of all withholding of sustenance or means of life from the enemy; of the appropriation of whatever an enemy's country affords necessary for the subsistence and safety of the army, and of such deception as does not involve the breaking of good faith either positively pledged, regarding agreements entered into during the war, or supposed by the modern law of war to exist. Men who take up arms against one another

1. *See* Instructions for the Government of Armies of the United States in the Field, General Order No. 100, art. 14 (Apr. 24, 1863) [hereinafter Lieber Code].

> in public war do not cease on this account to be moral beings, responsible to one another and to God.[2]

What then does military necessity *not* allow? The Lieber Code is clear on this as well, stating:

> Military necessity does not admit of cruelty—that is, the infliction of suffering for the sake of suffering or for revenge, nor of maiming or wounding except in fight, nor of torture to extort confessions. It does not admit of the use of poison in any way, nor of the wanton devastation of a district. It admits of deception, but disclaims acts of perfidy; and, in general, military necessity does not include any act of hostility which makes the return to peace unnecessarily difficult.[3]

In other words, the principle of military necessity prohibits acts that are gratuitous or superfluous in the sense that they do not confer a military advantage—that is, they are based in pure cruelty without practical advantage.[4] And clearly, killing enemy troops confers a large practical advantage insofar as it achieves, in the words of Article 14, "the legitimate purpose of the conflict, namely the complete or partial submission of the enemy at the earliest possible moment with the minimum expenditure of life and resources."[5] The mirror image of the principle of necessity is the principle of humanity, which restricts "suffering, injury or destruction not actually necessary for the accomplishment of legitimate military purposes."[6]

In applying these basic principles to particular situations, the ICRC's *Interpretive Guidance on Direct Participation in Hostilities* concludes that in conflicts between large, well-equipped armies, it will rarely prohibit any particular method of attack that is not already prohibited by a more specific rule of IHL.[7] However, in more asymmetrical conflicts such as

2. *Id.* art. 15.
3. *Id.* art. 16.
4. Gabriella Blum suggests that burgeoning domestic support for the war effort (by reporting high casualties of enemy troops) is not a legitimate military advantage for purposes of military necessity. Gabriella Blum, *The Dispensable Lives of Soldiers*, 2 J. Leg. Analysis 115, 142–43 (2010).
5. United Kingdom Ministry of Defence, The Manual Of The Law Of Armed Conflict § 2.2 (2004).
6. Practice Relating to Rule 14, Proportionality in Attack, *available at* http://www.icrc.org/customary-ihl/eng/docs/v2_cou_us_rule14 (quoting U.S. Dept. of the Air Force, Pamphlet 110–31: The Conduct of Armed Conflict and Air Operations §§ 1–3 (1976)).
7. *See* Mils Melzer, Int'l Comm. of the Red Cross, Interpretive Guidance on the Notion of Direct Participation in Hostilities under International Humanitarian Law 80 (2009) [hereinafter ICRC Interpretive Guidance].

non-international armed conflicts, the ICRC *Interpretive Guidance* concludes that the principles would yield substantive restrictions. It offers the following hypothetical:

> For example, an unarmed civilian sitting in a restaurant using a radio or mobile phone to transmit tactical targeting intelligence to an attacking air force would probably have to be regarded as directly participating in hostilities. Should the restaurant in question be situated within an area firmly controlled by the opposing party, however, it may be possible to neutralize the military threat posed by that civilian through capture or other non-lethal means without additional risk to the operating forces or the surrounding civilian population.[8]

The conclusion stands in stark contrast with the basic definition of the principle of necessity offered at the beginning of Section IX of the *Interpretive Guidance*: necessity only prohibits actions that do not advance "the complete or partial submission of the enemy at the earliest possible moment."[9] If this were the sole criterion, then perhaps the killing of an enemy terrorist who is lawfully targetable under IHL would not result in the submission of the enemy at an earlier moment than would his arrest and trial, because both killing and capture immobilize the threat. However, there is a second part to *jus in bello* necessity under both Lieber's formulation and the ICRC's: the "minimum expenditure of life and resources" of the attacking force.[10] Under this prong, the attempt to capture will inevitably result in a risk of greater damage to the assaulting force, and will offend the necessity principle's caveat that the assaulting force is permitted to achieve legitimate war aims "with the *minimum* expenditure of life and resources."[11] Consequently, risking *any* number of lives in an attempt to capture offends this principle as written. Indeed, even offering the *opportunity* to surrender might run afoul of this provision in certain circumstances, because it either eliminates the element of surprise or delays legitimate victory, or both.[12] The ICRC *Interpretive Guidance* offers little to explain why the principles of necessity and humanity would require capture, except for the conclusory statement that "it would defy basic notions of humanity to kill an adversary or to refrain from giving him or her an opportunity to surrender . . . ."[13]

8. *Id.* at 81.
9. *Id.* at 79 (citing UK Ministry of Defence Manual, *supra* note 5, § 2.2).
10. *Id; see also* Lieber Code, *supra* note 1, art. 15 (addressing military necessity in regards to the "unavoidable" destruction of persons).
11. ICRC Interpretive Guidance, *supra* note 7, at 79.
12. Indeed, Lieber explicitly recognized the importance of surprise. *See* Lieber Code, *supra* note 1, art. 19 ("Surprise may be a necessity.").
13. ICRC Interpretive Guidance, *supra* note 7, at 82.

We are left then with a disconnect between the ICRC's *formulation* of the principle of necessity and its *application* with regard to capture.[14] Given the principle of necessity's codified birth in the Lieber Code, proponents who argue that the principle means something more—a duty to pursue the least-harmful means—are insensitive to the historical context since Lieber codified the principle.[15] The following section explores that historical context.

II. LIEBER'S CONCEPTION OF NECESSITY

As noted above, necessity figured prominently in the work of Francis Lieber, who codified the first laws of war during the American Civil War, under the direction of President Lincoln. Although the Lieber Code was a legal document, Lieber was heavily influenced by philosophical texts, including those on natural law. He was also deeply Kantian in his orientation toward the law of war. In many respects, necessity was the conceptual cornerstone of his Code. As John Witt makes clear in his recent historical study of Lieber:

> Here then was a compelling but potentially ferocious framework for the laws of war. Outside of torture, virtually all destruction seemed permissible so long as it was necessary to advance a legitimate war effort. The law thus permitted the use of any weapon, including "those arms that do the quickest mischief in the widest range and in the surest manner." And it did so for a simple reason. As Lieber said more than once in the course of his lectures, short wars were more humane wars, and the way to ensure short wars was to fight them as fiercely as possible. The prospect of fierce wars might even prevent war from breaking out in the first place. It was thus critical that statesmen "not allow sentimentality to sway us in war," he warned. "The more earnestly and keenly wars are carried on, the better for humanity, for peace and civilization."[16]

This did not mean that there were no restrictions on warfare, however. Some prohibitions were categorical, regardless of whether necessity demanded

14. For an extensive critique, see W. Hays Parks, *Part IX of the ICRC "Direct Participation in Hostilities" Study: No Mandate, No Expertise, and Legally Incorrect*, 42 N.Y.U. J. INT'L L. & POL. 769, 805 (2010) ("The ICRC errs in its attempt to apply an inaccurate law enforcement paradigm in armed conflict.").

15. Indeed, the ICRC Interpretive Guidance concedes that military necessity is "strongly influenced" by the Lieber Code but includes no historical analysis of the development of the principle. ICRC INTERPRETIVE GUIDANCE, *supra* note 7, at 79 n.215.

16. JOHN FABIAN WITT, LINCOLN'S CODE 184 (2012).

it.[17] The use of torture was categorically impermissible, as was the use of poison and perfidy.[18] And today, the execution of captured POWs—even if taken during a reprisal to punish and induce a recalcitrant enemy to obey the laws of war—is impermissible under any situation (a categorical prohibition that emerged long after Lieber and was only recently codified).[19] But this just shows how little of the argumentative work is performed by the principle of necessity; the real prohibitory work in IHL is done by the specific prohibitions regarding outlawed methods of warfare, not the general principle of necessity, which allows prosecution of the war effort with maximum speed.[20]

As far as the general principle goes, what is outlawed by the principle of necessity is death and destruction not related to the war effort—actions performed purely out of cruelty, avarice, revenge, madness, or nihilism, one would suppose.[21] A rational actor has little reason to pursue such actions anyway, unless overcome by emotion, since they are not related to the war effort.[22] But the principle of necessity under IHL does not mean that the attacking force needs to sacrifice *more* in order to comply with the principle.[23] As Witt points out, Lieber wrote in an unfinished book that

17. *See* Gary Solis, The Law of Armed Conflict: International Humanitarian Law in War 260 (2010) (noting the situations that Lieber considered to be impermissible in war).

18. *See* Lieber Code, *supra* note 1, art. 16.

19. *See* Protocol Additional to the Geneva Conventions of 12 August 1949, and Relating to the Protection of Victims of International Armed Conflicts (Protocol I) arts. 11, 20, June 8, 1977, 1125 U.N.T.S. 3, at 11-12; Protocol Additional to the Geneva Conventions of 12 August 1949, and Relating to the Protection of Victims of Non-International Armed Conflicts (Protocol II) art. 13, June 8, 1977, 1125 U.N.T.S. 609, at 615. *But see* Michael N. Schmitt, *Military Necessity and Humanity in International Humanitarian Law: Preserving the Delicate Balance*, 50 Va. J. Int'l L. 795, 820–21 (2010) (citing the ICTY case, *Krupreskic*, which notes the "prohibition on belligerent reprisals against civilians that appears in Additional Protocol I had become customary." However, the author later indicates the United States and the United Kingdom consider these reprisals of military necessity under certain circumstances).

20. In his illuminating book, Witt argues that the Emancipation Proclamation was a war measure justified on the basis of military necessity—hence the greater social impact of Lieber's principle of necessity. *See* Witt, *supra* note 16, at 234.

21. *See* Lieber Code, *supra* note 1, art. 11 (stating that military necessity disclaims "all cruelty and bad faith . . . [;] all extortions and other transactions for individual gain; all acts of private revenge").

22. *See, e.g.*, Witt, *supra* note 16, at 184 (noting that Lieber believed that a brief and focused war effort is the best means of accomplishing military victory).

23. *See* Beth Van Schaack, *The Killing of Osama Bin Laden & Anwar Al-Aulaqi: Uncharted Legal Territory*, 14 Yearbook of Int'l Humanitarian L. 255, 292 (2011) (referring to as "revisionism" any interpretation of the necessity principle that requires capture before killing); *cf.* Blum, *supra* note 4, at 73 (arguing that the duty to capture based on military necessity could be enshrined as a legal obligation through amendment and

attacks were "lawful only as a means to obtain the great end for which a war is undertaken, and not for its own sake," and that this represented "the chief difference between the wars of barbarous ages and the armed contests of civilized people."[24] Witt concludes that "[i]n Lieber's hands, military necessity was both a broad limit on war's violence and a robust license to destroy."[25] Simply put, Lieber was not in favor of over-regulating warfare, because making wars too civilized would inevitably prolong them, potentially increasing the overall suffering.[26]

The resulting document that synthesized Lieber's theory of warfare and operationalized it into practice—what came to be known as the Lieber Code—is chock full of philosophical ideas regarding necessity. Unfortunately, the document remains a legal text with curt formulations unsuited to unpacking difficult philosophical concepts. Consequently, the Lieber Code provisions on necessity have been notoriously difficult to interpret. As noted in the previous section, the Code states that military necessity "admits of all direct destruction of life or limb of armed enemies" unless a specific prohibition applies, such as the one against causing unnecessary suffering or perfidy.[27] However, many scholars either ignore this aspect of the Code or refuse to recognize that it forms part of Lieber's definition of military necessity. Why is this insight ignored by modern human rights scholars tempted to redefine the principle of necessity?

The confusion stems in part from the structure of the Lieber Code itself. In Article 14, the Code states that "[m]ilitary necessity, as understood by modern civilized nations, consists in the necessity of those measures which are indispensable for securing the ends of the war, and which are lawful

supporting, like Melzer, a least-harmful-means test as a gloss on military necessity). However, Blum also has an innovative argument based on the principle of distinction. *See id.* at 127–31. Just as IHL requires attacking forces to use technology to distinguish between combatants and civilians, the same technology might be used to distinguish further *within* the category of combatants between threatening combatants and nonthreatening combatants. *See id.* at 120, 154–60. However, Blum fails to contend with the fact that the very concept of combatancy within IHL is based on the notion that all combatants are by definition threatening, hence their targetability based on status. *See id.* at 126 (conceding that IHL presumes that all soldiers are "seeking to kill"). To talk of "nonthreatening" combatants is a contradiction in terms unless one introduces a temporal element, that is, the combatant is not threatening at a discrete moment in time because he is sleeping or otherwise disengaged from direct fighting. *See id.* at 157–60.

24. *See* Witt, *supra* note 16, at 234. Witt refers to this as Lieber's "Clausewitzian perspective" on war (violence rationally related to the political objectives of the state). *Id.* at 236.

25. *Id.* at 234.

26. Lieber Code, *supra* note 1, art. 29 ("Sharp wars are brief.").

27. Lieber Code, *supra* note 1, article 15.

according to the modern law and usages of war." If one stops there and focuses exclusively on the phrase "*indispensable*," then the Code may indeed sound like it supports the least-harmful-means conception of military necessity. However it would be a mistake to stop after Article 14, because the definition of military necessity continues into Article 15 and its statement that "Military necessity admits of all direct destruction of life or limb of armed enemies . . . "[28] Consequently, the Code categorically establishes that destruction of enemy forces, in some cases including killing them, is clearly within the margin of military necessity. If that is the case, what *is* prohibited by military necessity? The following article of the Code provides the crucial answer to that question: "Military necessity does not admit of cruelty—that is, the infliction of suffering for the sake of suffering or for revenge . . . "[29] Taken together, these provisions make clear that necessity, at least as a historical matter during the Civil War, could not be used as grounds to establish a positive obligation to attempt capture prior to killing an enemy combatant.

The principle of necessity permits actions taken to secure the ends of the war, including killing enemy forces and destroying enemy installations, but not actions that violate specific prohibitions in the laws of war underlying the treatment of POWs or wounded soldiers receiving medical care. It does, however, outlaw all actions *unrelated* to the war aim, such as killing inspired by pure hatred or vengeance alone. These actions have no role to play in the decisions of the professional soldier. The full scope of Lieber's principle of necessity only becomes clear once one understands that the definition of necessity spans three whole articles of the Code.

Indeed, John Witt's study of Lieber and Lincoln details that whatever necessity meant, "it did not mean that armies were permitted to take only those actions that were necessary in the sense of leaving no other choice."[30] Hence by the nineteenth century Grotius's account of military necessity had been replaced by Lieber. Witt also notes that Lieber's version of necessity did not

> invoke a less restrictive but still demanding approach that would have prohibited acts of force for which there were less destructive substitutes. This has been an appealing notion for humanitarian lawyers ever since, some of whom have sought to adopt a least-destructive-means requirement to lessen the human suffering of war. But Lieber thought that the attempt to reduce the human suffering arising

28. *Id.*
29. Lieber Code, *supra* note 1, art. 16.
30. Witt, *supra* note 16, at 235.

> out of any one decision in wartime might well increase suffering in warfare more generally. "When war is begun," Lieber told his students, "the best and most humane thing is to carry it on as intensely as possible so as to be through with it as soon as possible." He repeated the same idea in the code. "The more vigorously wars are pursued, the better it is for humanity. Sharp wars are brief." If this was so, then the least destructive means were not necessarily the most humane. The opposite might be true. Indeed, if war was sufficiently terrible, there might be fewer wars. Human suffering from warfare might be reduced most by a rule that not only permitted but required the greatest possible destruction.[31]

Whether Lieber was correct or not when he claimed that sharp wars are brief is beside the point. It is a debatable empirical claim that may or may not be borne out by the facts; one need not subscribe to its veracity. The best way of describing Lieber's point is that there is an optimal level of regulation in wartime that reduces overall suffering. Under-regulating warfare will result in too much suffering, but counterintuitively, Lieber also teaches us that *over-regulating* warfare might also increase overall suffering if it unnecessarily prolongs the conflict and results in more death and destruction. Lieber's view suggests that philosophers and lawyers should find that optimal point of regulation. Whether this view is correct or not, there is a less controversial lesson to take from our discussion of Lieber: his vision of necessity represented the basic structure of the laws of war during the U.S. Civil War era. Necessity *permits* killing and destruction of enemy forces, whereas the specific prohibitions (distinction, proportionality, restrictions on various weapons, the prohibition on unnecessary suffering, perfidy, etc.) *restrict* the use of force. But it is important not to confuse the two, and one certainly cannot use the specific prohibitions as a rationale for reading the general principle of necessity in a wider fashion.

This analysis of the Lieber Code is strengthened by Lieber's own writings on military necessity. These writings are not widely available, perhaps contributing to the occasional misinterpretations of the Code. However, his unpublished manuscript on the *Law and Usages of War* makes abundantly clear that necessity simply means that the action in question is related to the object of the war. Although Lieber is not given his due as a theorist of war, his edifice is impeccably constructed, built from first principles inspired equally from Kant and von Clausewitz. He first defines war as "a protracted physical contest between large numbers."[32] Once there has been a resort to force, violence between the parties becomes lawful: "Physical destruction

31. *Id.* at 235–36.
32. Francis Lieber, Law and Usages of War (1861) (Notebook II).

and [stratagem] (not cruelty or treachery) are lawful." The major limitations on this right are the principles of reciprocity and retaliation. He defines the first as "what is right for the one, is right for the other (or perfect equality of the belligerents)." In the cases where the enemy violates these norms, the principle of retaliation creates a form of self-enforcement that helps ensure the principle of reciprocity. Simply put, the threat of retaliation itself enforces the principle of reciprocity, thereby ensuring that both sides of the conflict have the potential to suffer the same fate.

That being said, not all violence is permitted, Lieber maintains: "That no more hostility be resorted to, than necessary, and that the intercourse between the belligerents remains, even in war, that of honourable, truthful men."[33] But Lieber is quick to clarify that "necessary" in this context does not mean something akin to the least restrictive means, that is, the only avenue to achieve that particular result. Rather, he is clear that belligerents "may indeed inflict death or wounds—both may be, frequently are painful, but cruelty consists in inflicting pain for the sake of pain." In other words, cruelty is sadism, the act of being "*pleased with the pain of others*."[34] So for Lieber, the principle of necessity outlaws cruelty and "unnecessary infliction of pain, pain for its own sake to satisfy the lust of revenge or a fiendish hatred."[35]

Lieber could not be clearer that the killing of enemy combatants is consistent with the principle of necessity, and it is in this sense that he epitomizes the view of necessity as license: the licensing of soldiers to kill nearly any enemy soldier. "Simple infliction of death is not considered cruelty," he writes.[36] Lieber also thinks that the resort to cruelty is counterproductive: "Probably he who on principle abstains from treachery and cruelty will in the long run obtain the advantages generally attending a high-minded course, but whether or not, cruelty and treachery are not to be admitted in modern law of nations however provoking the enemy may be."[37] Although this may sound prima facie counterintuitive because refusing to follow the constraints of warfare would seem to place a fighting force in a better position, thus suggesting that rational self-interest would counsel in favor of violating the laws of war whereas only morality would counsel compliance. Not so, from Lieber's perspective.[38]

33. *Id.*
34. *Id.*
35. *Id.*
36. *Id.*, Notebook IV.
37. *Id.*
38. Lieber also notes: "War would be but destruction itself if treachery were adopted as a principle. It would be illogical; for how can we carry on transactions with the

Cruelty means engaging in violence and causing pain for its own sake, rather than engaging in violence in order to achieve the end result of war: causing the enemy to submit to one's conditions. Therefore cruelty *by definition* is rationally unjustified because it is unrelated to the external aim of the war and is tethered only to its purely internal logic of violence for its own sake. In fact, Lieber even translates the phrase military necessity as "*raison de guerre*,"[39] literally meaning the reason for war. The principle of military necessity is axiomatically satisfied by all actions that are performed in order to reach the goal of the war: submission of the enemy as quickly as possible to one's terms. "Peace of some sort must be the end of all war—a return to the normal state. Those who would carry on war for its own sake are enemies to civilization, to mankind," Lieber writes.[40] "War is not its own end; hence the battle—a portion of the war—neither. The object of the war and of each battle must lie beyond the war and beyond the battle."[41]

This represents the central and undeniable move of Lieber's ethical program. What separates murder from lawful belligerency is the collective nature of the conflict and the fact that the killing is performed in order to achieve the collective geopolitical aim of the war. Without that collective context, the killing becomes murder simpliciter:

> A word as to firing on centinels or single men of battle. All the principles which we have endeavoured carefully to lay down, and all the truths which we have endeavoured certain concerning the essence of war, must show you that firing upon single men, for no other purpose than killing them, is simple murder . . . The object of the war, and therefore, of the battle, lies *beyond* the war, and all killing which is not believed to be *conducive to the obtaining of this end*, is, as I have purposely so often stated, murder.[42]

So Lieber's collectivism runs deep. He views the soldier as implementing the will of the commander and the will of the political body under whose

enemy if we allow the principle of treachery to be acted upon. How could we conclude peace—a lasting, honest peace? On the ground of expediency, it would be better to abstain from treachery." *Id.*

39. *Id.*, Notebook VII.

40. *Id.*

41. *Id. See also* LIEBER, LAW AND USAGES OF WAR (1861) ("The object of all civilized war is either defence or the forcing of the enemy to conditions which we think necessary and just. It lies beyond the war and beyond the battle. Destruction of the hostile army is rarely the object of a land battle, but even when it is, it is only a means to obtain the [other] end of the war.").

42. *Id.*

authority he fights. The soldier is a professional, deserving the respect due generated by the relationship between opposing soldiers on opposite sides of the conflict. The soldier has distinct role responsibilities that are crucial for the licensing of killing enemy soldiers. Lieber even takes this point to its logical extreme, viewing the soldier as a "belligerent" in name only. The real "belligerents" are the nations the soldiers represent in warfare:

> Enemies are the contending parties. The contending parties are the political societies. *The hostile states are the real belligerents*. In regular wars the citizens of a warfaring state is [expected] to be an enemy to each citizens of the hostile state, but this is only because members of the hostile society, and not on account of individual hostility. The farther civilization advances the more distinctly are the two characters separated . . . Individual citizens cannot be made to suffer in person or property, as individuals. As such they are not enemies in truth.[43]

The soldiers themselves are therefore deserving of moral respect in their mutual combat.

The moral nature of combat flows from multiple sources. First, Lieber concludes that all nations belong to the same "family" of nations, not just a mere state of nature. This family is civilization itself—as opposed to mere savagery—that is represented by the international community of nations. The moral nature of combat stems from our *membership* in this family of moral nations. War represents a breakdown of peacetime relations, but human beings do not shed their "moral" or "social" character during war, because they all belong to the same family of nations, that is civilization. Consequently, the rules of warfare are designed to keep that family intact:

> War being a physical contest, yet man remaining forever a moral being, and peace being the ultimate object of war, the following conclusions [result]: (c) only so far as necessary for this object and (d) we must abstain from everything that would make the ulterior peace, the normal state, unnecessarily difficult or [unobtainable].[44]

This represents Lieber's Kantian impulses.[45] The goal of international discourse is to reach the normal state of peace (and ideally perpetual peace).

43. *Id.*
44. *Id.*
45. *See* Immanuel Kant, Perpetual Peace: A Philosophical Essay (1795). For a discussion, see Richard Baxter, *The First Modern Codification of the Law of War*, 3 Int'l Rev. Red Cross 171–89 (1963), *reprinted in* Richard Baxter, Humanizing the Laws of War 121, 124, 139 (2013).

Consequently, warfare should be conducted in ways that hastened the return to peace and do not needlessly frustrate its return. Prohibitions on treachery and cruelty fit nicely into this framework, since treachery and perfidy linger and foster distrust that extends well beyond the cessation of hostilities, making the return to peace difficult.[46] Similarly, cruelty inflames the passions with hatred that simmers long after the battle is over, thus preventing the establishment of a lasting peace—which is paradoxically the true goal of war: the *return* to peace.

Other *jus in bello* restrictions apply. For example, the prohibition against killing a soldier hors de combat follows the same logic. Soldiers who have effectively communicated their surrender are no longer a threat, and therefore their killing can only satisfy the demands of cruelty or vengeance. "A soldier on the field of battle makes known that he [submits] as prisoner of war, by laying down his arms and asking for quarter," Lieber writes.[47] "It must be granted except where there is an impossibility of making him a prisoner. Formerly some regiments would declare that they never give quarter and of course would receive none . . . This is now very rare, perhaps abolished in all organized armies. . . ."[48]

Similarly, wounded soldiers are also protected persons once they are hors de combat. Lieber even goes so far as to state: "*The wounded enemy is a sacred person.*"[49] He continues: "He is of course a prisoner, but must be provided for by him into whose hands he falls. No difference is to be made between him and the victor's own wounded."[50] This statement follows logically from Lieber's view that the real belligerents are the enemy collectives, and the soldiers are professionals working on behalf of their commanders and political leaders. Killing wounded soldiers who cannot fight is just as bad as declaring that no quarter will be given.[51]

Lieber's definition of belligerency is so well refined that it even provides him with an argument against slavery. As Witt explains in his history of the Civil War, President Lincoln used Lieber's concept of military necessity in order to justify Lincoln's executive actions to abolish slavery. However, there is another connection between Lieber's laws of war and

46. Lieber also says that "[w]ars of extirpation . . . wars of plunder, belong to the savage state of man." FRANCIS LIEBER, LAW AND USAGES OF WAR (1861).

47. FRANCIS LIEBER, LAW AND USAGES OF WAR, Notebook VII (1861).

48. *Id.*, Notebook VIII.

49. *Id.*

50. *Id.*, Notebook V.

51. Lieber also refers to the Battle of Balaclava (1854) during the Crimean War, in which an officer was charged for "having ordered his men, in battle, to bayonet wounded English and Frenchmen on the ground." *Id.*

the abolishment of slavery. For Lieber, slavery becomes possible when one nation vanquishes another and takes their enemies as slaves. This practice was once common, and even purportedly justified on the grounds that the victorious army was permitted to kill members of the vanquished people. Under this approach, enslaving the enemy population was a humane gift given to the enemy population: sparing their lives and taking their labor and freedom instead.

In Lieber's understanding, this argument for the legitimacy of slavery is fallacious because it starts from false premises about the spoils that are due to the victor:

> The victor has no primary or absolute right of killing the enemy. That is an idea belonging to the internecine period. We kill in battle to remove the opposing obstacle, that is the armed soldier in our way; when vanquished or disarmed he ceases to be the warlike obstacle in our way of obtaining the end of war. Granting him therefore to live is the very proof that the right of killing him has slipped from our hands, and, consequently, the right of enslaving founded upon the presumed right of killing . . . The right of killing ceases with the necessity of killing; hence the right of selling the life.[52]

Consequently, the prohibition against slavery stems from the basic principles of the laws of war: killing is permitted during warfare insofar as it is related to the aim of bringing hostilities to a close as quickly as possible. But once the hostilities are complete, the right to kill enemy combatants evaporates. So the putative right to enslave the enemy population is built upon a purely illusory right to kill the enemy population.

Lieber's version of the laws of war is incredibly progressive in some respects and less so in others. Lieber believed categorically that wounded soldiers incapable of fighting should not be killed, and that to do so was criminal. Wounded soldiers were sacred. Soldiers who laid down their arms and surrendered should be captured, although he apparently believed that the prohibition on declaring no quarter might be suspended in situations where the taking of prisoners was logistically impossible.[53] Civilians were generally protected from the horrors of warfare and could not be enslaved or killed simply because their side of the conflict was defeated. On the other hand, in his Lectures, he indicates that soldiers were not wholly immune from actions, such as the poisoning of drinking wells, which might

52. *Id.*, Notebook VI.

53. This rule has certainly changed. In the contemporary law of war, logistical limitations are not considered a justification for failing to take enemy soldiers as prisoners.

be taken by enemy forces as a method for securing the end of the war. This just shows how wide Lieber's early conception of military necessity was.

Why then do scholars think that Lieber's conception of military necessity is far more constraining than it actually is? First, they confuse the regulating function of the laws of war with its licensing function. The constraints regarding prisoners of war, wounded soldiers who are hors de combat, and the principles of distinction and proportionality that protect civilians—these are all regulating principles that constrain the behavior of combatants during armed conflict. But for Lieber the concept of necessity belongs most to the licensing function of the law of war, with only one small foot in the regulating sphere. Military necessity transforms, in warfare, what would otherwise constitute an immoral and illegal act of murder; but because the killing is performed in pursuit of the aim of winning the war, the killing is transformed into a lawful act of belligerency. This is the licensing function of the law of war, and the principle of necessity stands at its core. True, necessity also has a regulating function, but it is incredibly weak. It outlaws only acts of vengeance, cruelty, and sadism.

Of course, one might ask what the principle of necessity is good for if it always allows the killing and destruction of enemy forces unless another more specific prohibition applies. The answer is that in most cases the principle of necessity more closely tracks the *licensing* function of the law of armed conflict—that is that aspect of the law of armed conflict that changes the default rule that reigns in peacetime that says that killing is impermissible. Necessity is the expression of the law of armed conflict's changing of that default rule to one where the killing of enemy combatants becomes permitted. The one situation where necessity *does* provide a regulating function that restrains the use of force is when killing is performed for reasons that have nothing to do with prosecuting the war effort and getting the enemy to succumb as quickly as possible—a principle announced in Article 14 of the Lieber Code.[54] Think of killing for pure sadistic pleasure or vengeance, for example.[55] Necessity would not permit such killings because they were unrelated to the goal of winning the war.

One might also object that although this was Lieber's vision of the concept of necessity, the law of war has evolved substantially since then and has jettisoned Lieber's Clausewitzian notion of necessity. Perhaps we are

54. *See* Lieber Code, *supra* note 1, art. 14 ("Military necessity, as understood by modern civilized nations, consists in the necessity of those measures which are indispensable for securing the ends of the war, and which are lawful according to the modern law and usages of war.").

55. WITT, *supra* note 16, at 236.

no longer living in the era of Lieber? Although it is true that the laws of war have evolved, and perhaps gained rigor, codification, and theoretical sophistication in the process of adding new *specific* prohibitions on particular methods of warfare, its original structure remains relatively unchanged. The concept of necessity provides a license to kill enemy combatants, whereas specific prohibitions constrain that use of force against specific targets (civilians) and with specific methods (perfidy) or weaponry.

III. MILITARY NECESSITY AT THE NUREMBERG TRIBUNALS

Lieber's conception of military necessity survives to this day and is by no means a relic of American history. In fact, it was applied by the U.S. Military Tribunals sitting in Nuremberg in the *High Command Case* and to a certain extent in the *Hostages Case*, which included this famous definition: "Military necessity permits a belligerent, subject to the laws of war, to apply any amount and kind of force to compel the complete submission of the enemy with the least possible expenditure of time, life, and money."[56] This formulation replicates the conceptual structure of Lieber's definition of military necessity by linking it with the submission of the enemy and doing so as quickly as possible.[57] It is also codified in modern military manuals.[58]

Notice, however, that neither the Lieber nor the *Hostages* formulations of necessity permitted the concept to override the other, more specific, prohibitions contained in the law of war. In Article 14 of his Code, Lieber limited military necessity to actions "which are lawful according to the modern law and usages of war," whereas the *Hostages* formulation says the actions must be "subject to the laws of war." These formulations present a

56. *United States v. List (The Hostages Case)*, Case No. 7 (Feb. 19, 1948), *reprinted in* Trials of War Criminals Before the Nuremberg Military Tribunals under Control Council Law No. 10 1230, 1253 (1950).

57. David Luban argues that the *List* formulation of military necessity is even more permissive than Lieber's definition of military necessity. *See* David Luban, *Military Necessity and the Cultures of Military Law*, 26 Leiden J. Int'l Law 315, 341–42 (2013). However, Lieber's conception of military necessity was just as broad—permitting all military actions related to securing the ends of war and outlawing only sadistic and cruel killings inspired by vengeance and other evil emotions.

58. *See* UK Ministry of Defence Manual, *supra* note 5 (necessity is "that degree and kind of force, not otherwise prohibited by the law of armed conflict, that is required in order to achieve the legitimate purpose of the conflict, namely the complete or partial submission of the enemy at the earliest possible moment with the minimum expenditure of life and resources").

consistent framework: military necessity provides a broad licensing function for all actions designed to pursue the ends of war, and outlawing only those actions that are delinked from the aims of the war and are pursued for irrational or emotional reasons. Then, the analysis moves to the more specific prohibitions, including respecting the right of surrendered or wounded soldiers to be treated humanely. But the truly humane aspects of the law of war stem more from the specific prohibitions, not from the principle of military necessity, which since Lieber has been incredibly broad and probably remains so today.

To make this argument, let us examine in greater depth these post–World War II cases. First, consider the *Hostages Case*. The American Military Tribunal sitting in Nuremberg rejected the argument of the legality of reprisal killings of civilians by describing the general principle of military necessity, and then also describing its limits:

> Military necessity permits a belligerent, subject to the laws of war, to apply any amount and kind of force to compel the complete submission of the enemy with the least possible expenditure of time, life, and money . . . It permits the destruction of life of armed enemies and other persons whose destruction is incidentally unavoidable by the armed conflicts of the war.

Notice that this statement of the principle of military necessity does not set limits on the use of force needed to kill enemy soldiers, as long as those deaths are "incidentally unavoidable" to achieve military objectives. There is a kind of exception from the normal prohibition on killing that is part of the understanding of military necessity.

The term "incidentally unavoidable" bears some relationship to the common sense understanding of necessity. If something is unavoidable then it is fair to say that it is necessary, and necessity seems to be an appropriate label. But the qualifying term "incidental" raises suspicions that military necessity here is not really necessity as it would be understood in common parlance (or by metaphysicians, as we have seen in a previous chapter). Something can be "incidental" in that it is part of one way of accomplishing something, not the only way to accomplish the objective, as would seemingly be true if it were really necessary.

Yet, there is a second part of the *Hostages Case* where it is made clear that military necessity protects civilian lives and civilian property more strictly than it protects the lives of soldiers. Necessity

> does not permit the killing of innocent inhabitants for purposes of revenge or the satisfaction of a lust to kill. The destruction of property to be lawful must be

> imperatively demanded by the necessities of war . . . There must be some reasonable connection between the destruction of property and the overcoming of the enemy forces.[59]

Here we have the setting of constraints on destruction of lives and property in the use of the words "imperatively demanded" rather than "incidentally unavoidable," signaling that civilian life and property is to be valued more highly than the lives of soldiers, since "imperatively demanded" is much closer to the commonsense meaning of necessity than "incidentally unavoidable."

However, the other Nuremberg-era case uses different language from either parts of the *Hostages Case*. In the *German High Command Case*, military necessity is described as follows:

> A bare declaration that what was done was militarily necessary has no more probative substance than a statement contained in an answer or other pleading. In order to make out a valid defense of destruction or pillage on the ground of military necessity, the defendant must prove that the facts and circumstances were such at the time he ordered these measures that he would be justified in believing them to be necessary to save his troops from an imminent disaster.[60]

Here we have an account of necessity that is a kind of license that is much closer to commonsense understandings of necessity. The situation has to be one where if lethal force were not used the commander's troops would suffer "from an imminent disaster," with the understanding that the commander must be granted this license to satisfy his role.

The terminology employed in the *German High Command Case* sets the bar very high indeed, and seems to us to be quite close to what necessity should mean in IHL. Notice the use of two terms. First, there is the idea that a disaster would ensue if the lethal action were not taken. We are not merely to contemplate accomplishing a military objective, but only of one that would save the lives of one's own troops. And then there is also the term "imminent," signaling that if this particular lethal action is not taken *here*, the lives of one's troops will be lost.

59. *United States v. List (The Hostages Case), supra* note 56, at 1253–55. For a comment on this passage, see Schmitt, *supra* note 19, at 795–839.

60. *U.S. v. Wilhelm Von Leeb and Thirteen Others (The German High Command Case)*, United States Military Tribunal, Nuremberg, Dec. 30, 1947–Oct. 28, 1948, *reprinted in* THE UNITED NATIONS WAR CRIMES COMMISSION, XII TRIALS OF WAR CRIMINALS BEFORE THE NUREMBERG MILITARY TRIBUNALS UNDER CONTROL COUNCIL LAW NO. 10 125 (1949).

As we saw earlier, Hugo Grotius's "no other way" standard is stronger than either of the *Hostages Case* standards we find in international law from Nuremberg: the "incidentally unavoidable" standard, where "incidental" is the modifier, or the "imperatively demanded" standard, which seems to be restricted to civilian deaths. In Grotius's view, military necessity is not incidental but central to incidents of war, and military necessity is not restricted to lethal action taken against civilians, as it was for both of the Nuremberg *Hostage Case* decisions. Normatively, Grotius's standard for necessity seems to be more defensible than either of these two standards of necessity that we can find in the Nuremberg proceedings, while also being very similar to the *German High Command Case*. The understanding of necessity in the Lieber Code is closer to what necessity means in international law today, and in a restricted version can also be made plausible.

IV. WHAT'S RIGHT AND WHAT'S WRONG WITH LIEBER'S NECESSITY

One might object that IHL has moved beyond the Lieber Code, and that many of the customs of war permitted in Lieber's time have long since been outlawed by treaty or custom in the current post–World-War-II era of IHL. Although this is true—the Lieber Code was undoubtedly replaced by more modern codifications[61]—the question is more properly whether the principle of necessity has undergone a similar transformation. But based on the particular codification of the principle of necessity that one hears most often, and that has been adopted by the ICRC, it is clear that the principle of necessity has largely remained unchanged since Lieber.[62] Rather, it is the *specific* prohibitions that have changed in IHL.[63] Indeed, one of the reasons the specific rules on prohibited methods were adopted within the last fifty years is precisely because the principle of necessity—by itself—was

61. *See, e.g.*, Additional Protocol I, *supra* note 19, arts. 11, 20, 1125 U.N.T.S. at 11–12, 15; Geneva Convention (I) for the Amelioration of the Condition of the Wounded and Sick in Armed Forces in the Field, Geneva, 12 August 1949, art. 50, 6 U.S.T. 3114, 75 U.N.T.S. 31 ("Grave breaches to which the preceding Article relates shall be those involving any of the following acts, if committed against persons or property protected by the Convention: wilful killing, torture or inhuman treatment, including biological experiments, wilfully causing great suffering or serious injury to body or health, and extensive destruction and appropriation of property, not justified by military necessity and carried out unlawfully and wantonly.").

62. *See* Additional Protocol I, *supra* note 19, art. 54(5), 1125 U.N.T.S. at 27.

63. *See, e.g.*, Additional Protocol I, *supra* note 19, arts. 11, 20 1125 U.N.T.S. at 11–12, 15; Geneva Conventions, *supra* note 61, art. 13, 75 U.N.T.S. at 146.

ill-suited to the task.[64] Since military necessity means—and has meant since Lieber—that the attack is legitimately related to the expeditious pursuit of war aims with minimal risk of life and limb to the attacker, there is no possible way that the concept of military necessity could perform the wide-ranging normative work that some human-rights lawyers today have ascribed to it.[65] The concept is simply incapable of carrying that heavy a load in the argument.[66]

The more modern precedents support and extend this reading of military necessity as being essentially unchanged since the time of Lieber. As discussed above, the U.S. Military Tribunal sitting in Nuremberg concluded in *Hostages* that "[m]ilitary necessity permits a belligerent, subject to the laws of war, to apply any amount and kind of force to compel the complete submission of the enemy with the least expenditure of time, life, and money."[67] This formulation closely matches Lieber's insofar as it permits an unrestricted amount of force as long as it is rationally related to defeating the enemy, unless prohibited by a more specific rule. David Luban is correct when he concludes that the *Hostages* formulation of military necessity "includes any lawful act that saves a dollar or a day in the pursuit of military victory."[68] Some scholars are critical of such formulations on normative

64. *See* Luban, *supra* note 57, at 25 (noting that human rights advocates believe that humanitarian treaties were created "to break with the horrifying past").

65. *See id.* at 11–22 (describing the "Laws of Armed Conflict" approach to the laws of war wherein military necessity prevails over broader humanitarian concerns); *see also* Declaration Renouncing the Use, in Time of War, of Explosive Projectiles under 400 Grammes Weight, Nov. 29, 1868, *available at* http://www.icrc.org/ihl.nsf/FULL/130 [hereinafter St. Petersburg Declaration] (only legitimate war aim is "to weaken the military forces of the enemy; [t]hat for this purpose it is sufficient to disable the greatest possible number of men").

66. *But see* Burrus M. Carnahan, *Lincoln, Lieber and the Laws of War: The Origins and Limits of the Principle of Military Necessity*, 92 AM. J. INT'L L. 213, 231 (1998) ("Today, military necessity is widely regarded as something that must be overcome or ignored if international humanitarian law is to develop, and its original role as a limit on military action has been forgotten. As a result, the principle has not been applied in new situations where it could serve as a significant legal restraint until more specific treaty rules or customs are established."). Carnahan argues that the principle of military necessity has chastised military conduct, citing as examples the reluctance to bomb food crops during the Korean Conflict. *See id.* at 229.

67. *United States v. List (The Hostage Case)*, Case No. 7 (Feb. 19, 1948), *reprinted in* 11 TRIALS OF WAR CRIMINALS BEFORE THE NUREMBERG MILITARY TRIBUNALS UNDER CONTROL COUNCIL LAW NO. 10 1230, 1253 (2007); *see also* Luban, *supra* note 57, at 43 (referring to this as the Hostages formulation of military necessity). For a discussion of this standard in relation to the entire *List* case, see KEVIN JON HELLER, THE NUREMBERG MILITARY TRIBUNALS AND THE ORIGINS OF INTERNATIONAL CRIMINAL LAW (2011).

68. Luban, *supra* note 57, at 44. However, Luban views the *Hostage* formulation as a substantial expansion of Lieber's original formulation, mostly because Luban focuses

grounds because they do not require an attacker to give up even a trivial amount of marginal risk to its own troops in order to reduce the amount of casualties to the opposing force.[69] However, this just highlights the previous point: that military necessity often tracks the licensing function of IHL more than it tracks the regulating function of IHL, the latter being carried by more specific prohibitory rules.[70] As explained above, IHL involves two functions: it licenses the privilege of combatancy, permitting killing that would otherwise be illegal, and it then places constraints on that license, by virtue of specific prohibitions regarding methods and tactics.[71] Though it straddles both domains, the concept of military necessity belongs far more to the former than the latter.

The first question is what is meant by the term "indispensable" with regard to defining necessary actions as those that are indispensable for securing the ends of the war. First, if one reads only Article 14 of the Lieber Code, one might be left with the perception that "indispensable" means "left with no other choice."[72] But it certainly did not mean that for Lieber, as Articles 15 through 20 of the Lieber Code make clear.[73] A holistic reading of the entire first section of the Lieber Code makes clear that necessity allows not only the wholesale destruction of life and limb but also anything non-gratuitous.[74] Second, contemporary IHL commentators sensitive to

exclusively on Article 14 of the Lieber Code (defining military necessity in relation to actions that are "indispensable" to the war aims) but downplays Article 15 ("Military necessity admits of all direct destruction of life or limb of armed enemies") as well as the historical context, including the state practice and *opinio juris*, of Lieber's Code. *Compare id.* at 44–46, *with* Lieber Code, *supra* note 1, art. 14, 15. In fact, a complete reading of Lieber's notion of military necessity is impossible without considering in toto everything from Article 14 through Article 29 ("The more vigorously wars are pursued, the better it is for humanity. Sharp wars are brief."). *See id.* art. 14–29.

69. *See* Blum, *supra* note 4, at 124 (noting that necessity "justifies not only what is required to win the war, but also what reduces the risks of losses or costs of the war"); Seth Lazar, *Necessity in Self-Defense and War*, 40 PHIL. & PUB. AFF. 3, 39–42 (2012) (formulating necessity in terms of marginal risk).

70. *But see* Luban, *supra* note 57, at 40 (arguing that "necessity serves both a prohibitive and licensing function").

71. *See* Blum, *supra* note 4, at 123.

72. *See* Lieber Code, *supra* note `, art. 14.

73. *See* WITT, *supra* note 16, at 235 ("These were the key words: *Indispensable for securing the ends of the war*. . . . But what did [indispensable] mean? One thing was certain. It did not mean that armies were permitted to take only those actions that were necessary in the sense of leaving no other choice. Read this way, the necessity principle would have prohibited virtually every act of war, for it was rarely the case that any course of conduct (in war or otherwise) offered the only available path forward."); *see also* Lieber Code, *supra* note 1, art. 14–20.

74. Hays Parks, a member of the ICRC Direct Participation Working Group, also notes that the ICRC *Interpretive Guidance* fails to cite Article 15 and ignores its "life and

this nuance understand "indispensable" in a similar fashion, as proportionately related to prompt resolution of the war effort.[75] Provisions in the Additional Protocols also evidence this prohibition against superfluous suffering.[76]

One way of giving content to the notion of causing superfluous suffering is to think of marginal risk.[77] If the law were to impose a duty to capture, the burden imposed on the attacking party would take the form of additional risk; troops would be placed at risk that they would not otherwise suffer if they simply killed the target. Military necessity therefore insists on a form of Pareto optimality in which there is no Pareto-superior move that makes one side better off without making the other side worse off. Forgoing the use of lethal force (and using capture instead) would definitely benefit the target, but this advantage could only be secured by making the attacking side worse off (through the risk to its troops). Since there will always be risk associated with capture instead of kill (with the exception of enemy troops who have already surrendered and laid down their weapons), requiring capture would not be a Pareto-superior move. Consequently, Pareto optimality is reached at a rather low level in the necessity of armed conflict, since additional risk is always a potential burden for either side. That is why IHL offers so little protection to enemy combatants, other than against gratuitous suffering.[78]

limb" language, thus leading to the *Guidance*'s erroneous interpretation and application of military necessity. *See* Parks, *supra* note 14, at 805.

75. *See, e.g.*, Michael Bothe, Karl Josef Partsch & Waldemar A. Solf, New Rules for Victims of Armed Conflicts 194 (1982) (allowing relevant and proportionate action); Myres S. McDougal & Florentino P. Feliciano, Law and Minimum World Public Order 521–22 (1961) (equating Lieber's "indispensable" with "relevant and proportionate").

76. *See, e.g.*, Additional Protocol I, *supra* note 19, art. 35(2), 1125 U.N.T.S. at 21 ("It is prohibited to employ weapons, projectiles and material and methods of warfare of a nature to cause superfluous injury or unnecessary suffering."). For an example, see William Gerald Downey, Jr., *The Law of War and Military Necessity*, 47 Am. J. Int'l L. 251, 261 (1953) (discussing regulated weapon systems such as explosive bullets that aggravate "the recipient without furthering the military purpose of the projectile"); *see also* Robert D. Sloane, *On the Use and Abuse of Necessity in the Law of State Responsibility*, 106 Am. J. Int'l L. 447, 486–87 (2012); *cf.* Jean Pictet, Development and Principles of International Humanitarian Law 75 (1985) (noting change from "superfluous injury" to "unnecessary suffering").

77. For a discussion of marginal risk in this context, see Lazar, *supra* note 69, at 13. However, Lazar's analysis of necessity is more applicable for self-defense since his formulations all assume the wrongfulness of one side of the conflict—an assumption that is entirely inconsistent with contemporary *jus in bello* built around the equality of combatants.

78. *See id.* at 41 (noting that "the interests of enemy combatants are almost wholly discounted, and additional weight is given to the interests of civilians, regardless of their affiliation").

Several scholars, including Gabriella Blum,[79] have argued that there are good normative reasons to change the law going forward; some of these arguments are compelling, though even they must contend with Lieber's arguments. In particular, Blum points out that current international humanitarian law values civilian lives as hierarchically superior to combatant lives—an assumption that stands in need of moral justification. Consider that in some countries the division between a civilian and a conscript might be nothing more than thirty days in basic training and a standard-issue rifle that has never been fired. Are these facts sufficient to ground a categorical moral distinction between the two?

The legal debates surrounding the correct interpretation of necessity (as well as hors de combat) are hardly isolated; they sit within a broader philosophical debate regarding the nature of combatancy, distinction, and targeting that cuts to the very center of our modern system of legal regulation of warfare. Understanding and evaluating the normative appeal of the new definitions of necessity is impossible without first coming to terms with the broader philosophical positions of which they are a limited part.

Traditionally, Just War theory conceived of *jus ad bellum* and *jus in bello* as entirely separate—a position that gained renewed vigor after Michael Walzer's publication of *Just and Unjust Wars* in 1977. Given the canonical separation of the two spheres of justice, principles of *jus in bello* targeting were made without reference to the overall justice of the war effort—the so-called moral equality of combatants. For example, Nazi soldiers were subject to the same privilege of belligerency as Allied soldiers, despite the fact that the Nazis were engaged in a war of aggression and the Allies were engaged in a campaign of legitimate defense. Revisionist Just War theorists such as Jeff McMahan have argued that the moral equality of combatants is illusory, and that combatants participating in an unjust war have no right, ceteris paribus, to kill in battle. If this view were accepted, it would require wholesale revision of the principle of distinction as it is currently practiced in the law of war.

Janina Dill (individually and collectively with Henry Shue) has recently defended an intermediate position between the traditional Walzerian approach and the revisionist approach championed by McMahan.[80] Dill correctly notes that the revisionist view is almost impossible for individual soldiers to operationalize. In order for soldiers to determine whether they

79. *See, e.g.*, Blum, *supra* note 4, at 73.

80. *See* Janina Dill, *Should International Law Ensure the Moral Acceptability of War?*, 26 LEIDEN J. INT'L L. 253–70 (2013). *See also* Janina Dill & Henry Shue, *Limiting the Killing in War: Military Necessity and the St. Petersburg Assumption*, 26 ETHICS & INT'L AFF. 311, 313 (2012) ("It follows that the moral calibration of individual conduct

are permitted to launch an attack against a specific target, they would need to make the following determinations, each one of them without the crucial information to make an informed assessment: (1) whether the enemy's cause is just (or lawful), which requires access to information at the national and political level; (2) a subtle understanding of contested principles of *jus ad bellum* including the exact contours of self-defense, defense of others, imminence, preemptive force, and preventive attacks; and (3) the individual target's level of contribution to this effort, which may or may not be temporally removed from the time of the attack. Consequently, the attacking soldier faces what Dill refers to as an "epistemically cloaked forced choice" in war.[81]

Dill does not deny that an international legal system based on McMahan's individualistic principles would be, ceteris paribus, morally beneficial. Ideally, those fighting for unjust causes would be liable to attack, and those fighting for just causes would be immune from attack. But this outcome is impossible to operationalize, and an international legal system built around these principles would likely result in far greater deprivations of individual rights than the Walzerian system currently in place. So the current legal system is justified as the system that produces the very best moral outcome that can be achieved: the fewest deprivations of individual rights that can be achieved. With the principle of distinction currently in place, civilians are immune from attack. Though this prohibition is arguably overbroad (since some civilians contribute politically to unjust causes), the result is an overall system that limits the number of unjust killings during wartime. One might refer to this as a quasi-instrumentalist defense of the principle of necessity. It neither accepts the Walzerian moral position that soldiers are inherently subject to attack simply by their status as soldiers, nor does it accept the revisionism implied by moral individualism. It stakes out a middle ground, saying that the current system produces outcomes that reduce as far as possible the number of unjust killings.

We can now connect up this dispute with our particular concern about the principle of necessity. The key point here is that the modern principle of necessity is intimately connected with the more general principle of distinction. At a philosophical level, the question is what makes combatants

during combat operations on the basis of the rights of individual adversaries is not an achievable goal. Any set of rules that pretends to possess the virtue of conformity with an individual rights–based morality in fact permits the harming of individuals that are not (fully) liable to that fate. Individualized rules for the conduct of war are hypocritical and/or unworkable.").

81. *Id.* at 254.

subject to being killed in battle, even absent an individual claim of self-defense to justify their killing. The licensing version of the principle of necessity, where combatants are subject to killing at any time regardless of whether they might be captured instead, is a natural outgrowth of an extreme version of the principle of distinction. One might therefore distinguish between thick and thin versions of distinction. In the thick version of distinction, killing is permitted against all combatants, regardless of whether they might be captured instead, and not permitted against any civilians. In the thin version of distinction, killing is permitted against all combatants by virtue of their status, but only if there is no other means by which they might be disabled. The common philosophical issue is whether killings should be conducted according to pure status-based considerations regarding the target or whether they should be based on more sophisticated threat assessments regarding the target, including how dangerous the target might be if non-lethal force is used against him or her. So in order to tackle the normative question regarding necessity, one must also tackle the question of distinction itself. It is inevitable.

What moral principle could possibly justify the principle of distinction under either of its two manifestations? One might appeal to the soldier's decision to bear a weapon and fight—a decision that comes with the reciprocal risk of killing. Although this argument might be valid for volunteer armies, it by no means applies to conscripted armies, whose soldiers fight under various degrees of state-backed coercion. It is simply incorrect to suggest that all soldiers have voluntarily picked up their weapons and are therefore subject to the inherent risk from the principle of distinction. One might also appeal, as Walzer did, to the inherent dangerousness of the soldier—all soldiers represent a threat by virtue of their training. This seems like the most-likely candidate, but it requires that we confine the analysis to soldiers as a collective group. Indeed, soldiers *are* more threatening than civilians as a class, but by limiting the analysis to classes we just beg the question. As for any particular soldier, some are more threatening than others, and the proverbial sleeping soldier is hardly any threat at all, at least while he is sleeping (though he may certainly represent a future threat).

The better answer, which takes Dill's instrumentalism as its departure, is that a thin version of the principle of distinction may very well be morally preferable, but it is not an option on the table. Once we try to implement the thin principle of distinction, the very structure of the law of war may deteriorate, and we may ironically produce a situation that results in more immoral killings, not fewer. Here is why. The revisionist program requires a level of individual analysis that is simply unworkable in practice; soldiers would need to determine whether their enemy has contributed sufficiently to an unjust war cause to become liable to attack. Similarly, the least-harmful-means test requires that attacking soldiers engage in a threat analysis of their individual target to determine whether capture is feasible and whether killing as a last resort is justifiable. This requires complex assessments of the individual's capacity to engage in defensive force—a fraught analysis well known to any criminal lawyer. Instead of making lethal attack hinge on the military-status of the target, the least-harmful-means would require an individualized analysis much closer to the individual analysis required by the criminal law in cases of force by police officers and civilians exercising self-defense—judgments that even juries struggle with. If we moved to the least-harmful-means version of necessity, the law would require individualistic assessments much closer to the type of assessments that revisionist Just War theory might imply, but which instrumentalists would rightly fear as impracticable and morally problematic. At that point, one might as well simply move to an entirely individualistic version of self-defense of the type that some Just War theorists prefer. In short, the thin conception of distinction, as a halfway measure between thick distinction and moral individualism, is an implausible alternative: in practice it risks dissolving into the same type of operational assessments—an individual analysis of threat—that the revisionist position seems to require. At this point, one is thrown back into the civilian realm of police enforcement, rather than the collective world of armed conflict where status-based determinations guide targeting decisions.

It bears noting that among the supporters for the least-harmful-means interpretation of necessity, the international criminal lawyers are conspicuously absent. There are important international lawyers, human rights scholars, and even IHL experts among the supporters. But generally, bread-and-butter international criminal lawyers are underrepresented in the coalition that supports the least-harmful-means version of necessity. Why? International criminal lawyers are acutely concerned with fostering *actual* norm-compliance during armed conflict, and they also have a preference for norms whose violations are easy to adjudicate before courts of law. And these two points are connected. If a norm is comparatively more difficult to adjudicate in court, the norm is more likely to go unpunished and the offending conduct is likely to proliferate. To the extent possible, international criminal lawyers prefer enforceable norms, since enforcement is their stock-in-trade.

International criminal lawyers are also generally hostile to revisionist Just War theory and its rejection of the moral foundations for the classical principal of distinction. And that is because Just War revisionism (or at least its "deep morality"), tinkers with both sides of the principle of distinction. Yes, the revisionist position grants protective status to soldiers fighting for a just cause, but it also removes protected status for civilians who are responsible for (or causally connected to) the war effort. So civilians might become liable to attack under this conception—a fundamental weakening of the civilian protection that is one of the hallmarks of contemporary IHL and ICL. To conceive of a new system where civilians not participating in fighting are liable to attack is an unmitigated disaster from the point of view of most international criminal lawyers. Lawyers have been fighting for decades for militaries to confer protection on civilian targets, and now the deep morality suggested by revisionist Just War theory is undermining it.

Again, the two points are connected. Once one weakens the principle of distinction, one weakens it tout court and opens up the possibility for unrestricted warfare. IHL is built around status-based determinations, and the principles of distinction and necessity are the two most important elements of that structure. By pulling on the thread of necessity, one risks unraveling the entire tapestry of distinction, leading to a world where legal arguments about *jus in bello* violations now implicate precisely the type of considerations that they were designed to circumvent: contested determinations of *jus ad bellum* and deeply difficult threat assessments for individual targets. Under a revisionist legal order, it would become very difficult for the world community to criticize offending soldiers, who would be ignorant of the relevant *jus ad bellum* considerations. And it would also be difficult for the world community to criticize attacks that violate the least-harmful-means test of necessity, since the offending soldiers can always claim that the individual targets were acting dangerously, and third parties have difficulty standing in judgment of that assessment. The result is that attacking forces will *always* assert that their targets were dangerous.

An analogy might be appropriate here. Compare the principles of distinction and proportionality as they are currently understood in the law of war. The principle of distinction is widely understood and adhered to, and violations are relatively easy to police and adjudicate. When victims of an attack are not wearing uniforms or bearing weapons, tough questions about the lawfulness of the attack will be asked. In contrast, violations of proportionality (by killing too many civilians to achieve a military result) are almost never prosecuted,[82] because it requires determining the value

82. One small example is *Prosecutor v. Prlic* (ICTY Trial Chamber), which held that the destruction of a bridge was disproportionate to the value of the military objective. However, the case did not deal with disproportionality of civilian deaths, since no civilians were killed. The holding dealt solely with the disproportionality involved

of a military target—an inherently qualitative assessment that engenders widespread disagreement. It is no surprise that violations of distinction are so well prosecuted whereas the law of proportionality is so impoverished. It is because distinction is transparent, easy to apply and prosecute, and subject to independent confirmation with relative ease. On the other hand, the prohibition against disproportionate attacks requires highly contested determinations of military value that lack transparency and have played almost no role in the legal regulation of armed conflict. Tinkering with the modern principle of distinction—the shining star of modern IHL—will only bring it down to the level of proportionality: an important normative constraint whose lack of bright-line clarity has prevented it from having the operational influence that it deserves.[83] The criminal law has an important lesson to offer here, and it is one that IHL has traditionally heeded: that the legal and moral content of normative constraints cannot be entirely divorced from practical considerations regarding their adjudication and enforcement.

What we want to emphasize is that the instrumental argument does more than simply show that the deep morality suggested by revisionist Just War theory cannot be operationalized because it would undermine the modern principle of distinction. It also provides a rationale for rejecting attempts to radically redefine the principle of necessity, since necessity is one component of a thick version of distinction. Requiring individual threat assessments prior to the deployment of lethal force might sound like a good idea when considered at the level of abstract moral theory, but it fails when it is operationalized in institutional form.[84] With third parties unable to transparently determine whether individual targets were sufficiently threatening to warrant lethal force, soldiers will ignore the rule, and the principle of distinction—in either variation—will be undermined. With compliance undermined, the result might be a net moral deficit. These considerations should give us pause before uncritically adopting a radically restrictive version of necessity in IHL, which traditionally has operated with a necessity-as-license conception for the very reasons articulated in this chapter.

in destroying the bridge as a civilian infrastructure. For more discussion of the lack of prosecutions for the war crime of launching disproportionate attacks, see Jens David Ohlin, *Targeting and the Concept of Intent*, 35 MICH. J. INT'L L. 79 (2013).

83. *But see* MICHAEL NEWTON & LARRY MAY, PROPORTIONALITY IN INTERNATIONAL LAW (2014).

84. *See* Michael Schmitt, *Wound, Capture, or Kill: A Reply to Ryan Goodman's "The Power to Kill or Capture Enemy Combatants,"* 24 EUR. J. INT'L L. 855–61 (2013); Geoffrey S. Corn, Laurie R. Blank, Chris Jenks & Eric Talbot Jensen, *Belligerent Targeting and the Invalidity of a Least Harmful Means Rule*, 89 INT'L L. STUD. 536 (2013).

V. CONCLUSION

In this chapter, we have outlined notes of skepticism regarding the least-harmful-means interpretation of necessity. Are we on the wrong side of history? Why would anyone support an interpretation of the laws of war that permits more—rather than less—killing? Does this run counter to the animating impulse of *humanitarian* law? Does this run counter to the continuing and inevitable progressive development of human rights thinking in international law? As a general strategic matter, we would be pleased to live in a world where the current *jus in bello* prohibitions were adhered to by combatants on all sides of an armed conflict. A world without war crimes is a worthy goal, but we should not move the yardsticks to a potentially unattainable distance. Indeed, when the laws of war move too far beyond current state practice, they risk being ignored entirely—a potentially disastrous consequence for humanitarianism.

However, we are also aware that this analysis covers only one-half of the picture. In this chapter we have carefully articulated the dangers of tinkering with the principle of necessity and assigning it additional weight in the *jus in bello*. We hope to have persuaded some that the dangers are real and that they ought to have a cautionary impact on revisionist proposals. On the other hand, there is also something fundamentally odd about the current notion of military necessity that reigns in the laws of war. It allows battlefield killings in the situations that would not sound "necessary" in the commonsense understanding of the term. A major part of our argument has been to show that military necessity is a term of art in *jus in bello* with a particular conceptual meaning that diverges quite sharply from commonsensical understandings of the concept of necessity. And this is more than just a split between the layperson and the theorist. Lieber's conception of military necessity also conflicts with earlier philosophical accounts of necessity, such as Grotius's assessment that necessity means "no other way." Whatever is meant by military necessity in Lieber's sense, it is not the same as the Grotian idea of "no other way." Given that the Grotian definition hews much closer to common sense, we need to test the Lieber definition of military necessity to see if it could be tempered in some way so as to bring it closer in line with the commonsense definition. Even under the instrumentalist approach discussed above, this result would be salutary if it could be achieved in reality. In subsequent chapters we will make modest proposals to narrow the gap between military necessity as a term of art in the law of war and necessity as a commonsense idea that lethal action should be resorted to only if absolutely necessary. But before we can address any of those questions, we must first analyze the split between necessity as the term is used in the law of war and necessity as the term is used in human rights law. The latter is one legal domain where the concept of necessity does hew much closer to the commonsense and Grotian definition of necessity.

CHAPTER 5

Necessity in Human Rights Law and IHL

As we explained in prior chapters, necessity means different things in different contexts. The concept of necessity in international humanitarian law (IHL) is markedly different from how the concept is deployed in human rights law. The difference is more than just conceptual—it has actual consequences for the outcome of the moral and legal analysis. For example, the legality of a use-of-force operation might depend mostly on which body of law, and which normative regime, applies.[1] If IHL—and IHL alone—applies, then the principle of necessity will be permissive, though there may be legitimate arguments in support of changing that law as a matter of *de lege ferenda*. On the other hand, if international human rights law (IHRL) applies, then the rules regarding targeting and the use of force will be much more restrictive in nature. This chapter investigates the different senses of necessity in IHRL and IHL, and concludes that the concept of necessity is frequently misunderstood to mean the same thing as necessity is understood in civilian contexts. The two versions of the concept operate differently because the underlying legal assumptions of the two bodies of law are different: IHRL assumes that killing is illegal whereas IHL assumes that the killing of combatants is presumptively privileged. Moreover, the two bodies of law are designed for different purposes: IHL regulates the relationship between coequal belligerents in battle, whereas IHRL constrains the sovereign's treatment of subjects under its control.

1. *See* Beth Van Schaack, *The Killing of Osama Bin Laden & Anwar Al-Aulaqi: Uncharted Legal Territory*, 14 Yearbook of Int'l Humanitarian L. 255, 256–57 (2011).

Given these differences, can the two legal regimes be combined together in any meaningful way?

Resolving these questions requires a coherent account of necessity that spans across bodies of law, what the concept means in the abstract, and how the concept is applied in specific contexts. What emerges from this investigation is that necessity underlies all use-of-force questions in both armed conflict and peacetime frameworks, but the concept provides less cross-context unity than one might hope. Necessity, it turns out, means something quite different depending on the background legal norms that structure each particular body of law. In other words, it is not clear that the concept of necessity in the domestic law of self-defense can be transplanted, without significance alteration, to the domain of IHL. As we saw in previous chapters, the concept of necessity turns out to be something resembling a term of art in IHL, with a specific meaning that diverges from how the term is understood and applied in other normative regimes.

Consequently, this chapter has three aims. First, it seeks to briefly explain how necessity works in human rights law. Second, it investigates whether the human rights notion of necessity can be combined with—or co-applied with—the IHL version of necessity in times of armed conflict. The question is whether some hybrid notion of necessity as a normative constraint can be deduced from the two bodies of law—a methodology inspired by the Israeli Supreme Court's *Targeted Killings* decision.[2] In that case, Justice Barak argued that the principle of proportionality demanded that a targetable terrorist—as a civilian directly participating in hostilities—should be killed only if a "less harmful means" could not be employed.[3] Although the source of this exact interpretation of the principle of proportionality was listed as domestic (Israeli) source of law, it was also referred to as a "human right."[4] This phrase, coupled with the fact that the principle of proportionality clearly exists under customary international law, suggested to some that the analysis would be the same under international law.[5] The court concluded that "if a terrorist taking a direct part in hostilities can be arrested, interrogated, and tried, those are the means which should be

2. HCJ 769/02, *Pub. Comm. Against Torture in Isr. v. Gov't of Isr.*, 53(4) PD 459 [2006] (Isr.).

3. *Id.* ¶ 40.

4. *Id.*

5. *See* Marko Milanović, *Norm Conflicts, International Humanitarian Law, and Human Rights Law*, *in* INTERNATIONAL HUMANITARIAN LAW AND INTERNATIONAL HUMAN RIGHTS LAW 120 (Orna Ben-Naftali ed., 2011) (noting that although it was "not entirely clear whether the Court derived this rule from IHRL or from domestic constitutional law, but it is clear that it is a human rights norm that it was applying").

employed" because a "rule-of-law state employs, to the extent possible, procedures of law and not procedures of force."[6] (Although this was couched as a requirement of proportionality, it was really a discourse on the principle of necessity.) But IHRL can only be used to interpret the basic concepts of IHL if the two normative regimes are talking the same language. The following analysis asks whether the legal language is the same.

Finally, this chapter concludes with some speculative thoughts on when human rights necessity applies and when IHL necessity applies. One possibility would be to ask whether the government is acting as a sovereign or as a belligerent. If the former, then the normative constraints of human rights law certainly apply; if the latter, then the regulations of IHL should apply. We end with a discussion of what the implications of this framework would be for targeted killings.

I. HUMAN RIGHTS NECESSITY

Human rights courts often use the principle of necessity to evaluate the appropriateness of governmental action. The resort to necessity as a foundational principle of human rights law is evident not just in regional courts such as the European Court of Human Rights but also in domestic constitutional courts in Germany, Canada, and elsewhere. The concept of necessity shows up as a subcomponent of a larger test regarding proportionality analysis that largely dominates human rights adjudication across the globe.

Proportionality analysis is now so ubiquitous as a framework for adjudicating human rights that many commentators consider it to be constitutive of global constitutionalism—the convergence of different legal systems toward a common paradigm of constitutional human rights.[7]

6. HCJ 769/02, *Pub. Comm. Against Torture in Isr. v. Gov't of Isr.*, 53(4) PD 459 [2005] (Isr.), ¶ 40; *see also id.* (*citing McCann v. United Kingdom*, 21 Eur. Ct. H.R. (ser. A) at 91 (1995)) ("[T]he use of lethal force would be rendered disproportionate if the authorities failed, whether deliberately or through lack of proper care, to take steps which would have avoided the deprivation of life of the suspects without putting the lives of others at risk."). However, *McCann* is a problematic precedent for this point of law. *See also* Amichai Cohen & Yuval Shany, *A Development of Modest Proportions: The Application of the Principle of Proportionality in the* Targeted Killings *Case*, 5 J. INT'L CRIM. JUST. 310, 314 (2007) ("While it is hard to contest that the *McCann* formula should govern the conduct of law-enforcement agencies under human rights law in times of peace, its full application to situations of armed conflict is questionable.").

7. Mattias Kumm, *Constitutional Rights as Principles: On the Structure and Domain of Constitutional Justice*, 2 INT'L J. CONST. L. 574, 579 (2004).

Technically, proportionality analysis is used whenever a government has infringed upon an individual's liberty, but believes it has reason to do so. Proportionality analysis requires a four-prong test to evaluate the infringement's appropriateness. The first prong determines whether the governmental aim is legitimate. If the government has no business seeking that particular outcome in the first instance, then the infringement is already illegal before the rest of the analysis is performed. Second, a reviewing court should consider whether the *means* employed by the government to obtain its objective was suitable. Third, the government action must be "necessary" in order to achieve the suitable government aim, with "necessary" being defined as the least restrictive means to that end. Finally, the government action must be proportionate "in the narrow sense," such that the benefits are sufficiently great to withstand legal review.[8] In many instances the most scrutiny of the analysis will fall to the necessity prong as defined by the least-restrictive-means test. In most interesting and contentious cases, the governmental objective will be legitimate and its means suitable, though the way the means is carried out may not be the least restrictive means of vindicating the governmental objective. If that action infringes on the protected interest, then the governmental action is not truly necessary, and hence contravenes human rights law.[9]

One example of human rights adjudication under this model is *United Kingdom v. McCann* before the European Court of Human Rights.[10] In that case, the United Kingdom was alleged to have violated the Convention arising from its counterterrorism operations against the Provisional Irish Republican Army (IRA). The U.K., Spanish, and local police officials believed that the IRA was planning a specific terrorist bombing in Gibraltar. British security forces located the IRA suspects and planned an operation to stop the bombing. Believing that the suspects had a bomb, the military handled the operation and shot the suspects, though it was later revealed that they were not in possession of any weapon or bomb when they were killed. In resolving the complaint that the operation violated the human rights of the suspects, the Court analyzed the situation under Article 2 of

8. For a discussion of the four-pronged standard of proportionality analysis, see Alec Stone Sweet & Jud Matthews, *Proportionality Balancing and Global Constitutionalism*, 47 Colum. J. Transnat'l L. 73, 77 (2008).

9. For more discussion of the test, see Yutaka Arai-Takahashi, *Proportionality*, *in* The Oxford Handbook of International Human Rights Law 446, 452 (Dinah Shelton ed., 2013).

10. *Case of McCann and Others v. The United Kingdom*, Application No. 18984/91, Judgment (Sept. 27, 1995).

the European Convention on Human Rights (ECHR), which requires that the "derivation of life shall not be regarded as inflicted in contravention of this article when it results from the use of force which is not more than absolutely necessary . . . "

The Court determined that this necessity constraint was the strictest form of necessity, and one that imposed a higher burden than the necessity requirement governing political rights (which generally require that "there shall be no interference by a public authority with the exercise of this right except such as is in accordance with the law and is necessary in a democratic society . . . ").[11] The ECHR criticized the domestic U.K. inquest for not applying the stricter version of necessity when evaluating the operation, though the Court accepted the soldiers' contention that they honestly believed that it was absolutely necessary to shoot the suspects. The Court concluded that although the individual shootings by the soldiers did not violate the human rights of the suspects, the antiterror operation as a whole was problematic because there were other options at the authorities' disposal, including arresting them at the border.[12]

Although the ECHR had not fully developed a language of "proportionality analysis" by the time *McCann* was decided, the case nonetheless is emblematic of the strict version of necessity applied in human rights cases where questions of force are concerned. For a more contemporary example of the same analysis, consider *Al-Skeini*, which involved the killing of Iraqi citizens by British soldiers on the streets of occupied Iraq.[13] Again applying Article 2(2) of the ECHR and its requirement that the use of force be "no more than absolutely necessary," the Court concluded that the provision also implied that the government must conduct a meaningful investigation (independent of the chain of command) of allegations of inappropriate use of force—a procedural defect of the United Kingdom's conduct in this case. These cases, and others, show how powerful the human rights notion of necessity really is. Whether a human rights case is explicitly governed by a "least-restrictive-means" test or a test of "absolute necessity," both involve the strictest scrutiny over the government's behavior. In order to justify its actions, the government needs to show that it had no other alternative to secure its legitimate aim; if other, less injurious alternatives existed, the government action or policy violates human rights law.

11. *See, e.g.*, ECHR, arts. 7(2), 8(2), 9(2), 10(2), 11(2).
12. *McCann, supra* note 10, para. 203.
13. *See Case of Al-Skeini and Others v. The United Kingdom*, Application No. 55721/07, Judgment (7 July 2011).

II. COMBINING HUMAN RIGHTS NECESSITY WITH IHL NECESSITY

Now we deepen the analysis. Many lawyers believe that the legality of military operations can be adjudicated under human rights law. Given that military operations during an armed conflict are also governed by IHL, the application of human rights law would require harmonizing the two fields. Under this view, there are more than two options: apply IHL with its broad notion of military necessity, or apply IHRL with its highly restrictive notion of necessity.[14] There is a third possible route that would result in strict constraints on government action: both IHL and IHRL apply *at the same time*. Co-application of the two normative regimes is possible only if one rejects IHL as a *lex specialis* regime that completely knocks out other legal rules from application.[15]

Lex specialis is a legal maxim that states that the more specific law should prevail over the more general one. Take a simple example from a statue. Imagine that a government law says in subsection A that "no one will be allowed in the public park after dark." Then, later in the same law, subsection F says that "police officers shall be empowered to operate on all public property to complete their law enforcement duties." These two provisions are in conflict. A sensible reading would be that the first prohibition is *lex generalis*, but that subsection F is a more specific exception to it, a *lex specialis* that applies just to police officers in spite of the general prohibition announced in the earlier subsection. However, the maxim cannot be mechanically applied without reflection because it is by no means obvious how broadly or how narrowly one should define the specific law. Even if IHL is deemed to be *lex specialis* and in some deserving of legal priority, it is not clear whether that means that IHL as a whole should receive priority and knock out the application of other bodies of law, or whether *lex specialis* only means that *specific rules* of IHL should receive priority over

14. *But see* NILS MELZER, TARGETED KILLING IN INTERNATIONAL LAW 91–139 (2009) (exploring the right to life under different courts and jurisdictions); Robert Chesney, *Who May Be Killed? Anwar al-Awlaki as a Case Study in the International Legal Regulation of Lethal Force*, 13 Y.B. INT'L HUMANITARIAN L. 3, 47 n.195 (2010) (concluding that even assuming IHL requires capture if feasible, the killing of al-Awlaki was lawful because capture was not practicable in his case).

15. *See* Jordan Paust, *Self-Defense Targetings of Non-State Actors and Permissibility of U.S. Use of Drones in Pakistan*, 19 J. TRANS. L. & POL'Y 237, 274 n.94 (2009) (referring to *lex specialis* as "Latinized nonsense," and concluding that "I know of no relevant human right that would needlessly inhibit lawful conduct on the battlefield"). The text of the maxim is *lex specialis derogat legi generali*.

the *lex generalis*. The difference here is between IHL knocking out human rights law entirely in situations of armed conflict, or a particular rule of IHL taking precedence over a general principle of human rights law.

If IHL is not a *lex specialis*, this opens the door to apply the rules of IHRL in two manners: first, when there is no IHL rule on point, and second, when the governing IHL rule has little content and can be interpreted in light of a relevant IHRL rule. In either situation, co-application of IHL and IHRL functions as a gap-filling exercise, plugging the holes left by the skeletal nature of IHL. The need to fill gaps is allegedly especially acute in non-international armed conflicts (including civil wars), which have comparatively fewer codified rules as compared against their international cousins (international armed conflicts), which are well regulated by the Geneva and Hague Conventions and other treaty regimes.[16]

If both IHL and IHRL apply *at the same time*, this would potentially displace the licensing version of military necessity that dominates in modern IHL. In co-applying human rights and law of war norms together, the normative prescriptions of IHRL are viewed as universal and applicable in all situations, including armed conflict. Of particular relevance are the IHRL protections involving the right to life and the general notion of proportionality analysis (including necessity as one component) that has swept human rights discourse and global constitutionalism. As for the first—the right to life—it is generally taken as axiomatic that, in the words of the International Covenant on Civil and Political Rights (ICCPR), "[e]very human being has the inherent right to life . . . [that] . . . shall be protected by law."[17] With regard to proportionality, most European constitutional courts generally recognize that the balancing of interests implied in cases of conflicting rights is to be governed by proportionality analysis.[18] In such

16. *See, e.g.*, MARKO MILANOVIĆ, EXTRATERRITORIAL APPLICATION OF HUMAN RIGHTS TREATIES 43 (2011) (discussing the *Tadić* case, and noting that the court had to have recourse in the general rules of state responsibility, "since the rules of international humanitarian law did not provide an answer").

17. *See* International Covenant on Civil and Political Rights, art. 6 ¶ 1, *opened for signature* Dec. 19, 1966, 999 U.N.T.S. 171 (entered into force Mar. 23, 1976) [hereinafter ICCPR].

18. For a discussion of proportionality, see generally Moshe Cohen-Eliya & Iddo Porat, *Proportionality and the Culture of Justification*, 59 AM. J. COMP. L. 463, 465 (2011) (tracing the spread of proportionality from Prussian administrative law to its later adoption by the European Court of Human Rights); Sweet & Mathews, *supra* note 8, at 72 (noting that proportionality balancing has become a dominant technique of rights adjudication, discussing its genealogy, and theorizing about why it has become attractive to judges worldwide). *See also Dudgeon v. United Kingdom*, 45 Eur. Ct. H.R. (ser. A) at 24 (1981) ("On the issue of proportionality, the Court considers that such justifications as there are for retaining the law in force unamended are outweighed by

cases, the government can infringe the right of the individual no more than is necessary to achieve its legitimate interest; anything beyond this level would be impermissibly disproportionate.[19] Implicit in the notion of proportionality is the notion of necessity, in the sense that actions that are unnecessary to achieve the government interest become disproportionate and become responses requiring judicial intervention on the basis of human rights law.[20] As applied to targeted killings, the argument would be that the inherent right to life of the individual terrorist suspects can be infringed only if it is truly necessary to achieve the government result. Since capture would disable the foreign terrorist as much as killing him, the decision to forgo capture in favor of military killing represents a disproportionate response by the government.[21]

Although this view is uncontestably the correct analysis for situations governed wholly by human rights law, the question is whether a situation could be governed by *both* IHL and IHRL, such that they are co-applied in the analysis, each one enriching the other and filling in the gaps left by the other's normative regime.[22] Given the general paucity of codified rules governing non-international armed conflicts—Common Article 3 and Additional Protocol II being two of the most notable exceptions—one might look to IHRL to fill in the gaps left by IHL.[23] With the co-application strategy, the concepts of proportionality and necessity as used by IHRL would be imported into situations already acknowledged as being governed by IHL.[24]

the detrimental effects . . . ."); *Handyside v. United Kingdom*, 24 Eur. Ct. H.R. (ser. A) at 23 (1976) (explaining that penalties imposed "must be proportionate to the legitimate aim pursued").

19. *See* Thomas M. Franck, *On Proportionality of Countermeasures in International Law*, 102 Am. J. Int'l L. 715, 752 (2008) ("[I]n matters ranging from the regulation of property to constraints on human rights, the proportionality principle has emerged as 'one of the most important principles invoked' . . . to challenge the effect of regulations on the rights of persons," *quoting* Axel Desmedt, *Proportionality in WTO Law*, 4 J. Int'l Econ. L. 441, 442 (2001). *See also* Mattias Kumm, *Political Liberalism and the Structure of Rights: On the Place and Limits of the Proportionality Requirement*, *in* Law, Rights, and Discourse: The Legal Philosophy of Robert Alexy 131, 136–41 (George Pavlakos ed., 2007).

20. *See Isayeva v. Russia*, App. No.57950/00, 41 Eur. Ct. H.R. 40 (2005) ("Consequently, the force used must be strictly proportionate to the achievement of the permitted aims.").

21. *See* Gabor Rona, *Interesting Times for International Humanitarian Law: Challenges From the "War on Terror,"* 27 Fletcher F. World Aff. 55, 64–65 (2003) (noting that drone attacks violate human right to life).

22. *See* Louise Doswald-Beck, *The Right to Life in Armed Conflict: Does International Humanitarian Law Provide All the Answers?*, 88 Int'l Rev. Red Cross 881, 888–903 (2006).

23. *See* Milanović, *supra* note 5, at 95–96.

24. *Cf.* Norm Lubell, Extraterritorial Use of Force Against Non-State Actors 236–42 (2010) (arguing that IHL proportionality would apply during

It is important to distinguish between different flavors of co-application. In the *Nuclear Weapons* case, the ICJ famously concluded that the human right not to be arbitrarily deprived of life "falls to be determined by the applicable *lex specialis*, namely, the law applicable in armed conflict which is designed to regulate the conduct of hostilities."[25] In other words, although human rights are universal and apply in some abstract sense in every situation, including armed conflict, their *content* is determined exclusively by reference to IHL, which simply is a human rights framework for armed conflict. Consequently, the full scope of a party's legal obligations is determined by the operative legal rules of IHL, not the formal rules of IHRL. This mildest form of co-application has little or no practical consequences above an IHL-only view, because IHL remains the *lex specialis* that expresses what human rights law requires during armed conflict.

In contrast, a stronger flavor of co-application assumes that the operation of both fields of law *would* have practical consequences because the content of universal human rights norms is not exclusively determined by the relevant rules of IHL.[26] Instead, the norms and doctrines of IHRL apply when there is no direct IHL rule on point, and even when there is an IHL rule on point, its interpretation is to be influenced in the background by the universal IHRL norm.[27] When there is no direct IHL rule on point, this flavor of co-application has huge practical consequences because it allows extraterritorial operation of an IHRL norm during an armed conflict through its gap-filling function.[28] And even when there is an IHL rule on point, this flavor of co-application provides a canon of interpretation that has the potential to strongly influence the outcome of the analysis, depending on the relevant norms in question.[29] For example, under this analysis,

full-blown armed conflicts but situations falling below that threshold might require IHRL principles of proportionality).

25. *See Legality of the Threat or Use of Nuclear Weapons*, Advisory Opinion, 1996 I.C.J. 226, 240 (July 8); *see also Legal Consequences of the Construction of a Wall in the Occupied Palestinian Territory*, Advisory Opinion, 2004 I.C.J. 136, 178 (July 9) (describing IHL as the *lex specialis* applicable during armed conflict).

26. *See* Milanović, *supra* note 5, at 95–96.

27. *See* Cordula Droege, *The Interplay between International Humanitarian Law and International Human Rights Law in Situations of Armed Conflict*, 40 Isr. L. Rev. 310, 338–40 (2007).

28. *See generally* Noam Lubell, *Parallel Application of International Humanitarian Law and International Human Rights Law: An Examination of the Debate*, 40 Isr. L. Rev. 648 (2007) (generally discussing co-applicability of IHL and IHRL and highlighting some discrepancies); William A. Schabas, Lex Specialis? *Belt and Suspenders? The Parallel Operation of Human Rights Law and the Law of Armed Conflict, and the Conundrum of* Jus ad Bellum, 40 Isr. L. Rev. 592 (2007) (arguing that IHL and IHRL are incompatible, and a seamless integration of the two should not be attempted).

29. A prime example is the ECHR case involving Chechnya, which applied human rights law directly, in spite of the existence of an armed conflict. However, as Blum and

the IHRL rule against arbitrary detention without due process of law might require some amendments to the detention regime that is usually contemplated in IHL, which allows indefinite detention of all POWs until the end of hostilities. This conclusion is upsetting for some IHL lawyers, because it potentially unwinds a very carefully crafted legal regime for detention that IHL lawyers negotiated and implemented. Similarly, rules on targeting during armed conflict might be influenced by the co-application of human rights principles. The laws of war generally permit unlimited targeting of all combatants on the sole basis of their status as enemy combatants. In contrast, human rights law requires a heightened level of necessity (exigency) before the police may conduct lethal operations. Consequently, the co-application of IHRL to situations previously thought to be governed by IHL could, at least in theory, mitigate the extreme permissiveness of the IHL rules on targeting.

Although the co-application approach arguably fills gaps, there are several arguments that are frequently made to suggest that IHL is an independent body of law—*a lex specialis*—that either knocks out all other governing legal regimes, including IHRL, or provides the decision rule for the content of human rights during situations of armed conflict (as the ICJ suggested in *Nuclear Weapons*).[30] First, the basic foundational norms of the two regimes stand in some tension, at least at the level of codified law.[31] Whereas IHRL is based on the foundational norm that everyone has the right to life, IHL is based on the reciprocal risk of killing, or the idea that each soldier has the right to kill other soldiers with impunity, and in so doing opens herself up to a reciprocal risk of killing.[32] In other words, a universal right to life does not seem to exist in IHL; the entire body of law

Abresch both correctly note, neither Russia nor Turkey argued that it was derogating from human rights law due to the existence of an armed conflict and the triggering of IHL. It is thus unclear whether the ECHR would render the same rulings when faced with a State, such as the United States, that insists that its actions are justified by IHL. *See Isayeva v. Russia*, 41 Eur. Ct. H.R. 35–55 (2005); *see generally* William Abresch, *A Human Rights Law of Internal Armed Conflict: The European Court of Human Rights in Chechnya*, 16 Eur. J. Int'l L. 741 (2005) (analyzing ECHR application of human rights law in Chechnya cases); *see also* Gabriella Blum, *The Dispensable Lives of Soldiers*, 2 J. Leg. Analysis 115, 132 n.39 (2010); *Ergi v. Turkey*, 1998-IV Eur. Ct. H.R. 59 (1998) (applying human rights law).

30. *See, e.g.*, Nuclear Weapons, *supra* note 25, at 240.

31. *See* Schabas, *supra* note 28, at 593–94 (arguing that there is a fundamental incompatibility between the two systems stemming from the law of war's separation of *jus in bello* and *jus ad bellum*, a distinction which is not replicated in human rights law); *see, e.g., Isayeva*, 41 Eur. Ct. H.R. at 46 (referring to the "legitimate aim" of the action); Schabas, *supra*, at 607 (noting correctly that legitimate aim is irrelevant under IHL proper).

32. *See* Droege, *supra* note 27, at 313 (discussing reciprocity).

is based on its *rejection,* because IHL assumes that killing in warfare can be regulated by distinguishing between lawful and unlawful targets.[33] So the incompatibility goes straight to the core of the two fields.

One answer to this objection is that the right to life, even in IHRL, is hardly universal. Article 6 of the ICCPR goes on to qualify the inherent right with "[n]o one shall be *arbitrarily* deprived of his life."[34] Perhaps the central rule of distinction in IHL—killing combatants and protecting civilians—is a principled rule that is non-arbitrary.[35] However, the concept of "arbitrariness" in IHRL usually means something more substantial than this. In wartime under IHL, a combatant wearing a uniform is legally targetable at almost any moment in time, with only a few exceptions (when he is hors de combat, injured, providing medical services, etc.), including when he is asleep. These seemingly arbitrary killings are permissible simply by virtue of the target's enemy uniform—his status alone—yet undeniably lawful under IHL.

The potential incompatibility with the two bodies of law has led to anxiety that their co-application will necessarily involve a watering down of human rights law and its constraining version of the principle of necessity.[36] Nowhere is that anxiety in greater display than in the right to life; in order to reconcile itself with the central privilege of combatancy at the core of armed conflict, IHRL must radically scale down its ambitions regarding the right to life. For some, this is a deal with the devil that IHRL and its

33. *See* Doswald-Beck, *supra* note 22, at 882 (noting that Human Rights Courts adjudicating the right to life must make reference solely to the Human Rights Conventions that created these courts, partially explaining the absence of IHL from these decisions); Gloria Gaggioli & Robert Kolb, *A Right to Life in Armed Conflicts? The Contribution of the European Court of Human Rights*, 37 ISR. Y.B. HUM. RTS. 115, 134–36 (discussing the right to life in IHL); *see also* Noëlle Quénivet, *The Right to Life in International Humanitarian Law and Human Rights Law, in* INTERNATIONAL HUMANITARIAN LAW AND HUMAN RIGHTS LAW: TOWARDS A NEW MERGER IN INTERNATIONAL LAW 331, 338–40 (Roberta Arnold & Noëlle Quénivet eds., 2008) (discussing grounds for deciding on the justification of the use of force in IHL); *cf.* Doswald-Beck, *supra*, at 882 n.2 (noting that one exception includes *Abella v. Argentina*, Case 11.137, Inter-Am. Comm'n H.R., Report No. 55/97, OEA/Ser.L/V/II.95 rev. 271 (1997)). *But see* G.I.A.D. Draper, *Human Rights and the Law of War*, 12 VA J. INT'L L. 326, 338 (1972) (concluding that Article 15 of the European Convention on Human Rights incorporates, by reference, all of IHL); *see also* Abresch, *supra* note 29, at 745 ("The drafters of the ECHR presumably envisioned that states involved in armed conflicts would derogate to humanitarian law with respect to the right to life.").

34. ICCPR, *supra* note 17.

35. *See* Abresch, *supra* note 29, at 745 ("Most human rights treaties provide that the right to life is non-derogable, leaving the word 'arbitrary' as the only hook for humanitarian law.").

36. *See* Milanović, *supra* note 5, at 97.

proponents ought to stay as far away from as possible.[37] As Milanović puts the point sharply, "[F]or all its humanitarian ethos, IHL is still a discipline about killing people, albeit in a civilized sort of way."[38]

A good example of the incompatibility of the two normative regimes is the previously discussed *McCann* case, decided by the ECHR. The Israeli Supreme Court relied on *McCann* when it concluded that civilians directly participating in hostilities could be killed only if capture, arrest, and trial were not feasible.[39] In *McCann*, the Court applied Article 2 of the ECHR, which provides strict criteria for when the right to life can be infringed, and noticeably fails to exclude armed conflict from its provisions.[40] Article 2, Section 1 starts by proscribing that "[n]o one shall be deprived of his life intentionally save in the execution of a sentence of a court following his conviction of a crime for which this penalty is provided by law," thus carving out capital punishment from the article's scope.[41] Section 2 then goes on to catalog areas where a killing is not considered a violation of Section 1, including self-defense and defense of others (legitimate defense), lawful arrest or preventing escape from custody, and lawfully quelling riots and insurrection.[42] There is no mention of the privilege of combatancy in armed conflict against lawful targets.[43]

Most important, these three categories (defense, arrest, and riots) are only excluded if *absolutely necessary*.[44] Not only is the concept of absolute necessity much more demanding than the concept of military necessity, as we explained above, but the ECHR concluded that absolute necessity is a far more demanding legal test than the notion of "necessary in a democratic society," which governs many other rights provisions in the ECHR.[45]

37. *See, e.g.*, Schabas, *supra* note 28, at 593–94. In a sense, this is the mirror image of the anxiety that IHL lawyers have regarding the importation of human rights law into their discipline, which will unravel the carefully structured deal that yields success in IHL. *See, e.g.*, Yoram Dinstein, *Concluding Remarks: LOAC and Attempts to Abuse or Subvert It*, 87 INT'L L. STUD. 483, 488 (2011) ("[O]ften today we encounter the unpleasant phenomenon of human rights-niks who, hoisting the banner of human rights law, are attempting to bring about a hostile takeover of LOAC."). The institutional conflict between human rights and military lawyers is explored in David Luban, *Military Necessity and the Cultures of Military Law*, 26 LEIDEN J. INT'L L. 315 (2013). Luban notes that though Dinstein's rhetoric is "exaggerated and unusually belligerent," the phenomenon he describes is real. *Id.* at 318.

38. Milanović, *supra* note 5, at 98.

39. *See McCann v. United Kingdom*, 21 Eur. Ct. H.R. (ser. A) ¶ 97 (1995).

40. *Id.* ¶ 150.

41. ICCPR, *supra* note 17, art. 2(1).

42. *Id.* art. 2(2).

43. *Id.*

44. *See McCann*, 21 Eur. Ct. H.R. ¶ 149.

45. *See id.*

Moreover, the Court noted that a domestic U.K. inquest after the killings examined their lawfulness under the standards of "reasonable force" and "reasonable necessity," both of which were incapable of expressing the highest form of exigency required by absolute necessity.[46] The Court concluded that, although the actions of the individual soldiers did not violate the absolute necessity standard, the planning of the operation by commanders, and other actions by government officials, did violate the standard.[47] The standard therefore requires that the underlying situation left the government with *no other alternative* than the use of lethal force.[48]

This notion of absolute necessity is far different than the concept of military necessity as it was formulated by Lieber and in more modern formulations. Recall first that Lieber defined it as "measures which are indispensable for securing the ends of the war, and which are lawful according to the modern law and usages of war," and concluded that necessity "admits of all direct destruction of life or limb of *armed* enemies" but outlawed cruelty, "the infliction of suffering for the sake of suffering or for revenge," as well as anything that, such as perfidy, "makes the return to peace unnecessarily difficult."[49] In the more modern ICRC formulation—influential though not binding—military necessity allows actions "required in order to achieve the legitimate purpose of the conflict, namely the complete or

46. This is arguably similar to the U.S. standard of reasonableness governing domestic law enforcement cases. *See, e.g.*, Scott v. Harris, 550 U.S. 372, 376 (2007); Tennessee v. Garner, 471 U.S. 1, 11–12 (1985); Plakas v. Drinski, 19 F.3d 1143, 1149 (7th Cir. 1994). For a criticism of the standard, see George M. DeryIII, *The Needless "Slosh" through the "Morass of Reasonableness": The Supreme Court's Usurption of Fact Finding Powers in Assessing Reasonable Force in* Scott v. Harris, 18 GEO. MASON U. C.R. L.J. 417, 436–48 (2008). *But see* Matthew C. Waxman, *Detention as Targeting: Standards of Certainty and Detention of Suspected Terrorists*, 108 COLUM. L. REV. 1365, 1413 (2008) (supporting reasonableness as the operative principle governing targeting in international law).

47. *See McCann*, 21 Eur. Ct. H.R. ¶ 213 (1995) ("In sum, having regard to the decision not to prevent the suspects from travelling into Gibraltar, to the failure of the authorities to make sufficient allowances for the possibility that their intelligence assessments might, in some respects at least, be erroneous and to the automatic recourse to lethal force when the soldiers opened fire, the Court is not persuaded that the killing of the three terrorists constituted the use of force which was no more than absolutely necessary in defence of persons from unlawful violence within the meaning of Article 2(2)(a) of the Convention.").

48. This is also sometimes referred to as the "least-harmful-means" or "least-restrictive-means" test. *See* Blum, *supra* note 29, at 120; *see also* Mehrdad Payandeh, *The United Nations, Military Intervention, and Regime Change in Libya*, 52 VA. J. INT'L L. 355, 385 (2012) (arguing that transplanting least-restrictive means test from constitutional law to IHL is not advisable).

49. *See* Instructions for the Government of Armies of the United States in the Field, General Order No. 100, arts. 14–16 (Apr. 24, 1863) [hereinafter Lieber Code].

partial submission of the enemy at the earliest possible moment with the minimum expenditure of life and resources," and disclaims attacks that are not "actually necessary for the accomplishment of legitimate military purposes."[50] Although *actual necessity* may sound like a stringent citerion—and tonally similar to *absolute necessity*—in fact the far more relevant element is the *ends* for which the action must be necessary. Unlike in human rights law, where the action must be absolutely necessary to save the life of another, here the action need only be actually necessary for the accomplishment of the conflict, which includes defeating the enemy as quickly as possible with the fewest risks to one's own personnel.[51] It is precisely for this reason that, under existing law, the destruction of the enemy's "life or limb" is presumptively consistent with this standard, at least as far as IHL is concerned.[52] (In the final section of this book, we will ask whether existing law should be modified on this score, and whether other normative principles might counsel in favor of a slightly more restrictive notion of necessity).

So the two notions of necessity, though closely related, are worlds apart, leading to the anxiety of watering down human rights law. As Milanović puts the point, "allowing the state to kill combatants or insurgents *under human rights law* without showing an absolute necessity to do so, or to detain preventively during armed conflict, might lead to allowing the state to do the same outside armed conflict, with one precedent leading to another, and then another, and yet another."[53] Milanović argues that *lex specialis* is a rule of conflict avoidance rather than conflict resolution, so that if one could make IHL and IHRL simpatico with each other, one ought to do so rather than viewing IHL as taking precedence when its rules conflict with IHRL.[54] Regardless of whether this is right as a general matter,

50. *See, e.g.*, Int'l and Operational Law Dep't, U.S. Army, Law of War Deskbook 8 (2011); Melzer, *supra* note 14, at 78–79; U.S. Dept. of the Army, The Law of Land Warfare ¶ 3 (July 1956); United Kingdom Ministry of Defence, The Manual Of The Law Of Armed Conflict § 2.4 (2004).

51. *See* Seth Lazar, *Necessity in Self-Defense and War*, 40 Phil. & Pub. Aff. 3, 43 (2012) ("The problem is essentially that identified in 57(2.a.ii): minimizing risks to civilians often involves imposing additional risks on friendly combatants.").

52. *But see* Marco Sassòli, Antoine A. Bouvier & Anne Quintin, How Does Law Protect in War?: Cases, Documents, and Teaching Materials on Contemporary Practice in International Humanitarian Law 1–2 n.16, 2 (3d ed. 2011), *available at* http://www.icrc.org/eng/assets/files/publications/icrc-0739-part-i.pdf (stating on the one hand that "[i]n order to 'win the war' it is not necessary to kill all enemy soldiers; it is sufficient to capture them or to make them otherwise surrender," but on the other hand, conceding that IHL "does not prohibit the use of violence").

53. *See* Milanović, *supra* note 5, at 97.

54. The warrant for this position is that no treaty expressly gives IHL this power over human rights law. *See id.* at 115. *But cf.* Draper, *supra* note 33 (finding that IHL

the fact remains that on standards of necessity in the realm of targeting, IHL and IHRL *do* conflict, and no amount of interpretation can square the circle. As Milanović concedes, "It is questionable . . . whether this necessity requirement could be effectively applied in a more traditional battlefield setting," and "[t]here is perhaps no other area of potential conflict where the infusion of IHLR with IHL could lead to a greater slide into utopia, with a consequent slide into irrelevance."[55]

Second, there are other ways to go about solving the alleged codification gap sparked by the paucity of rules governing non-international armed conflicts. Importing the rules of IHRL is one solution, but one might also apply the rules from international conflicts, either on the basis of analogy or because these rules have become customary in non-international conflicts as well.[56] Whether applied by analogy or custom, there are strong prudential reasons to import rules from within IHL rather than look outside to another body of law to fill the gap.[57] The rules of IHL applicable in international conflicts are, at the very least, engineered to deal with the very particular situation of warfare. Moreover, IHL as a field is moving in a direction whereby the rules of warfare are becoming insensitive to the distinction between international and non-international conflicts; the rules of the former are gradually being adopted to apply to the latter.[58] This is a preferable solution especially as essential building blocks such as the

as *lex specialis* is implicitly incorporated by human rights provisions recognizing state parties' power to "derogate" from the right to life).

55. *See* Milanović, *supra* note 5, at 121. Presumably, this leaves open the possibility of using co-application in cases *away* from the traditional battlefield. However, it is unclear if the analysis can be segmented in this fashion. If the two forms of necessity are inconsistent, why should they be co-applied in cases on the traditional battlefield either?

56. *See, e.g., Prosecutor v. Tadić*, Case No. IT-94-1-I, Decision on the Defence Motion for Interlocutory Appeal on Jurisdiction, ¶¶ 128–35 (Oct. 2, 1995), *available at* http://www.icty.org/x/cases/tadic/acdec/en/51002.htm (applying rules of IAC on the basis of customary law); *see also* Abresch, *supra* note 29, at 742 (noting three methods, including analogy and custom, that international lawyers have used to borrow the rules from IAC to apply them to NIAC); Christopher Greenwood, *International Humanitarian Law and the Tadić Case*, 7 EUR. J. INT'L L. 265, 280 (1996).

57. For a list of customary rules applicable in NIAC, see generally CUSTOMARY INTERNATIONAL HUMANITARIAN LAW (Jean-Marie Henckaerts & Louise Doswald-Beck eds., 2005) (outlining 161 rules related to IHL).

58. *Tadić Defence Motion*, ¶ 126; Review of Indictment, *Prosecutor v. Martic*, ICTY Trial Chamber, 8 Mar. 1996, ¶ 11; *see also* KNUT DÖRMANN ET AL., ELEMENTS OF WAR CRIMES UNDER THE ROME STATUTE OF THE INTERNATIONAL CRIMINAL COURT 444 (2003) (discussing the ICTY's application of rules to internal armed conflicts); John Cerone, *Jurisdiction and Power: The Intersection of Human Rights Law & the Law of Non-international Armed Conflict in an Extraterritorial Context*, 40 ISR. L. REV. 398, 398 (2007) (substantial convergence between rules of IAC and NIAC); Marko Milanovic & Vidan Hadzi-Vidanovic, *A Taxonomy of Armed Conflict*, *in* RESEARCH HANDBOOK ON

principle of necessity mean different things in IHL and IHRL (as this section has explained), but at least the principle of necessity means the same thing in IAC (international armed conflict) as NIAC (non-international armed conflict), and its borrowing between them will not be subject to the same failures of translation.

Third, the rules of IHL, from Geneva to Hague Conventions, were already designed with the purpose of protecting innocent civilians and their rights.[59] The central building blocks of IHL—the principles of necessity, proportionality, distinction, and humanity—were designed so as to balance the interests of the relevant parties and achieve a humanizing result that reduced the amount of suffering caused by armed conflicts. The importation of IHRL rules, designed to protect rights during peacetime, might upset the carefully calibrated rules that were designed to do the same thing during armed conflict.[60] That is the reason that rules of IHL are often considered *lex specialis*.[61] In fact, the humanizing rules of IHL are designed to achieve practical results because they consider their compliance and self-enforcement as well as their normative pull. Throughout the whole field—including notions of *tu quoque* and reprisals—the field has explicitly grappled with how to impose normative restraints on the conduct of warfare even in the absence of a global sovereign to demand compliance.[62] At least one example is the immediate notion that the rules of armed conflict are bilateral and apply to both sides of the conflict; the collapse of IHL as a normative regime will harm one's own soldiers as well, thus giving each side of the conflict some self-interested reasons to comply with its prohibitions.[63]

INTERNATIONAL CONFLICT AND SECURITY LAW 256, 256 (Nigel D. White & Christian Henderson eds., 2013).

59. *See* GARY SOLIS, THE LAW OF ARMED CONFLICT: INTERNATIONAL HUMANITARIAN LAW IN WAR 23 (2010) ("Like its fraternal twin, LOAC, IHL refers to the body of treaty-based and customary international law aimed at protecting the individual in time of international or non-international armed conflict."); Blum, *supra* note 29, at 127 (stating that the animating principle of IHL is the "sparing of all those who do not partake in hostilities.").

60. *See, e.g.*, Blum, *supra* note 29, at 120 ("The obvious advantage of the existing paradigm has been its purportedly straightforward applicability to the battlefield: In reliance on a status-based rule of distinction, soldiers need not engage in a costly and dangerous process of ascertaining the merits of each individual target.").

61. See W. Hays Parks, *Part IX of the ICRC "Direct Participation in Hostilities" Study: No Mandate, No Expertise, and Legally Incorrect*, 42 N.Y.U. J. INT'L L. & POL. 769, 797–98 (2010).

62. *See, e.g.*, ROBERT E. SCOTT & PAUL B. STEPHAN, THE LIMITS OF LEVIATHAN 33–35 (2006) (discussing prisoner's dilemma problems in international law).

63. *See generally* Eyal Benvenisti, *Customary International Law as a Judicial Tool for Promoting Efficiency*, *in* THE IMPACT OF INTERNATIONAL LAW ON INTERNATIONAL COOPERATION 85 (Eyal Benvenisti & Moshe Hirsch eds., 2004); Jens David Ohlin,

Fourth, and finally, the co-application of IHRL and IHL is fraught with difficulties because the two legal regimes govern different *relationships*.[64] IHL is based on reciprocity, on co-equal belligerents meeting each other on the battlefield, each one subject to the same rules as the other.[65] Although the belligerents may not be equal in military strength, their equality as a formal matter is undeniable under the law of war, because the concept of reciprocity governs their relationship. Unfortunately, contemporary asymmetric conflicts between states and nonstate actors, in particular terrorist organizations and networks, have placed unparalleled pressure on the principle of reciprocity. It is an open question whether our current reciprocity-based system of IHL is up to the task of regulating the asymmetrical conflicts of today and tomorrow, a question that we will more fully answer in Chapter 8. But it would be an overreaction to the emergence of asymmetric conflicts to run to the other side of the spectrum and expect human rights principles, on their own, to adequately regulate asymmetric conflicts with terrorists.

International Human Rights Law is based on a completely different relationship between the sovereign and her subject. As a body of law, IHRL constrains how a government treats its own citizens (and other noncitizen subjects) internally.[66] These rules do not reciprocally apply against the citizen in his or her dealing with the sovereign; this would be a category mistake. To the extent that there is any reciprocity at all it is completely different: each sovereign reciprocally promises to other sovereigns to treat his own subjects (not just foreign nationals) in accordance with certain codified standards of human rights.[67] But it is important to distinguish between, on the one hand, the source of the promise (reciprocally bilateral or multilateral at the level of sovereigns) and on the other hand, the object of the regulation in question, which is the sovereign's internal treatment of her subjects as constrained by IHRL. Although this relationship clearly applies to civilian life, we question whether it alone can effectively regulate asymmetric conflicts between states and nonstate actors. Although these new wars are fundamentally different from those that Grotius or even Lieber saw, it would be wrong to completely deny the applicability of *jus in bello* to them.

Nash Equilibrium and International Law, 96 Cornell L. Rev. 869, 880–90 (2011) (finding the source of international legal obligations in self-interested contractarianism).

64. *See* Schabas, *supra* note 28, at 607 (stating that these legal regimes are incompatible because human rights law's "fundamental concern is not with finding a fair and balanced approach to a conflict between two combatant parties but rather with regulating the essentially unequal relationship between state and individual").

65. Solis, *supra* note 59, at 9–10.

66. *See, e.g.*, Louis Henkin, The Age of Rights 13–14 (1996).

67. *Id.*

III. CONCLUSION

In this chapter we have explored and explained how the concept of necessity operates differently in human rights law and *jus in bello*. It should come as no surprise that their legal operation is substantially different—the two fields of law are different enterprises with different background conditions. However, as we will explore in other chapters, there may be some room for human rights *principles* in armed conflict. In other words, our analysis in this chapter was meant to excavate the incompatibility between human rights necessity and *jus in bello* necessity in today's law. But this was not meant to sanctify the current state of IHL as inevitable or incapable of revision. It is an open question whether today's *jus in bello* displays an appropriate balance between the interests of attacking forces (to kill enemy soldiers without limitation) and our desire to reduce war's cruelty. This is often described as the balancing act between military necessity and humanity—a relationship capable of piecemeal or wholesale revision if necessary—which we will explore in more detail in Chapter 7. Tomorrow's IHL might strike a new balance: one that is more weighted to the principle of humanity than the current state of affairs.

Part of the warrant for rebalancing IHL back toward the principle of humanity (and away from the principle of military necessity) might be an appeal to *human rights principles*—the rights of enemy soldiers to be free from certain treatment or outcomes.[68] This might even take the form of a new principle regarding unnecessary killing in some contexts. However, it is important to be clear about the different ways that human rights principles might affect the law of armed conflict. One manner is the direct application of human rights law in situations of armed conflict, so that human rights law and IHL cross-fertilize each other, producing a humanizing effect on the latter based on rules of law emanating from the former. Although this procedure might have some humanizing effects on IHL, the procedure itself is fraught with difficulty for all of the reasons we have identified in this chapter—the two fields of law have radically different conceptions of necessity.

However, it is possible for human rights principles to affect IHL in a more subtle and abstract way. At the level of moral theory, basic principles of human rights might affect how we understand IHL's current balance

68. For a discussion of how such thinking might work in *jus in bello*, see David Luban, *Human Rights Thinking and the Laws of War*, in THEORETICAL BOUNDARIES OF ARMED CONFLICT AND HUMAN RIGHTS (Jens Ohlin ed., 2016).

between necessity and humanity and lead us to question that current state of affairs, in particular the almost complete forfeiture of the right to life that IHL foists upon combatants during armed conflict. If a rebalancing is required, however, it will then need to be operationalized and codified in law. It is at this point that it is crucial to understand the interplay between human rights necessity and *jus in bello* necessity that we have outlined in this chapter. There are many ways of rebalancing the law through new codifications, and not all approaches will be equally successful. Only by understanding the schism between the varieties of necessity will it be possible to imagine changes in tomorrow's IHL and implement them in a coherent doctrine. The key will be to humanize IHL and protect the rights of soldiers while still being sensitive to its underlying and inescapable impulse: to permit combatant killings in order to return as quickly as possible to a state of peace.

CHAPTER 6

Necessity in Criminal Law

Allowing perpetrators to excuse their wartime conduct by pleading necessity represents the most powerful exemplar of the principle of necessity as a state of *exception*. The application of the defense in the criminal context (whether international or domestic) allows a defendant to be justified or excused—based on the exigency of the immediate situation—from the demands of a generally applicable criminal prohibition.[1] The normative structure of the defense is a utilitarian or consequentialist balancing that suggests that the overall benefits of the defendant's conduct outweigh the resulting harm caused by violating the criminal prohibition.[2] That is why the principle is also sometimes referred to as the lesser-evils justification because it implies that the defendant has selected the all-things-considered better outcome. However, this description is only accurate if one defines the "better outcome" in explicitly consequentialist—as opposed to deontological—terms. In other words, the defendant is rewarded for imposing harm on the victim of his crime so as to improve the lot of a larger number of third parties—a distributive problem that would seem to ignore the separateness of persons.[3] It

1. *See* JEROME HALL, GENERAL PRINCIPLES OF CRIMINAL LAW 426 (2d ed. 1960).
2. *See* MARKUS DUBBER & TATJANA HÖRNLE, CRIMINAL LAW: A COMPARATIVE APPROACH 441 (2014) (discussing necessity's utilitarian rationale and asking how it can be squared with jurisdictions, such as Germany, that are generally hostile to utilitarian approaches).
3. The idea of the "separateness of persons" was introduced by John Rawls to explain his discomfort with utilitarian balancing. *See* JOHN RAWLS, A THEORY OF JUSTICE 164–67 (rev. ed. 1999).

is little consolation to the victim that his inherent moral dignity was violated in order to benefit others.[4]

This is precisely what makes the necessity defense so dangerous and why the criminal law has evolved different strategies for *containing* the application of the defense—a defense that, if allowed to run wild, might quickly swallow up the criminal law into a sea of exceptions so numerous and so vast that they quickly unwind the rule itself. Consequently, the present chapter takes a novel approach to necessity in international criminal law by cataloging and evaluating the containment strategies that the law might use to limit the application of the necessity defense. To start, Section II looks at the situation when no viable constraint exists by examining the legality of torture and the possibility of arguing a state of necessity as a justification or excuse for torture. Although torture has been roundly criticized as a prohibited method under domestic criminal law, international humanitarian law, and international human rights law, these pronouncements also leave open the small possibility that despite the prohibition against it even in a state of necessity, defendants might be permitted to argue necessity in an ex post criminal prosecution.[5]

Section III then surveys international criminal law's most popular containment strategy that might apply even in a criminal prosecution: the rule disallowing necessity and duress claims in cases involving the killing of innocent civilians. This rule, originally borrowed from common law systems of criminal law, was applied by the International Criminal Tribunal for the Former Yugoslavia (ICTY) in the famous *Erdemović* case, although its status as binding law for future cases is somewhat in doubt. First, the blanket exclusion conflicts with the rule applied in many civil law systems of criminal law, where the necessity defense is permitted at least in theory even in murder cases. Second, the more pressing problem with the containment strategy is its fundamentally ad hoc nature—why exclude the defense for one category of cases but not another? Is this different treatment, based on the particular crime, philosophically or normatively defensible?

Finally, Section IV considers the most aggressive containment strategy—a wider prohibition on the necessity defense for *principled* reasons. This containment strategy is rather unlikely if understood as a blanket prohibition,

4. One could describe this as a problem of distribution of harm. *See* DUBBER & TATJANA HÖRNLE, *supra* note 2, at 442.

5. For a discussion, see Paola Gaeta, *May Necessity Be Available as a Defence for Torture in the Interrogation of Suspected Terrorists?*, 2 J. INT'L CRIM. JUST. 785 (2004).

but its underlying structure becomes more plausible once it is described as a principled but not universal containment strategy. The most promising example of this strategy is the German case of the hijacked airliner, where the German Constitutional Court concluded—in a startling and principled defense of deontological values—that giving the country's prime minister the authority to order the downing of a hijacked airliner was a violation of the most fundamental right in the German Constitution (GG): the right of human dignity.[6] The court's reasoning was both elegant and devastatingly simple: shooting down a plane to prevent it from being used as a weapon against a skyscraper would involve deliberately killing the passengers on the plane in order to save a greater number of civilians on the ground. According to the court, this represented an impermissible form of utilitarian balancing that violated the inherent moral worth of the civilians on the airplane. In essence, the court concluded that the German Constitution protected the deontological moral worth of the human beings on the airplane—a principled result that goes much further than the ad hoc containment strategy deployed by the ICTY in *Erdemović*. Unfortunately, the German court left open the possibility (by refusing to pronounce on the issue) that the necessity defense might be invoked afterward in a criminal prosecution for shooting down an airliner. If it had followed through on its argument to its logical conclusion, it should have explicitly concluded that even the criminal law defense of necessity represented an impermissible infringement of the inherent moral worth of the human beings on the airplane.

I. NECESSITY IN DOMESTIC CRIMINAL LAW

In domestic U.S. law, the Model Penal Code, Section 302, defines the criminal defense of necessity as follows:

> Conduct the actor believes to be necessary to avoid harm or evil to himself or to another is justifiable, provided that:
>
> (a) the harm or evil sought to be avoided by such conduct is greater than that sought to be prevented by the law defining the offense charged . . . [7]

6. *See Aviation Security Case*, Federal Constitutional Court (Germany), Judgment of the First Senate of 15 February 2006, *available at* http://www.bverfg.de/entscheidungen/rs20060215_1bvr035705en.html.

7. Model Penal Code § 302, and Comment (1985).

Stated so boldly, this defense seems to give a very broad defense to actions that would otherwise be punishable. It is common to understand this defense as a "choice of evils defense,"[8] that is, a defense based on the idea that although it would normally be prohibited to do a certain act, in certain situations it is justifiable to do the act than not given the negative consequences that will undoubtedly result from not doing the act. In Just War theory, necessity is also often discussed under the label of the "lesser of two evils."[9] Indeed, one can find such discussion extending back at least as far as the early seventeenth century.[10]

Notice though that even in its bold statement, the Model Penal Code authors build into the defense a restraint in terms of proportionality. For after it is said that there is subjective determination that a certain action is necessary to avoid a harm, there is then a second consideration, namely a weighing of harms. The harms or evils avoided by the act necessary to prevent them are weighed against the harms or evils caused by so acting. So, from the beginning, it is clear that necessity alone will not function to relieve from guilt or punishment without an assessment of proportionality, at least in this nearly canonical view of United States' criminal law. Indeed, LaFave and Scott say that "necessity" is actually a misnomer, for it is not literally necessary "that a policeman speed after a fleeing criminal," but only that the law regards it as preferable for the policeman to do so rather than to let the criminal escape.[11]

We have quoted Grotius as requiring that a harm be imminent for a State to be justified, in *jus ad bellum* considerations, in attacking on grounds of self-defense. So, the idea of imminence is not all that new, although it is certainly true that it has not played a large role in the principle of necessity in the *jus in bello* context.[12] The requirement of imminence makes it much harder to get to the stage of using the weighing considerations of the principle of proportionality than it might first appear. This is very similar to the idea of imminence in discussions of preemptive attacks.

8. *See* Wayne R. LaFave & Austin W. Scott, Jr., Criminal Law 442 (2d ed. 1986).

9. *See* Michael Ignatieff, The Lesser Evil: Political Ethics in the Age of Terror (2004).

10. Francisco Suarez is well known for advancing such arguments. *See* his treatise *On War, in* Selections from Three Works (Disputatione XIII, De Triplici Virtute Theologica: Charitate) (Gwladys L. Williams, Ammi Brown & John Waldron trans., 1944) (c. 1610).

11. *See* LaFave & Scott, *supra* note 8, at 441.

12. *See* Emanuel Gross, *Legal Aspects of Tackling Terrorism: The Balance between the Right of a Democracy to Defend Itself and the Protection of Human Rights*, 6 UCLA J. Int'l L. & For. Aff. 107 (2001).

Nonetheless it is true that imminence is often hard to define. Is sinking "imminent" when sailors discover a small hole that will eventually sink the ship? Such questions are often hard to answer, although some have bitten the bullet and said that in the ship case this was already a clear case of imminence.[13] Here is how one author summarizes the conditions necessary for the common law defense of necessity:

> The defense involves a reasonable belief that an individual confronts an imminent and irreparable harm, a lack of legal avenues to avoid the evil, the commission of a criminal act which is reasonably calculated to eliminate the harm; and a proportionality between the crime and the threat.[14]

Here we have a clear statement of how necessity is limited only to cases where serious harm is imminent. Although important, imminence is not the only limitation on the principle of necessity, for proportionality is also a major limit.

Military necessity is normally restricted to certain kinds of emergency situations. Indeed, the Nuremberg trials seemed to limit considerations of military necessity to cases of self-defense emergencies.[15] The Nuremberg court said that there must be an "instant and overwhelming necessity for self defense" that is imperative, where this means that there is "no choice of means and no moment of deliberation."[16] Such emergency cases will be few and far between. However military necessity can be claimed even when the war being fought is not just. The self-defense considerations are localized ones, not considerations of *jus ad bellum*. Either side to a war can claim necessity. Necessity is restricted to *jus in bello* considerations of tactical emergency, as the Nuremberg court says, and must be of the sort that would "be necessary to save his troops from an imminent major disaster."[17]

There is a time constraint as well, as we saw in the previous section. The requirement of imminence means that there must be a preponderance of evidence for thinking that the serious harm will occur, and that it will take place soon, normally in a few hours, unless the tactic is employed. The standard way to think about this requirement is in terms of *The Caroline*

13. *Id.* at 108.
14. Matthew Lippman, *Conundrums of Armed Conflict: Criminal Defenses to Violations of the Humanitarian Law of War*, 15 DICKINSON J. INT'L L. 66 (1996).
15. *See The German High Command Trial, reprinted in* XII LAW REPORTS OF TRIALS OF WAR CRIMINALS 124.
16. *Id., quoting The Caroline* case.
17. *Id.* at 125.

case's requirement of an "instant and overwhelming necessity for self defense leaving no choice of means and moment of deliberation."[18]

In addition, we are to consider whether there are other avenues open to us, within the time frame when we can still prevent the harm, and that these avenues are themselves legal or at least less problematical than the means under consideration. There are two sorts of weighing that must be done: first, weighing the chosen conduct against other options that could achieve the same result, and then weighing the consequences of the means to be employed against the harm to be prevented by those means. But in any event, the requirement of imminence makes it harder to even get to the weighing of harms required by the principle of proportionality.[19] Sometimes the analysis will simply fail at the level of the imminence requirement.

We must not allow the invocation of military necessity to become merely "a callous way of violating basic human rights."[20] To make sure that necessity does not swamp other very important considerations that are at least if not more important, necessity is restricted in domestic law to some kind of an emergency, where the only acceptable way out of the emergency is to use tactics that would otherwise be considered inappropriate. And here the term "emergency" is meant to signal that it will only rarely be true that a certain tactic can be employed. No large category of exceptions is hereby created, but only a rare exception to an otherwise rather firm rule. Indeed, we will now explore the various and competing doctrines that the law employs to restrict the number or scope of the necessity defense in both domestic and international criminal law. Although there are a number of different legal devices, they all share a common intuition: the necessity defense, left unconstrained, would be a dangerous and morally unsupportable doctrine. Necessity is not a blanket justification that can transform any rule into one that admits of an endless class of exceptions. The neorealists were simply wrong to think that military necessity could be employed to explode the restraints of the Just War theory and its rules of war.

Similarly, the requirement of imminence is meant to restrict the cases that can fall under the justifying spotlight of the principle of necessity. Imminence is supposed to signal the idea that the emergency is truly upon us, and there is very little time for us to contemplate other, more palatable options. But if there is more time, then it is quite likely that there

18. *See id.*, *quoting* II MOORE'S DIGEST OF INT'L L. 414.
19. *See* Gross, *supra* note 12, at 107.
20. Allen Gewirth, *War Crimes and Human Rights*, *in* WAR CRIMES AND COLLECTIVE WRONGDOING 53 (Aleksandar Jokic ed., 2001).

are other tactics that could be pursued to achieve the same military objective. And, in addition, proportionality then enters into the picture to urge that the costs of the strategy must be outweighed by the value of that which is to be achieved by the strategy. The idea is that imminence forces us to think about whether there was a serious emergency that could not be averted in any other less lethal way than the way that was indeed chosen at the moment, and proportionality forces us to assess what is the goal to be achieved by the otherwise prohibited tactics.

II. NO CONSTRAINTS ON THE NECESSITY DEFENSE

No issue arising from the U.S. armed conflict with al-Qaeda has prompted more criticism and more soul searching than torture, or what U.S. security officials for some time were euphemistically calling "enhanced interrogation techniques."[21] But the debate over torture in the United States, which began in earnest after 9/11, was philosophically far behind the Israeli experience—for the security services, the judiciary, and Israeli academics, all of whom have worked out in detail the various legal and moral positions regarding the permissibility of torture.[22]

The Israeli Supreme Court was the first court to offer a really sophisticated treatment of necessity and torture.[23] The Court specifically considered the so-called ticking time bomb scenario made famous by the philosophical literature, but now also a concern in real-like counterterrorism operations. Assume that agents know that a terrorist plot is imminent and a suspect in custody has the information they need to foil that plot. Can the agents torture him to get the information from him?

At first glance, the necessity defense would suggest yes. The normative structure is largely utilitarian.[24] Although one individual will be horribly mistreated, the harm to him or her is outweighed by the benefit to others, in this case the innocent civilians whose lives will be spared when the terrorist bombing is foiled. This suggests that the security operatives

21. *See* Kai Ambos, *May a State Torture Suspects to Save the Life of Innocents?*, J. INT'L CRIM. JUST. 261 (2008).

22. *See* Adam Raviv, *Torture and Justification: Defending the Indefensible*, 13 GEO. MASON L. REV. 135 (2004); Michael S. Moore, *Torture and the Balance of Evils*, 23 ISR. L. REV. 280 (1989).

23. *Judgment Concerning the Legality of the General Security Service's Interrogation Methods*, Supreme Court of Israel, 38 I.L.M. 1471 (1999).

24. *See, e.g.*, GEORGE P. FLETCHER, BASIC CONCEPTS OF CRIMINAL LAW 83 (1998).

are justified in torturing the detainee to save the putative victims of the terrorist attack.

The central move in the Israeli *Torture* decision was to distinguish between an *ex ante* policy decision and an *ex post* exemption offered by the criminal law.[25] The court rejected any attempt to infer the former from the latter. In other words, just because an interrogator would be entitled to argue necessity as a defense to a criminal prosecution for torturing a detainee did not mean that the court could infer that it would be justified to craft a *policy* in favor of torturing detainees in counterterrorism operations. Why not? It would seem logical that if necessity exculpates a defendant for torturing a detainee under these (admittedly extreme circumstances), then necessity would also justify the creation of a bureaucratic policy that would structure how and when the torture would be conducted.

However, something is lost when necessity moves from a criminal law defense to an affirmative policy guidance. Specifically, what is missing is the *urgency* of the particular decision. The criminal law defense of necessity is premised, at least in theory, on the idea that violating the criminal law prohibition is the only possible solution (or rather the *best* possible solution) given the time pressure facing the agent. Because the situation is urgent, he has no opportunity to find other alternatives, thus making the violation of the law a true necessity. Aquinas famously wrote that necessity knows no law.[26] One way of interpreting that statement is that necessity counsels exceptions or departures from the law, which is precisely what makes the defense so dangerous. But there is another way of interpreting Aquinas's statement. Because necessity knows no law, it is by its nature outside of the law and incapable of being reduced to a law-like formulation, which is precisely what a bureaucratic *policy* of torture seeks to do.[27] By reducing torture to a state-like policy, where many alternatives and the cool

25. *See* HCJ 5100/94, *Public Committee against Torture in Israel v. Israel*, Supreme Court of Israel, Judgment of 6 September 1999, para. 36 ("In the Court's opinion, the authority to establish directives respecting the use of physical means during the course of a GSS interrogation cannot be implied from the 'necessity defense.'"). For a discussion of these issues, see Youngjae Lee, *The Defense of Necessity and Powers of Government*, 3 Crim. L. & Phil. 133 (2008).

26. St. Thomas Aquinas, Summa Theologica, Part II, 1st part, que. 96.

27. *See* Alon Harel & Assaf Sharon, *What Is Really Wrong with Torture?*, 6 J. Int'l Crim. Just. 241, 250–51 (2008) ("By stating that torture, even when mandatory, ought never to be rule-governed we imply that the agent can never justify the performance of torture on the basis of a rule permitting, requiring or authorizing it. Instead, the agent always ought to make a fresh judgment, attuned to the specific circumstances, whether performing it here and now is appropriate. Even if endorsing such a guideline and relying on it would generate better choices on the part of the agent, the agent ought never to rely on such a guideline. Torturing a person must be based on a

reflection of day reign, the true state of necessity has evaporated. For that reason, necessity can never be a true justification for a state policy of torture, though it could be used in a criminal law trial.[28]

The very same argument appeared in the torture memos produced by the Office of the Legal Counsel during the Bush administration. The Yoo and Bybee Memorandum argued that the president could authorize the torture of suspected detainees, based on a whole series of interwoven arguments (many of them now discredited), including that the president had the authority to ignore international law.[29] One of the arguments detailed the availability of the necessity defense under the criminal law, thus suggesting (without explicitly saying) that one could infer an ex ante policy authorization from an ex post criminal law justification.[30] In other words, since the president or one of his advisors could claim necessity if ever prosecuted, then the president had the lawful authority to authorize torture in the first place. This was precisely the argument rejected by the Israeli Supreme Court in the *Torture* case.

In order to understand why the necessity defense cannot be used as a doctrinal hook for an ex ante policy decision, it is important first to clarify the nature of the necessity defense and whether it constitutes a justification or an excuse—two terms that are only now gaining widespread currency in international law through their frequent use in international criminal law where the categories are central. A justification negates the wrongfulness of the criminal act, transforming what would otherwise be a wrongful act in contravention of an established legal prohibition.[31] In contrast, an excuse negates the culpability of the actor.[32] By implication, justifications are general in nature since they apply to the act in question regardless of who performs it; excuses are personal in nature since they attach to the individual agent whose situation is somewhat compromised and thus not deserving of punishment.[33]

particular judgment—a judgment concerning the appropriateness of torture here and now. Such a judgment ought not to be based on a rule permitting torture, even not one using vague terms such as 'reasonableness' or 'necessity.'").

28. *Id.* at 252 ("By turning the singular case of practical necessity into a rule, one turns a categorical prohibition into one that is conditional on circumstances.").

29. *See* Jay Bybee, Assistant U.S. Attorney General, Office of Legal Counsel, Memorandum to Alberto Gonzales, *Standards for Conduct for Interrogation under 18 U.S.C. 2340–2340A* (Aug. 1, 2002).

30. *Id.* (discussing both necessity and self-defense arguments).

31. George P. Fletcher, Basic Principles of Criminal Law 89–90 (1998).

32. *Id.*

33. Paul Robinson, *Criminal Law Defenses: A Systematic Analysis*, 82 Colum. L. Rev. 199, 221 (1982). *See also* Sarah Finnin, Elements of Accessorial Modes of Liability 110 (2012).

Is necessity a justification or excuse? The issue has plagued comparative criminal law (and international criminal law) theory for decades.[34] American legal scholars generally view necessity as a justification and duress as an excuse. In the classic duress case, the defendant's autonomy is compromised by a third agent who threatens to harm either the defendant or his family if the defendant does not perform the agent's bidding (some criminal act such as a murder). Since this is an autonomy-reducing threat that negates the culpability of the actor (because the law cannot reasonably expect him to sacrifice his family in order to live up to the demands of the law), most scholars have correctly viewed duress as an excuse.[35] Necessity involves the defendant's commission of a criminal act in order to respond to some environmental threat; the illegal act is performed as a *response* to the environmental threat, not as a *submission* to the threat as is the case in duress. Because necessity requires that the defendant select the lesser of the evils (the better result from a consequentialist perspective), necessity has generally been viewed as a justification.

So the general scheme in the common law is that the necessity defense requires a justified response to an environmental threat, whereas the duress defense requires an excused response to a threatening agent who demands that the defendant perform an illegal act on his behalf. The problem with this scheme is that it is under-inclusive. There are other possibilities. What if the defendant is facing an environmental threat but fails to select the lesser of two evils? The threat's origin in the environment suggests that the necessity defense applies, but he does not meet the criteria for a criminal law justification. But the only available excuse does not apply either because the threat was not from a third party individual imposing her will on the defendant. Some jurisdictions, including Germany and other civil law jurisdictions, recognize another category of "excused necessity" to respond to precisely this situation.[36] For this defense, the defendant need not show that he selected the lesser evil; it is an excuse, after all. However, many jurisdictions limit the defense to situations where either the defendant himself

34. For a recent discussion, see Dwight Newman, *Theorizing Duress and Necessity in International Criminal Law*, *in* RETHINKING CRIMINAL LAW THEORY 291, 300–02 (Francois Tanguay-Renaud & James Stribopoulos eds., 2012). *See also* Kent Greenawalt, *The Perplexing Borders of Justification and Excuse*, 84 COLUM. L. REV. 1897 (1984).

35. *See, e.g.*, Kyron Huigens, *Duress Is Not a Justification*, 2 OHIO ST. J. CRIM. L. 303 (2004); Joshua Dressler, *Exegesis of the Law of Duress: Justifying the Excuse and Searching for Its Proper Limits*, 62 S. CAL. L. REV. 1331 (1989).

36. For an explanation of the doctrine, see MICHAEL BOHLANDER, PRINCIPLES OF GERMAN CRIMINAL LAW 123 (2009) (though using the language of duress instead of the language of excused necessity).

or a close family relative will be harmed by the environmental threat.[37] With this doctrinal limitation, excused necessity remains unavailable as a defense for a security interrogator who tortures a detainee in order to stop a terrorist bombing that will kill some distant and unknown civilians with no personal connection to the interrogator.[38] Presumably, the law expects the interrogator to evaluate the situation with cool, detached logic, since no family members or close associates are threatened by the terrorist act.

Why should we care about the categorization of necessity as a justification or excuse?[39] We care in part because of the different messages that they send to the world. Since a justification is general in nature and speaks to the lawfulness of the *act* in question, by logical entailment it tells others that they too can commit the same act or render assistance to the defendant or those in similar situations.[40] In contrast, an excuse makes no such announcement to the world. If a defendant is excused by virtue of some personal circumstance, he has still performed an unlawful act—one that others may not assist or replicate.[41] The mistake of the White House torture memos is that they took this point one step too far; one cannot move from the general nature of justifications to the further ex ante policy authorization that the memo was purporting to find for the president of the United States. That is because even though necessity may be a justification, it always requires ex post consideration of the particular facts giving rise to the lesser-evils dilemma faced by the defendant.[42]

Even though the White House torture memos were eventually recalled and revised by the Office of Legal Counsel,[43] and even though the Israeli Supreme Court rejected the possibility of pre-authorizing torture on the basis of the necessity defense, it is nonetheless still striking that *neither* explicitly rejected necessity as a defense to torture in a criminal prosecution. In other words, although there is widespread recognition that the necessity defense cannot be used as a doctrinal bootstrapping device to create

37. This issue is discussed in Jens David Ohlin, *The Bounds of Necessity*, 6 J. INT'L CRIM. JUST. 289 (2008).

38. This situation is described by Florian Jessberger in *Bad Torture—Good Torture? What International Criminal Lawyers May Learn from the Recent Trial of Police Officers in Germany*, 3 J. INT'L CRIM. JUST. 1059 (2005).

39. *Contra* Greenawalt, *supra* note 34, at 1920 (arguing that the distinction is unhelpful).

40. *See* Lee, *supra* note 25.

41. *Id.*

42. This point is nicely explained in Harel & Sharon, *supra* note 27.

43. *See* JACK GOLDSMITH, THE TERROR PRESIDENCY: LAW AND JUDGMENT INSIDE THE BUSH ADMINISTRATION 153 (2007) (discussing a conversation with Ashcroft regarding Goldsmith's intention to withdraw OLC memo and noting that Ashcroft "was not terribly surprised and did not resist").

a policy authorization, very few courts or commentators are willing to say that an interrogator who engages in torture should actually be convicted and punished for his actions. At least in the torture context, the general consensus is that there are few constraints on the application of the necessity defense in this context.[44] This produces a disturbing situation and one that speaks to the great power of the necessity doctrine as an exception to generally applicable criminal prohibitions. Even if one cannot infer the existence of an ex ante policy authorization from it, it is nonetheless disturbing that the necessity doctrine remains available as a potential defense that operates as an exception to generally applicable criminal prohibitions. This is especially surprising since the United Nations Convention Against Torture specifically states that "[n]o exceptional circumstances whatsoever, whether a state of war or a threat of war, internal political instability or any other public emergency, may be invoked as a justification for torture."[45] Incidentally, this "no justification" provision does not apply to cruel, inhumane, or degrading treatment (CIDT)—a distinction that was suggested by the United States delegation in 1979 based on their concern that want counts as CIDT was subjective and likely to change during an emergency situation.[46]

One possible outlier to this general conclusion is the *Daschner* case in Germany.[47] The local police in Frankfurt were investigating the abduction of a child, and detained a suspect in the case, though the police could not find the child. Fearing that time was running out, Daschner (the police official in charge of the case) directed the interrogators to threaten to torture

44. For different approaches to this question, *compare* Mirko Bagaric & Julie Clarke, *Not Enough Official Torture in the World? The Circumstances in Which Torture Is Morally Justifiable*, 39 U.S.F. L. Rev. 581 (2005) and Michael S. Moore, *Torture and the Balance of Evils*, 23 Isr. L. Rev. 280 (1989), *with* George C. Christie, *The Defense of Necessity Considered from the Legal and Moral Points of View*, 48 Duke L.J. 975, 1031 (1999) and Paola Gaeta, *May Necessity Be Available as a Defence for Torture in the Interrogation of Suspected Terrorists?*, 2 J. Int'l Crim. Just. 785 (2004). *See also* Adam Raviv, *Torture and Justification: Defending the Indefensible*, 13 Geo. Mason L. Rev. 135, 151–53 (2004).

45. Convention Against Torture and Other Cruel, Inhuman or Degrading Treatment or Punishment, art. 2(2), Dec. 10, 1984, 108 Stat. 382, 1465 U.N.T.S. 85 [hereinafter Convention Against Torture].

46. *See* Manfred Nowak & Elizabeth McArthur, The United Nations Convention Against Torture: A Commentary 118 (2008) (concluding "In retrospect, one might wonder whether the US delegation had already foreseen a situation such as its 'global war against terror' which has more than anything else undermined the absolute and non-derogable prohibition of torture and cruel, inhuman or degrading treatment.").

47. *See* Landgericht Frankfurt a.M. [LG] [Regional Court] Dec. 20, 2004, Neue Juristische Wochenschrift 692 (692–96), 2005 (F.R.G.) [hereinafter *Daschner*].

the detainee unless he divulged the information they needed to locate the boy. After the threat, the detainee divulged the information though it was of little use to the police; the child was already dead.[48] Even though the interrogators only *threatened* the detainee with torture, this threat was illegal under local law, and Daschner was prosecuted for ordering the threat. A Frankfurt court concluded that justified necessity was unavailable as a defense for two reasons, one contingent and the other principled. First, the court concluded that the torture threat was not the only means available to the interrogators, and that other avenues were possible to find the required information—in other words the illegal act was not truly "necessary" to avert the harm in question. For the second and more principled objection, the court concluded that the necessity defense in this context would infringe on the inherent human dignity of the suspect in custody. We will discuss this constraint in more detail in Section III. But in short, the court invoked a deeply Kantian notion codified in Article 1 of the German Constitution, which protects the rights of all individuals to be free from utilitarian balancing. Since this is precisely what torturing the suspect would involve, the defense was not appropriate in this case. The court also concluded that excused necessity was inapplicable because Daschner had acted to save an unknown and unrelated boy—not a family member or close associate.[49]

Unfortunately, the court did not have the courage of its convictions. Although it found that Daschner was not entitled to any criminal law defense for his behavior (neither self-defense, justified necessity, nor excused necessity applied), the court nonetheless concluded that Daschner was not an appropriate subject of punishment. In short, the court created an entirely new category: guilty but not punishable—a somewhat innovative but perhaps incoherent category that infringes upon the conceptual terrain of excuses that usually occupy the same conceptual space as a way to prevent punishment of non-culpable defendants.[50] In *Daschner*, the court extended the idea to say that even some *culpable* defendants should not be punished.

The takeaway message from these cases is that although there is substantial resistance and discomfort associated with the great power of the necessity defense, especially in cases of torture, criminal lawyers are generally very uncomfortable with courts actually convicting or punishing defendants who engage in torture under a state of necessity. In this line of

48. *Id.*
49. *See* Ohlin, *supra* note 37, at 296–97.
50. *See* Jessberger, *supra* note 38, at 1065–66.

cases, few legal doctrines constrain the application of the defense, even though the application of the defense involves a substantial infringement of a Kantian right of human dignity on the part of the victim who is tortured and used as a means to an end. We now turn to how international criminal law has resolved these issues.

III. AD HOC CONSTRAINTS

Given the danger associated with necessity as a criminal law defense, domestic courts have generally sought ways to constrain its application. Criminal courts in common law jurisdictions have traditionally deployed a decidedly ad hoc constraint on its application: the exclusion of necessity and duress as defenses to the killing of innocent civilians.[51] However, civil law jurisdictions have traditionally not excluded necessity and duress but rather have allowed them in all cases regardless of the criminal charge, as long as the defendant meets the stringent requirements of the defense. During its earliest years, the ICTY was forced to decide whether it would adopt the common law view (ad hoc constraints on necessity and duress), or whether it would adopt the civil law perspective (no ad hoc constraints on necessity and duress at least in theory).[52] As we will discuss in this section, the issue is fraught with danger because the necessity and duress defenses are so powerful that they risk unraveling the most central norm of international humanitarian law: the prohibition on killing innocent civilians. The judges of the ICTY were ultimately concerned about the policy implications of this unraveling, and ultimately held that necessity and duress were unavailable in war crimes cases dealing with the killing of innocent civilians. They left open the possibility that the defense might apply to other war crimes (that do not involve killing), and it is also unclear whether other international tribunals will follow the ICTY's precedent.[53] The issue is a live and enduring doctrinal controversy.

The case began in 1995, when Drazen Erdemović was a young member of the 10th Sabotage Detachment of the Bosnian Serb Army. After the Srebrenica massacres, Erdemović did not escape into hiding as Radovan

51. It is somewhat unclear whether the exclusion applies only to murder cases or in prosecutions for manslaughter as well.

52. The Model Penal Code in Sections 2.09 and 3.02 takes the civil law approach and allows the necessity and duress defenses for all crimes.

53. For a discussion, see Rosa Brooks, *Law in the Heart of Darkness: Atrocity & Duress*, 43 VA. J. INT'L L. 861 (2003).

Karadzic and other suspects eventually did, but instead spoke openly and remorsefully about his participation in the massacres. While out drinking one night at a bar, he talked about the painful events with another soldier who was apparently displeased about the prospect that Erdemović might confess. The night ended when the soldier shot Erdemović, though he survived. Erdemović was not deterred: he found a television reporter and willingly confessed on camera, telling the reporter that he wanted to cooperate with the tribunal. He was then arrested and brought before the ICTY, where he tearfully recounted what had happened.

According to Erdemović, his unit was deployed to a farm near the town of Pilica. On July 16, 1995, busloads arrived with Bosnian Muslim men who had been captured by the Bosnian Serb Army either in Srebrenica or while escaping from Srebrenica after it fell to Bosnian Serb forces. The buses contained men who were considered to be of "fighting age"—between seventeen and sixty—and they were escorted in groups of ten and lined up against the side of a farm building for execution by Erdemović and his unit. Erdemović initially refused to shoot the prisoners. This is what he later told the judges at the ICTY during his formal testimony:

> Your Honour, I had to do this. If I had refused, I would have been killed together with the victims. When I refused, they told me: "If you are sorry for them, stand up, line up with them and we will kill you too." I am not sorry for myself but for my family, my wife and son who then had nine months, and I could not refuse because then they would have killed me.[54]

On a previous occasion, Erdemović had seen a commander order the summary execution of another insubordinate soldier who had refused to fire. Erdemović believed his commander when he said that Erdemović should line up with the victims if he wanted to share their fate. He was also worried that his family would be harmed if he was branded a traitor. So he complied. He used a machine gun and killed them in groups of ten, killing a total of about seventy men over the course of the afternoon. When it was finished, though, he knew that he could not do it again. Later that day he was ordered to participate in the execution of five hundred Bosnian Muslim men in a local cultural center. He got away with the insubordination this time because three of his fellow soldiers backed him up when he refused to kill the detainees, and other soldiers ended up doing the job for him.[55]

54. *Prosecutor v. Erdemović* Trial Transcript (on file with author).
55. *Id.*

The judges were convinced that Erdemović was genuinely plagued by his conscience, and a court-appointed psychiatrist determined that he was suffering from post-traumatic stress disorder. This made his case especially difficult to resolve. Generally speaking, claiming "superior orders" is rarely a successful defense for committing a war crime, but Erdemović's situation was slightly different. Erdemović was claiming that he acted under necessity or duress—that he only committed the killings because he feared for his own life.

The duress defense has long been controversial, ever since the British case of *Dudley and Stephens* in 1884.[56] The two men were sailors on a shipwrecked boat, slowly succumbing to thirst and hunger. Dudley and Stephens killed the cabin boy on their boat and resorted to cannibalism in order to keep themselves alive. They were prosecuted for murder but claimed that their actions were necessary to avoid the greater evil—the death of everyone on the boat. The British court adjudicating their fate ruled that although English law recognized necessity as a defense, it could not be applied in cases of murder. This rule survives to this day in most common law countries—that is, countries such as the United States and other former British colonies that trace their legal systems back to Britain. But other European legal systems—so-called civil law countries such as France or Germany—have generally allowed the defense (or at least the possibility of it) in all circumstances, even in cases of murder.[57]

The question for Erdemović was which rule should apply at international tribunals. The issue came down to a question that was simple to state but very difficult to resolve: When faced with a threat to his life or his family, can the law of war demand that a soldier engage in an act of moral heroism and stand up for what is right? When faced with a choice—his own death or committing a crime—does the soldier have a duty to sacrifice himself? Does it matter if the civilians are going to be killed anyway by other soldiers? Perhaps the law should treat the soldier charitably and view his dilemma with compassion. In a close 3-2 vote, the judges of the ICTY Appeals Chamber concluded that recognizing the defense of duress would have disastrous consequences in wartime and send the wrong message to soldiers in the field.[58] According to the Appeals

56. *See* Elies van Sliedregt, Individual Criminal Responsibility in International Law 246 (2012).

57. *See* Antonio Cassese, International Criminal Law 287–89 (2d ed. 2008); Sliedregt, *supra* note 56, at 247.

58. Judgment, *Prosecutor v. Erdemović*, ICTY Case No. IT-96-22-A, Appeals Chamber (Oct. 7, 1997).

Chamber, Erdemović did have a duty to sacrifice himself in order to protect the captured civilians.[59]

Even so, the judges were sympathetic to Erdemović's predicament, and concluded that although duress could never offer a complete defense to the charges, it could be considered as a mitigating factor when he was sentenced. He received a five-year sentence, which he served in a Norwegian prison.[60] He was released early after only three years and entered into the ICTY's version of a witness protection program after agreeing to cooperate with the tribunal in future prosecutions, including testifying against Milosevic at his trial. At his hearing when he pled guilty, Erdemović, dressed casually in a striped shirt, looked forlorn and summed up his situation this way:

> I have lost many very good friends of all nationalities only because of that war, and I am convinced that all of them, all of my friends, were not in favour of a war. I am convinced of that. But simply they had no other choice. This war came and there was no way out. The same happened to me.[61]

After discussing his decision to confess and approach the tribunal, he concluded: "Because of everything that happened I feel terribly sorry, but I could not do anything. When I could do something, I did it. Thank you. I have nothing else to say."[62]

Although duress provided Erdemović with an argument to support a short prison sentence, the excuse is unavailable for leadership-level defendants who—by definition—are always in control of the situation; their autonomy is never compromised by a third party.[63] However, even leadership-level defendants might sometimes be able to appeal to necessity as a defense, which only amplifies the importance of the ad hoc constraints announced by the ICTY in the *Erdemović* case. For leadership-level defendants charged with responsibility for a massacre, the fate of necessity as an available defense is of prime importance.

The legal reasons for the ICTY's adoption of the old *Dudley and Stephens* rule were that the court was tasked with determining the content of customary international law. The court concluded that the world's legal

59. *Id.*
60. *Id.*
61. Erdemović Trial Transcript, *supra* note 54.
62. *Id.*
63. We say "by definition" since international tribunals often define the leadership-level defendants as those who had control over the crime (or "hegemony over the act") as those terms are understood by Claus Roxin's Control Theory.

cultures were hopelessly conflicted on the issue because common law jurisdictions apply the rule from *Dudley and Stephens* (rejecting the necessity defense for murder) whereas civil law jurisdictions have no similar exclusion. Consequently, the three-judge majority of the Appeals Chamber concluded that the issue was one of first impression for the tribunal and ought to be decided on sui generis grounds.[64] In finding that necessity and duress should be unavailable as defenses to the killing of innocent civilians, the court found that the policy reasons behind *Dudley and Stephens* applied with even greater force in the context of armed conflict. Soldiers have higher duties to follow the dictates of international humanitarian law, which is specifically designed to protect innocent civilians and minimize their exposure to war's horrors. If that means that soldiers should be required to sacrifice themselves in order to protect those innocent civilians, then so be it. The law should demand this much and more of professional soldiers who owe a moral and professional obligation to follow the dictates of international criminal law.

The majority's conclusion stood in sharp contrast with the Rome Statute, which explicitly codifies necessity and duress defenses as long as the defendant "acts necessarily and reasonably to avoid this threat, provided that the person does not intend to cause a greater harm than the one sought to be avoided."[65] A two-judge minority in *Erdemović* issued a strongly worded dissent that argued that necessity and defense could—in theory—constitute defenses under international criminal law. The schism between the majority and minority involved not just substance but also methodology, with the dissent concluding that the absence of agreement between legal cultures suggested that there was no rule of customary international law that *prevented* the tribunal from considering the necessity and duress defenses. There being no rule of customary international law prohibiting the defense, it should at least be entertained.[66] The methodological controversy involved the appropriate background conditions: Does one need to find a rule of customary law to *allow* the defense or a rule of customary law to *prohibit* the defense?

64. *See Erdemović, supra* note 58.

65. Rome Statute, art. 31. For a discussion, see Albin Eser, *Article 31 Grounds for Excluding Criminal Responsibility, in* COMMENTARY ON THE ROME STATUTE OF THE INTERNATIONAL CRIMINAL COURT (Otto Triffterer ed., 2d ed. 2008).

66. *See* Separate and Dissenting Opinion of Judge Cassese, *Prosecutor v. Erdemović*, ICTY Case No. IT-96-22-A, Appeals Chamber (Oct. 7, 1997), para. 47 ("Law is based on what society can reasonably expect of its members. It should not set intractable standards of behaviour which require mankind to perform acts of martyrdom, and brand as criminal any behaviour falling below those standards.").

If we step back, the dispute in *Erdemović* involves a characterization of the common law and civil law divide on necessity that may no longer be accurate. Both the majority and minority apparently agreed that the common law imposes ad hoc constraints on the application of the necessity defense, whereas the civil law tradition does not. As we saw in our discussion of the *Daschner* case above, however, even some civil law jurisdictions such as Germany are moving toward a *rejection* of the necessity defense in a great number of cases. If this is correct, then at least some civil law jurisdictions have flipped from permitting the necessity defense in more cases than the United States allows, to a new situation where they permit the necessity defense in *fewer* cases than in the United States. In an American courtroom, the necessity defense would be available in all cases except murder, whereas in a German courtroom, the necessity defense would not be available in any case that involves the infringement of the victim's human dignity.

The difference between the two approaches is not just in the scope of the necessity defense, but the nature of the legal mechanism used to constrain it. The *Dudley and Stephens* rule adopted by the ICTY is an ad hoc constraint applied to a random group of cases (involving murder and killing). In contrast, the German constraint is principled and deeply Kantian, and would apply in a whole range of different cases. We now elucidate the nature and specifics of this Kantian constraint in the following section. As a case study for understanding this principled constraint based on Kantian dignity, we consider whether the necessity defense should apply to a government official who orders the downing of a hijacked airplane.

IV. PRINCIPLED CONSTRAINTS

In 2006, the German Constitutional Court was asked to consider the constitutionality of new antiterrorism legislation (provisions of the Aviation Security Act) that authorized the prime minister to order the military to shoot down a hijacked airliner that was being aimed at civilian populations on the ground.[67] The legislation was enacted specifically to respond to the threat posed by two recent incidents. The first was the 9/11 attacks when hijackers used airplanes to destroy the World Trade Center and the Pentagon. The second was a German incident involving a man threatening to crash an airplane into the commercial district of Frankfurt unless

67. *See* Aviation Security Act of 11 January 2005, § 14.3.

his demands were met.[68] Faced with the realization that such situations might be repeated, German legislators wanted to make it explicitly clear that the prime minister had the authority to order a military resolution to the threat. Presumably the impulse behind the legislation was largely utilitarian: if the military was capable of saving more lives than it condemned by shooting down the airplane, then all other things being equal the military ought to fire a missile at the airplane.

Litigants challenged the legislation on the grounds that it contravened the German constitutional protection of human dignity—a protection deeply embedded in the post–World War II legal structure of the country.[69] The Constitutional Court concluded in the affirmative that the provision was unconstitutional because it conflicted with the inherent dignity of the passengers on the plane who would be used as mere means to a particular end. In other words, they could not be condemned simply to save a greater number of civilians on the plane. This violated their Kantian dignity.[70]

The Constitutional Court considered and ultimately rejected several objections to its controversial conclusion. Perhaps the passengers had consented in some hypothetical way to being shot down by virtue of their purchasing of plane tickets and boarding the airplane. The argument here would be that the passengers were implicitly aware that their aircraft might be turned into a weapon of mass destruction, and that in such a case firing on the airplane would be the only way of preventing the disaster. This would constitute a risk—albeit an unpredictable and unlikely one—that they had tacitly consented to when they boarded the plane. The Court found this argument fanciful and referred to it as an "unrealistic fiction." The second objection is that the passengers were doomed anyway, and that shooting down their airplane only killed the hijackers without really changing the fate of the passengers. In the absence of government intervention, the plane would crash into a target on the ground and the passengers would die anyway.[71] Their fates are sealed whether the government acts or not.

68. *See* Aviation Security Case, Federal Constitutional Court (Germany), Judgment of the First Senate of 15 February 2006.

69. *Id.*

70. *See* Oliver Lepsius, *Human Dignity and the Downing of Aircraft: The German Federal Constitutional Court Strikes Down a Prominent Anti-terrorism Provision in the New Air-Transport Security Act*, 7 German L.J. 761 (2006).

71. This argument mirrors one often heard in discussions about the *Dudley & Stephens* case. If the shipwrecked passengers were all likely to die anyway, then the fate of the cabin boy (the victim) was not placed in a worse situation when he was killed in order to feed the other survivors. Under this argument, committing the crime improved the situation of some passengers while not worsening the situation of the victim. In the words of modern economics, this was a Pareto superior move. Of course, this argument was complicated by the fact that a rescue ship arrived shortly after the murder.

The Court rejected this argument and found that the government action would violate the passengers' inherent right to dignity regardless of what happens next. Just as killing an individual falling from a building would constitute a murder, so too making the passengers a mere means to an end would violate their Kantian dignity even if they would inevitably die anyway. Doomed passengers still have rights.[72]

The Constitutional Court's decision provides a roadmap for a deeply principled constraint on necessity arguments in international law. If the argument is generalized, it suggests that the power of the necessity defense should be curtailed—and indeed denied—in any situation where doing so would infringe on the human dignity of the victim.[73] Although the Constitutional Court specifically refused to consider whether its argument applied to a criminal law prosecution against a government official, its argument would seem to apply with equal force to the criminal context as well. Indeed, this was the argument in the *Daschner* case. If authorizing the destruction of the airplane violates the dignity of the passengers, then arguably excusing this conduct does as well.

If one were to apply this principled Kantian constraint against the necessity defense, it would severely curtail its application in armed conflict situations and go even further than the *Dudley and Stephens* ad hoc constraint. However, there would still be some residual application of the necessity defense in cases where human dignity is not infringed by the criminal act. Consider, for example, a domestic crime that involves destruction of property, a regulatory offense, traffic offenses, or a victimless crime such as drug possession. In all of these situations the crime does not involve an infringement of someone's human dignity, so the necessity defense could be applied even under the principled approach that we have described. In the armed conflict scenario, however, it is hard to see what is left after the principled constraint is applied against the necessity defense. Almost *all* international offenses involve an infringement against someone's human dignity, which is precisely why the offenses were criminalized in the first instance.[74]

72. It should be noted that the Constitutional Court held that shooting down a plane with *only* hijackers onboard would be permissible and would not violate the constitutional protection of human dignity. Although in some sense one would be killing the hijackers in order to save the potential victims on the ground, the hijackers would not be "mere means" but rather would be agents of the threatening action and thus morally liable to be killed.

73. For a discussion, see Luis Ernesto Chiesa, *Duress, Demanding Heroism and Proportionality: The Erdemovic Case and Beyond*, 41 VAND. J. TRANSNAT'L L. 741 (2008).

74. *See, e.g.*, Christopher Macleod, *Towards a Philosophical Account of Crimes against Humanity*, 21 EUR. J. INT'L L. 281 (2010).

V. CONCLUSION

In light of the prior considerations, we support a broadly Kantian constraint on the application of the necessity defense in international criminal law. The constraint is justified for multiple reasons.

First, as the majority recognized in *Erdemović*, there are grave policy reasons in support of it. The one mistake made by the *Erdemović* majority was instituting an ad hoc constraint rather than a principled one. Armed conflict presents near-constant situations of unimaginable pressure on the individuals involved. If international law were to view defendants with the same level of charity as domestic criminal law, many of the prohibitions codified in international law would lose their salience. Indeed, the basic assumption in domestic criminal law is that threats are *exceptional*, thus suggesting that a defendant faced with a threat should be viewed as having engaged in conduct that is truly at the outer boundary of normal experience. It is for that reason that domestic criminal law treats the defendant's decision-making and behavior with such charity. Who among us should criticize the defendant when he or she acted contrary to the demands of the law in such exceptional situations? In war, however, the presumption is reversed. Threats are everywhere in a situation of armed conflict. If a risk to life and limb should trigger the application of the necessity excuse, then much of armed conflict would be governed by a state of exception. But that seems wrong. In armed conflict, all concerned come to expect the risks that are implicit in war, which by its very definition involves a constant risk and fear of death. What seems exceptional in domestic law becomes ordinary in armed conflict. It is against this new backdrop that threatening situations should be evaluated with a more demanding standard.

Second, participants in an armed conflict have a higher duty to uphold the deep moral principles on which international criminal law is based. The basic conception of international humanitarian law is that civilians are *protected persons* under the law of war and demand moral protection even if that protection requires greater risks to soldiers involved in the fighting.[75] Although there is great uncertainty and controversy over what level of force protection a military unit may rightly prioritize over the risk to enemy civilians who might be collateral damage, no one questions that international law demands at least *some* prioritization of enemy civilians over the needs of individual soldiers, as we discuss in Chapter 11. If this

75. The same could be said of captured soldiers who are hors de combat (they too are *protected persons* under the law).

were not the case, then the rule against disproportionate collateral damage could be jettisoned entirely; it cannot, precisely because military forces are required to protect enemy civilians even if doing so imposes some burdens on their conduct of hostilities.

All of this suggests that international criminal law should place higher demands on soldiers in combat than those who are not. If that means the soldiers sacrificing themselves rather than violating the core prohibitions of international criminal law, then that seems morally correct, at least in some cases. Indeed, many domestic legal systems already recognize that some professionals bear special duties to those under their care, including sailors responsible for the lives of their passengers. In the same way, soldiers belong to a *profession* that requires an oath to protect innocent civilians during conflict. Requiring soldiers to sacrifice themselves rather than violate international criminal law is simply one manifestation of the higher duty of that profession.

Should the same considerations apply when the defendant is not a soldier? Although war crimes are usually committed by combatants, crimes against humanity and genocide are sometimes committed by civilians who do not belong to the same "profession" of soldiers with their associated ethical duties to those under their charge. However, it would be wrong to conclude that civilians have *no* higher duty to other civilians who can be victimized by crimes against humanity or genocide. Indeed, the obligation not to commit international crimes is an *ergo omnes* obligation—a duty owed to everyone in the world community. Even if not a soldier, a civilian is bound to bear some burdens and sacrifice himself or herself rather than violate international criminal law. The source of this obligation is the universal duty that all members of the human race have to other members of the world community to be free from genocide and crimes against humanity. Although the burdens are high (sometimes requiring death rather than violating the law), the potential harm created by international crimes is so high that the extra burden is justified.

Just to be clear: this Kantian proposal for a principled constraint on the necessity defense represents a normative change in international law, albeit one that we believe is morally justified. The Rome Statute is clear that necessity is a valid defense under international law as long as "the person does not intend to cause a greater harm than the one sought to be avoided."[76] In short, the Rome Statute is explicitly utilitarian in nature, and one can find no inkling of a Kantian constraint in the *travaux preparatoires*

76. Rome Statute, art. 31(d).

to the Statute.[77] The only avenue for reading a Kantian constraint into the Rome Statute is to focus on the Article 31(d) requirement that the defendant must act "necessarily and reasonably" to avoid the threat. One could, therefore, interpret "reasonably" to invoke a Kantian constraint, in line with the same argument made by the Frankfurt Court in the *Daschner* case. One should recall that in that case the court concluded that violating the human dignity of the victim was not an "appropriate means" of averting the disaster, and therefore the German criminal code provision on justified necessity did not apply. Similarly, one could argue that Article 31(d) of the Rome Statute does not confer a necessity defense in cases involving the violation of a victim's human dignity because such actions are not "reasonable" as that term is used in the Rome Statute provision. However, we see no reason to believe that "reasonable" in the Rome Statute is some special code word for Kantian impulses, though we wish that it were so. Therefore, we would support an amendment to the Rome Statute that would explicitly impose a Kantian constraint on the necessity defense and demand more of defendants who are faced with difficult choices. We also support a Kantian argument in defense of extending to soldiers the right not to be unnecessarily killed.

The one serious objection to this proposal is that it would conflict with the principle of culpability (or *Schuldprinzip*).[78] If defendants are faced with an extreme existential threat, then their autonomy is compromised and they lack the necessary prerequisites in order to be valid subjects of punishment.[79] This is where the distinction between justifications and excuses might play a part. Given the lack of culpability of the defendant, one might split the difference by saying that his actions are not justified but nonetheless his conduct ought to be excused. However, even this produces a worrisome result because that result is the same: the exculpation of the international criminal law violator. The deeper question is whether there is, in fact, a deprivation of the defendant's autonomy that is so severe that it negates the defendant's culpability. This is not clear. Certainly in necessity cases the autonomy deprivation is not a *literal* or *complete* impingement on his or her freedom, as might be the situation in an insanity case. Rather, the question is whether the demands of the law are so unreasonable that one should view the defendant as having no *reasonable* choice at all.[80] But

77. *See* Eser, *supra* note 65, at 887–88.

78. *See* Separate and Dissenting Opinion of Judge Cassese, *Erdemovic, supra* note 66, para. 46.

79. *Id.*

80. See Chiesa, supra note 73, at 741–50.

that is precisely what our analysis has questioned, that is, whether it is reasonable for international law to demand compliance even in the face of difficult choices on the part of the defendant. This is where the Kantian argument does its work: making an individual victim a mere means to an end constitutes an impermissible choice made by a defendant under an admittedly severe threat; even if the choice is a difficult one, the law can rightly stand in judgment over a defendant who violates international law under these conditions.

CHAPTER 7

Striking a Balance between Humanity and Necessity

In this chapter we pose the question of whether the principle of necessity can be reconciled with the principle of humanity without extending to soldiers greater protections than they are currently granted in international law. The principle of humane treatment is one that calls both for the minimizing of suffering and for merciful treatment, as a way of displaying honor. At its core, humane treatment is related to the principle of humanity that involves treating another person as a fellow human, as a member of the same group, the human race, rather than in any number of other ways that take account of his or her differences with others. What it means in any particular situation to treat another person as a fellow human is not always easy to see. Restraint is crucial because there are so many competing interests that people have that they will often not see themselves as primarily fellow humans instead of oppressors and victims, for instance.

When we conform to the principle of humanity, we disregard many of the particularities and differences of our lives, and give to others the benefit of the doubt, as if we were all pretty much the same. But humane treatment also calls for sensitivity to context, not so that we can disregard our common humanity, but rather so that we can identify how a fellow human should be treated in a situation of vulnerability, rather than seeing the person as stripped of any particularity, or as an enemy rather than a fellow human. Humanitarian considerations, as Grotius acknowledged over three hundred years ago, call for discounting what it is alleged that that soldier did on the battlefield, but not disregarding the fact that this person was a prisoner completely under the care of the capturing army. Humane treatment in accordance with the Geneva Conventions sees a person as a prisoner, for instance, and treats him or her as much like a fellow human as one can. In this sense, the contemporary principle of humane treatment combines consensual and universal moral considerations.

In this chapter we examine how the principle of humanity relates to the principle of necessity. Section I examines what humanity is. Section II explains the connection between dignity and humanity. Section III provides a minimalist understanding of humane treatment. Section IV connects dignity to the unique vulnerabilities of humans. Section V attempts to provide a relatively new account of humanitarian rights. And in the last section we draw some general conclusions about how humanity relates to necessity.

I. HUMANITY

Humanity is a value and an ideal. Humanity is often referred to as a kind of principle, where the principle of humanity is the principle that all humans are deserving of respect because of the dignity that is found in each member of humanity. Dignity has been variously understood to be grounded in the idea of a will or soul that is unique to humans among all other creatures and is of ultimate value. Humans were seen to be special because they could do something that no other creatures could do, and this was something that had high instrumental value, namely thinking and problem solving.

The concept of humanity has had an increasingly prominent role in the origination and justification of legal institutions. The most significant of these contemporary institutions is the United Nations. The Preamble of the Charter of the United Nations says:

> We the People of the United Nations determined
>
> - to save succeeding generations from the scourge of war, which twice in our lifetime has brought untold sorrow to mankind, and
> - to reaffirm faith in fundamental human rights, in the dignity and worth of the human person, in the equal rights of men and women and of nations large and small, and
> - to promote social progress and better standards of life in larger freedom.[1]

1. Preamble, Charter of the United Nations (1945).

This preeminent international legal institution declares as its grounding idea the faith in human rights and dignity. This founding goal has proven to be more important than the first mentioned goals, namely, to end war, or to promote social progress.

In addition to the United Nations, and quite a bit earlier, the idea of humane treatment during war was espoused at least as early as Hugo Grotius's seminal work, *De Jure Belli ac Pacis* (1625).[2] Humaneness is the idea that people should act toward one another with restraint, especially with the restraint that would come from being compassionate or having sympathy for another person's plight. This idea was especially significant in the development of the laws of war that would restrain the activities that could bring suffering to soldiers and civilians alike.

The idea of humaneness spawned another idea that is at least as significant especially today: the idea of humanitarianism. Humanitarianism is the idea that people should be ready to go to one another's aid when human need exists due to such events as famine, natural disaster, or war. Michael Walzer has recently described humanitarianism as a "two in one, a gift that we *have* to give," combining aspects of charity and duty in a single concept.[3] Humanitarianism is the key concept in the institutions that deal with relief efforts after major catastrophes such as civil wars or typhoons. And humanitarianism has been especially prominent in discussions of whether there is a duty of States to go to the aid of people in other States who are being abused by their States. The term "humanitarian intervention" has been coined to refer to especially military operations to stop a civil war or an atrocity.

The idea of humanitarianism is also the guiding idea behind such organizations as the International Committee of the Red Cross and Doctors Without Borders. These groups send their members into some of the most inhospitable situations in order to minister to fellow humans who have become incapable of providing for their own needs or fending for themselves. These organizations support human staff members who put themselves at great risk in order to help those who are especially vulnerable to dying or suffering greatly.[4] And the staff of these humanitarian organizations put themselves in such risk simply because there are other humans who are in dire need, not people they know, but total strangers often living in countries as distant from the aid workers' home countries as possible. And the connection between these people who give and those who receive

2. Hugo Grotius, De Jure Belli ac Pacis (On the Law of War and Peace) (Frances W. Kelsey trans., 1925) (1625).

3. Michael Walzer, *On Humanitarianism*, 90 Foreign Affairs 69–80 (2011).

4. *See* Michael Barnett, Empire of Humanity: A History of Humanitarianism (2011).

aid is merely that they are fellow humans, where human vulnerability is one of the key things that brings them together. The link here is provided by the concept of *solidarity* between fellow human beings as legitimate objects of moral concern.

In addition, the idea of humanity has spawned the even larger source of contemporary institutions, through the idea of human rights. Human rights are rights that individual humans have by virtue of being human. It is the proliferation of human rights institutions that has fueled some of the interest in figuring out what it means to be human such that one could have rights simply by satisfying the conditions for being human. Here there is a clear move to connect the descriptive status of being human with a normative status, being the bearer of rights.

As we will see as this chapter proceeds, humanity is also referred to as a principle: "the principle of humanity," which seems to stand in opposition to the military necessity of winning a battle or a war. The principle of humanity, although controversial, reminds us that the people whose lives are taken in battle are humans who have dignity that must be respected. Yet, the question that emerges is whether humans can intentionally kill other humans during war and still respect each other's dignity as humans.

Aquinas held the view that "if a man in self-defense uses more than necessary violence, it will be unlawful."[5] And Hugo Grotius famously regarded the principle of necessity as a strongly restrictive principle: "War in defense of life is permissible only when the danger is immediate and certain . . . The danger again must be immediate (*praesens*) and imminent (*hic*)."[6] And a bit later in the text, Grotius adds: "I maintain that he cannot lawfully be killed, either if the danger can in any other way be avoided, or if it is not altogether certain that the danger cannot be otherwise avoided."[7] Over the centuries the principle of military necessity has been considerably weakened with respect to the killing of soldiers. But humanity calls for a different understanding of the principle of necessity.

II. HUMANITARIANISM AND HUMAN DIGNITY

The rights of soldiers are often described in international law as humanitarian rights. By this is meant, in part, rights to be treated humanely—where

5. THOMAS AQUINAS, SUMMA THEOLOGICA II-II, qu. LXIV, art. 7, at 1465 (Fathers of the English Dominican Province trans., 1948).
6. GROTIUS, *supra* note 2, at 173.
7. *Id.* at 175.

a soldier is not supposed to be subjected to unnecessary or overly severe adverse treatment, even as it is generally acknowledged that in many situations soldiers can be killed without violating their rights. And in this sense, it is odd that humanitarian rights of soldiers are often defended on grounds of dignity since there are at least two major dignity considerations that would seem to apply to armed conflict. The first is how a soldier is treated in terms of his or her suffering, and the rules or laws of war have addressed this directly with proper restraints on tactics and weapons used during war. But the second aspect of the dignity of soldiers concerns how the right to life is regarded. For human beings generally, the right to life is normally thought to be the most significant of the human rights, rather than the right not to suffer, although certainly these two rights are very close to the top of any rights hierarchy. But traditionally a soldier in armed conflict is thought to have a much more heightened right not to suffer than a right to life. And the question is whether this is consistent with calling the rights of soldiers humanitarian.

The label "humanitarian" makes reference, among other things, to the idea of certain types of treatment being humane. In this sense, someone can be executed humanely even though that person is being intentionally killed. Here humaneness is seen as equivalent to "not cruel" or "not unnecessarily causing suffering among humans." And these are laudable goals. But the question is whether promoting human dignity is exhausted by this relatively narrow understanding of humanitarianism. Why does humanitarianism, and its cousin humaneness, not call for respecting the soldier's right to life? Or if soldiers should not have their rights to life protected, aren't there still related special rights that need to be recognized so that the dignity of soldiers can be protected?

It seems to us that the notion of humanitarian rights should extend beyond what is called for from a concern that people are humanely treated in the narrow sense of not suffering unnecessarily. In some respects all humans should be treated humanely, that is, they should be treated in a way that does not cause them unnecessary suffering. But there are other special rights that are important for the protection of human dignity. Dignity seems to require taking account of special roles and circumstances of humans beyond what is required for protecting the dignity of all humans.

Humans, qua humans, are vulnerable in many ways. As David Hume once pointed out, if humans had hard shells, like some other creatures, they would not be so vulnerable to so many kinds of bodily injury.[8] If

8. David Hume, Treatise on Human Understanding (1739).

humans had a stronger sense of smell, they would not be vulnerable to factors that cause impaired vision since they would be better able to compensate for loss of one sense by the use of another. Humans are also uniquely intentional creatures whose dignity, or worth, is largely associated with the higher mental faculties. The Merriam-Webster Dictionary says this about dignity: "a way of appearing or behaving that suggests seriousness and self-control."[9] It is the self-control of the will associated with humans, and paradigmatically so, that makes them uniquely vulnerable to factors that would impair the ability to exercise their intentional decision-making.

Kant famously put the dignity of humans at the center of his moral philosophy. Here is a passage from his *Metaphysics of Morals*, Part II:

> But man as a person, i.e., as the subject of a morally-practical reason, is exalted above all price. For such a one (*homo noumenon*) he is not to be valued merely as a means to the ends of other people, or even to his own ends, but is to be prized as an end in himself. This is to say, he possesses dignity (an absolute inner worth) whereby he exacts the respect of all other rational beings in the world, can measure himself against each member of his species, and can esteem himself on a footing of equality with them. The humanity in one's person is the object of the respect which he can require of every human being, but which he must not forfeit.[10]

For Kant, human dignity is the value of a human life as an end in itself. This value is premised on the idea that humans have a noumenal life, a certain kind of higher mental capacity including intentionality, which distinguishes them from all other animals.

Interestingly, Kant does recognize that a person can, to a certain extent, forfeit his or her dignity: primarily by not fulfilling his or her moral duties. And many of these duties are grounded in showing respect for other humans as themselves having dignity in their humanity. Kant says that he has in mind the person who attempts suicide. So, we should be reluctant to jump too quickly to draw conclusions about the case of a soldier who takes up arms. Indeed, there is no reason to think that Kant has in mind that a soldier forfeits his or her dignity, because it is not immediately evident

9. The Oxford English Dictionary defines dignity as "The quality of being worthy or honourable; worthiness, worth, nobleness, excellence." Although the OED definition simply explains the effect of dignity, the Merriam-Webster definition goes further and offers a potential ground for it.

10. Immanuel Kant, The Metaphysics of Morals, *in* Immanuel Kant's Ethical Philosophy 97 (James W. Ellington trans., 1983) (1797).

what duty the soldier violates. Indeed it is somewhat notorious that serving in the military is often associated with paradigmatically doing one's duty, rather than failing to do one's duty.

To treat people with dignity is to treat them as responsible agents. This means that we should not ignore the bad things that a person does, just as we should not ignore the good things that a person brings into the world. A society can punish a person and still respect that person's dignity, and a society might even be able to execute a person and still respect that person's dignity, if the means of execution minimizes suffering. It has sometimes been thought that it is sufficient in such cases that the society not make the person suffer unnecessarily for the society to show that it still respects the person's dignity. But from a Kantian perspective, and from other deontological perspectives, humanitarianism means more that not making people suffer unnecessarily—the life of the person also needs to be taken seriously.

In international law there is a movement in favor of strengthening the principle of humanity so that the domains of international humanitarian law and human rights law come closer together, as we saw in the previous chapter.[11] Yoram Dinstein has challenged the idea that there is a principle of humanity that is a principle similar to the principle of distinction or the principle of proportionality. Instead he argues that:

> There is no overarching, binding, norm of humanity, that tells us what we must do (or not do) in wartime. What we actually encounter are humanitarian considerations . . . these considerations do not by themselves amount to law: they are meta-juridical in nature . . . If benevolent humanitarianism were the only factor to be weighed in hostilities, war would have entailed no bloodshed, no human suffering, and no destruction of property; in short war would not be war. IHL [International Humanitarian Law] must be predicated on a subtle balance—and compromise—between conflicting considerations of humanity, on the one hand, and the demands of military necessity on the other.[12]

We find a major international legal theorist supporting the idea of balancing, even recognizing that combatants should be protected in such a

11. *See generally* SEARCHING FOR A "PRINCIPLE OF HUMANITY" IN INTERNATIONAL HUMANITARIAN LAW (Kjetil Mujezinovic Larsen, Camilla Guldahl Cooper & Gro Nystuen eds., 2013).

12. Yoram Dinstein, *The Principle of Proportionality*, *in* SEARCHING FOR A "PRINCIPLE OF HUMANITY" IN INTERNATIONAL HUMANITARIAN LAW 72, 73 (Kjetil Mujezinovic Larsen, Camilla Guldahl Cooper & Gro Nystuen eds., 2013).

balancing, and yet not willing to move away from the traditional idea that soldiers' rights to life count for very little.

The principle of humanity is more than "meta-juridical"; it permeates the law in ways both profound and subtle, though it is often unclear how the principle should apply in tandem with the other core principles of the laws of war. Indeed, there certainly is legal precedent for seeing a principle of humanity as a strong principle in international law. We earlier cited a decision by the High Court of Israel in 2005. Here the Israeli Court held that terrorists needed to be treated humanely. The High Court held that "a civilian taking part in direct hostilities cannot be attacked at such time as he is doing so, if a less harmful means can be employed."[13] The idea is gaining strength that not only human rights norms but a principle of humanity should be held to be applicable to soldiers and other combatants. The real dispute is not over whether the principle is juridical or not—it clearly is—but rather what doctrinal consequences might flow from our recognition of that principle.

Last, the famous Martens Clause, originally appended to the 1899 Hague Convention, and often incorporated into other international law documents, holds as follows:

> Until a more complete code of the laws of war is issued, the High Contracting Parties think it right to declare that in cases not included in the Regulations adopted by them, populations and belligerents remain under the protection and empire of the principles of international law, as they result from the usages established between civilized nations, from the laws of humanity, and the requirements of public conscience. [14]

As Dinstein and others have pointed out, the reference to the "laws of humanity" is rather vague and not defined. Yet the principle of humanity has become an entrenched part of international law.

The principle of humanity overlaps with various human rights principles, but the idea of humanitarian rights can be kept separate from human rights during armed conflict. The rights of soldiers should be seen as role-based rights, as soldiers are not humans standing alone but humans occupying a specific social role—this is also one source of a soldier's license

13. *Public Committee Against Torture in Israel and Palestinian Society for the Protection of Human Rights and the Environment v. Israel*, ILDC 597 (IL 2006), para. 40.

14. See the Preamble to the 1907 Hague Regulations, all four Geneva Conventions of 1949, the Preamble of the 1977 Additional Protocol II, art. 1, para. 2 of the 1977 Additional Protocol I, and the Preamble of the 1980 Conventional Weapons Convention.

to kill that we have discussed. The rights and dignity afforded to fellow soldiers, as soldiers, is not the same as the more general rights and dignity afforded to fellow humans. The principle of humanity in wartime carries with it the idea of humanitarian rights not yet full-scale human rights. Yet, perhaps the humanitarian rights of soldiers should be expanded from the traditional model of understanding humanitarian law. And a minimum of dignity should be afforded to those who occupy the role of soldiers.

III. HUMANE TREATMENT

In this section, we develop a minimalist conception of the principle of humane treatment. Minimalism is meant to be deflationary in two respects. Minimalism is supposed to minimize the number of assumptions that one begins with. And this is then also supposed to minimize the likely objections to the place where one starts. A minimalist principle of humane treatment provides the least controversial way to understand the norms governing the appropriate behavior during war. When we speak of humane treatment we refer to greater restraint than that which is called for due to considerations of justice and what we strictly owe to each other. While still operating within the domain of minimalist principles, a soldier's sense of honor dictates that she do more than provide what is due. In following the principle of charity, she is quick to forgive or pardon rather than to punish.

The difficulty is that in war, it seems especially dangerous to give to the enemy the benefit of the doubt. If there are to be restraints in war, it seems less controversial to restrict ourselves by the principle of justice only rather than the principle of humaneness. And since we owe very little if anything to people who are attacking us, or who have tried to attack us, justice-based laws of war will provide very minimal restraints indeed. But there are good reasons to think that most enemy soldiers have not done anything wrong in attacking, since most soldiers act merely because they have been ordered to act, and hence even enemy soldiers are not owed a lethal response on our part. Indeed, for many centuries philosophers have accepted the moral equality of soldiers, that whether they serve on the aggressing or defending side, the soldiers themselves are no more or less guilty. Even in war, justice does call for restraints, and we would argue that more than justice is required: soldiers also seek honor during killing.

Humaneness morally *requires* compassion and mercy, but only in certain circumstances. The most obvious case concerns confinement. The less obvious cases concern other statuses that a person has been thrust into, such as the vulnerable status of not having a weapon at all when others do, or of not having a certain type of weapon when others do. Even confinement is best seen as a special vulnerable status that changes what is morally required. On the other hand, soldiers who have no special vulnerabilities are not owed compassion or mercy as a matter of humaneness, although it is still often a very good thing for compassion and mercy to be displayed toward them. Humaneness becomes a duty, the violation of which counts as a war crime, only in special circumstances of vulnerability.

The general idea here is that justice does not exhaust all of our duties. For justice typically concerns what is owed as a matter of what we have done, that is, our conduct. Justice often dictates what is owed as a matter of our equality, and thus justice can concern status, although normally only universal status, such as what is owed as a matter of our human rights. But there is no human right to be treated with compassion or mercy. Such considerations have to do with special status, not universal status. Thus, we will talk of humaneness rather than humanity to make sure that we do not think of the duties of humaneness as extending to all human beings in all circumstances. Compassion and mercy are duties only in special circumstances, primarily when one person is vulnerable to another. It would indeed be good to display compassion and mercy to all humans, but this becomes a duty only when special circumstances of vulnerability obtain.

To say that the principle of humane treatment is the cornerstone of humanitarian law is to place it over the more traditionally recognized principles of discrimination, necessity, and proportionality.[15] These principles are often understood as forming the entire basis for the laws of war. But unless we stretch these principles, it will be hard to make sense of the kind of prohibitions that are involved in many of the provisions in Common Article III of the Geneva Convention, what is sometimes called the "Convention in Miniature."[16] Necessity clearly calls for balancing or weighing restraining considerations against lethal conduct. And the principle of proportionality also involves a weighing or utilitarian calculation that seems very different from the prohibitions of the "Convention in Miniature." The principle of discrimination or distinction, which is clearly not about balancing, does call for completely different treatment of civilians and combatants. So, if we are right to think that the principle of humane treatment cuts across

15. For a good preliminary philosophical discussion of these three principles, see Douglas P. Lackey, The Ethics of War and Peace 58–68 (1989).

16. Kenneth Watkins, *Controlling the Use of Force: A Role for Human Rights Norms in Contemporary Armed Conflict*, 98 Am. J. Int'l L. 25 (2004) (quoting the International Committee of the Red Cross's Commentary on the Geneva Convention).

this divide between civilians and combatants, then the principle of humane treatment is not merely derived from, or a combination of, these other three principles.

If humanitarian law, or the law of war, is to have a grounding or cornerstone at all, the three traditional principles will not do the job. It is possible that the rules or laws of war have no underlying principle of justification. Indeed, it sometimes seems as if what we have is merely a list of rules from different eras, cobbled together into increasingly lengthy instruments, where there is so little agreement about their basis that the lists merely repeat previous lists verbatim, lest the original consensus about them be jeopardized by minor changes in wording.[17] Perhaps, there is no cornerstone to humanitarian law. But then that branch of international law will be significantly more infirm than people generally think. The Geneva Conventions, for instance, at least until quite recently, have been considered the least controversial of all aspects of international law.[18] It would be odd if there were to be no underlying normative rationale for the various provisions of such a well-accepted document.

IV. DIGNITY AND VULNERABILITY

At this stage, we have two important concepts on the table, vulnerability and dignity. In this brief section we wish to explore the relationship between these two concepts that are so important in understanding the rules and laws of war. One way, explored in this section, is that humans are especially vulnerable because they have the ability to choose how to live their lives and are not constantly driven by instinct and other forces of natural necessity. The ability to choose how to lead a person's life is at the center of both a person's dignity understood as one's ultimate worth ("beyond price," as Kant put it) but also one's uniquely human vulnerability.

The ability to make choices, concerning how one wants to live one's life, has both positive and negative aspects. The positive aspect is obvious—humans are the only creatures that have this capacity, and it allows them to form intentions and act on those intentions to create short-term and

17. This seems especially apparent when examining the Rome Statute that lifts verbatim from previous documents such as the Geneva Conventions' Common Article III.

18. Members of George W. Bush's administration have cast doubt on whether it is still true that the Geneva Conventions are uncontroversial. One member of this administration said that the Geneva Conventions were antiquated due to the rise of terrorism.

long-term, individual and coordinated, enterprises. The negative side of making choices is that the human person is accountable for what he or she does in ways that are not true of the creatures that lack this ability. And so if humans make bad choices they are vulnerable in that they are responsible for the consequences of those choices, such as the death of other humans. In the context of war, this vulnerability is often described in terms of being liable to punishment, or even liability to be harmed or killed, because of what they have chosen to do on the battlefield.

Vulnerability for bad, or good, choices is especially important in the context of war and armed conflict. Even in cases of conscription, a person makes a choice of whether to resist or not. In cases of volunteering for military service, the person is responsible for what results from such a choice. The human person cannot claim to be relieved of liability or even from responsibility due to natural necessity, the forces of natural instinct etc., which would be the motivator for nonhuman animals.

And even in cases of volunteering for military service, we must investigate what considerations moved the person to volunteer. In some cases, the "volunteer" may have felt compelled by economic or family circumstances to join, seeing no other reasonable options at that point in his or her life. And similar things can be said about those who are conscripted. It will matter how severe the consequences were of resisting the conscription. In some cases, the penalty for resisting conscription may be so low that acquiescing in the conscription is closer to being a volunteer than in some cases of "volunteering" where there was intense pressure to enlist but no conscription.

In addition, part of a human's vulnerable nature is that he or she can lose the capacity for choice in a myriad of injuries that would not have been anything so nearly catastrophic if experienced by nonhuman animals. Head injuries are especially likely to affect capacity for choice, and yet humans are not well protected by nature in their heads. And once one realizes that the center of dignity for humans is connected to choice over how to live one's life, there is a sense that humans are vulnerable to certain kinds of injury because those injuries affect choice and hence also the dignity of these humans.

The dignity of humans is not exhausted by considerations of their choices—the sheer capacity for choice, rather than the actualization of choice, may be sufficient for establishing the minimal dignity of a human life. But as one loses one's ability to choose, there is a diminishment in the kind of dignity that Kant spoke of, and that has animated most discussions of this topic, including those at the time of the drafting of the United Nations Charter.

Dignity is also affected by a loss or diminishment of one's ability to make choices for the better in one's life. Soldiers who return from battle and who are "shell shocked" or suffering from a "post traumatic stress disorder" often feel incapable of making decisions about how to make their lives better.[19] In addition, returning soldiers often have trouble adjusting to the mundane decisions of ordinary life after having spent a long time in a realm where all choices seemed extraordinary and consumed with basic survival. Here again dignity, as understood in first personal terms, is affected by vulnerabilities that are exacerbated by wartime situations.

Not all people who experience combat are adversely affected in the ways we have been indicating. What is important, though, is that anyone in combat is much more at risk, than they normally would be, of being so harmed due to the vulnerabilities that all humans have by virtue of being human. So, although soldiers qua soldiers should not be said to have general human rights, the special rights they have by virtue of their roles will warrant strong protections, even if those protections are not as sweeping as such things as the absolute human right to life.

It is in these ways that we can begin to see how vulnerability and dignity are linked, especially in the context of war and armed conflict. The dignity and vulnerabilities of humans affects how they are treated in terms of their human and humanitarian rights. These rights are supposed to protect people in the most vulnerable of circumstances. Yet, humanitarian rights in particular have not lived up to the promise of protecting some of the most vulnerable during war, namely soldiers and other combatants.

Humanitarian rights protect the dignity of certain people, especially those who are in precarious situations in terms of vulnerability. This is because sentience is not the key consideration for human dignity. Humans are not unique in being able to suffer—for many nonhuman animals can also suffer. Rather, humans are unique in terms of the capacity for intentional acts of willing, and it is the denial or abrogating of that feature that would be a paradigmatic assault on a person's dignity. It is true that a human can experience suffering more deeply in some cases than is true for a nonhuman animal, because of the human's capacity for self-reflection. But even this characteristic is not unique to humans, and in any event is not at the core of a human's dignity, the person's ultimate worth.

For dignity to be respected for those who assume certain highly vulnerable roles, there must in most cases be some specific right that is recognized and granted special protection in a given society. The reason for

19. *See generally* NANCY SHERMAN, STOIC WARRIORS (2007).

this is that there must be something dignity-enhancing that offsets the dignity-diminishing situation. The prisoner, who has had his or her liberty restricted, has had a dignity-diminishing experience. And although punishment may be justified in a host of ways including retribution, deterrence, expressivism, etc., in addition there must be something dignity-affirming that would not normally be extended to persons who are not imprisoned. Instead, what often happens is that the prisoner is treated in multiple ways that are dignity-diminishing, or there is no special consideration given so that the dignity of the prisoner is affirmed even as he or she has liberty restricted.

V. HUMANITARIAN RIGHTS

The idea behind humanitarianism is that people who are in special situations or roles, where they have a heightened vulnerability to risk, should be seen as having rights that protect them in their dignity. But these humanitarian rights are not the same as human rights, which apply to every human in every situation, which attach to humans qua humans, and which do not take account of special circumstances or roles. Indeed, for human rights, the only role that matters is being human. Yet, protecting the dignity of humans may need different or additional protection when these humans are in situations of increased vulnerability, where their vulnerability is not merely due to the fact that they are human.

Humanitarian rights should not be seen as a competing domain of rights to the domain of human rights. In our view a properly humanitarian view of war puts soldiers at the center of concern since soldiers and combatants are those most directly affected by war and armed conflict. The U.N. document that is most directly relevant to these issues sees civilians and noncombatants as those most directly affected by armed conflict. In the 1970 Report of the Secretary-General on Respect for Human Rights in Armed Conflict there was a very strong statement about the intended effect of having the General Assembly examine armed conflicts in human rights terms:

> It is an endeavor to provide a greater degree of protection for the integrity, welfare, and dignity of those who are directly affected by military operations pending the earliest possible resolution of such conflicts.[20]

20. Respect for Human Rights in Armed Conflict, Report of the Secretary-General, A/8052, para. 13 (1970).

Yet the United Nations' examination of the effects of human rights in battlefield situations was mainly restricted to the protection of civilian lives, even though the lives of soldiers are certainly those that are most directly affected by military operations. Although civilians are increasingly attacked, even targeted, in wars, the direct targeting of people is most often directed at soldiers rather than at civilians even in today's asymmetric wars.[21]

Even if it were true that soldiers forfeited some of their most basic rights by becoming soldiers, it may still be true that soldiers need extra protection due to assuming this role. (Many soldiers are forced into their role via conscription.) On the assumption that soldiers can be killed, or are liable to be killed, because they have assumed a different, more dangerous status from other humans, what this also means is that soldiers are more vulnerable than all other humans who retain the right not to be killed. Because soldiers are at increased vulnerability to be killed, it would make sense also to say that soldiers should have special rights that minimize the harm that is likely to occur to them because of their loss, even if only temporarily, of basic rights. In some respects, this is what humanitarian law has traditionally sought to do: to provide a set of special rights not to suffer unnecessarily, that are especially apt for soldiers who are more vulnerable to such suffering because they lack the protections of basic human rights such as the right to life and the right not to be attacked.

There is a kind of special vulnerability that occurs for soldiers in wartime circumstances even if it is true that soldiers have forfeited basic general rights. But specifically how vulnerable soldiers are varies, as does the specific ways soldiers are vulnerable. This variability is due to the changing character of war and armed conflict over the ages. In traditional ways of thinking of humanitarian law, the key right is that soldiers not suffer unnecessarily. What counts as necessary, as we argued above, is and has been contentious. But what the specific vulnerabilities are is not so contentious.

Consider that now concern for the rights of civilians during war has meant that they can be directly attacked only if it is clear that these civilians pose a threat to other civilians or soldiers. It is our view that when directly attacked, the special rights of soldiers must be expanded to protect the soldiers in their special vulnerabilities. This protection is needed due to the increased vulnerability that these soldiers face, which is itself due to the restrictions on the rules of engagement aimed at protecting civilians. Or consider a situation where the soldiers must first announce themselves

21. *See generally* MICHAEL GROSS, MORAL DILEMMAS OF MODERN WAR (2010).

before entering a building believed to be occupied by enemy warriors.[22] This restriction on the rules of engagement again would warrant an expanded set of role-based rights for soldiers aimed at protecting the soldiers in their now more vulnerable states.

We here raise the question of why the rules of war should not change in a limited way to protect the vulnerabilities of soldiers. In cases where soldiers face increased vulnerability, it would make sense to say that soldiers should only take on this increased risk if it were clear that taking on a risk of death was strictly necessary for achieving a legitimate military objective. And in this way we could see the moral argument for a strengthened principle of necessity, perhaps of the sort contemplated by the ICRC in its 2009 Interpretive Guidance. Indeed, the fact that soldiers are supposed to risk their lives while in combat does not make them have less special rights. Rather, their increased vulnerabilities should be seen as supporting increased special rights. The special rights are extended at least in part to compensate for the decrease in general rights that they face because of their supposed forfeiture of basic general rights when they assume the role of soldier.

This is an appropriate place to say that the forfeiture idea is weakened in many cases where the soldier is coerced into taking on the dangerousness of fulfilling the soldier's role. The idea of forced forfeiture is itself peculiar. The idea of forfeiture makes the most sense in terms of the choices a person makes that are not coerced—where one is held responsible for one's choices, and if those are especially bad choices then one loses some of one's previous rights or status in the society. But since many soldiers are conscripted, the idea that they could forfeit their rights, or their dignity, by these acts is to say the least hard to justify. Of course it will matter what the options were to acquiescing in one's conscription, but in general something seems suspicious about the idea that all soldiers, even those who have been conscripted, have by their own coerced acts forfeited their rights.

VI. CONCLUDING THOUGHTS ON THE PRINCIPLES OF HUMANITY AND NECESSITY

At the beginning of this chapter, we discussed various meanings of the term "humanity," one of which was that humanity is a source of norms

22. *See* Michael Walzer's fascinating discussion of this case in JUST AND UNJUST WARS (1977).

and values.[23] In this final section we will now discuss one of the most significant norms associated with humanity, a principle that calls for people, especially during war or armed conflict, to exercise special vigilance in how fellow humans are treated. As we have been arguing in this chapter, the special humanitarian protections of humans during times of war should extend to soldiers and other combatants.

Kant characterized one of the versions of the categorical imperative as the "formula of the end in itself" or "the principle of humanity." In Kant's view, there is a practical imperative for all people, namely: "Act in such a way that you treat humanity, whether in your own person or in the person of another, always at the same time as an end and never simply as a means."[24] This principle is deeply connected to Kant's notion of the dignity of a human person. To respect the dignity in each person, we must treat each person as an end in itself, not simply as a means to our own ends.

In situations of war or armed conflict, it is hard to understand how the various participants, especially the soldiers shooting at enemy soldiers, could still treat the enemy soldiers as ends in themselves. Indeed, the idea of military necessity, in its traditional formulation, saw the soldier's role to be one of killing as many enemy soldiers as possible. It is also true that this military goal was related to the further goal of bringing the war to an end as soon as is possible so as to have the least number of casualties in the long run. But there is no denying that the traditional principle of military necessity was aimed at using enemy soldiers as a means to ending the war as quickly as possible, and did not see enemy soldiers as ends in themselves.

Yet, it is also part of the more modern understandings of military necessity that this principle is to be balanced against the principle of humanity. Indeed, this is why Michael Schmitt gives his essay "Military Necessity and Humanity" the subtitle "Preserving the Delicate Balance."[25] Schmitt characterizes the principle of humanity in international humanitarian law as an imperative "which operates to protect the population (whether combatants or noncombatants) and its property."[26] Yet, the question to consider is

23. Dinstein has argued that humanity is not a principle of law, but only a "meta-juridical" principle. *See* Yoram Dinstein, *The Principle of Proportionality*, *in* SEARCHING FOR A "PRINCIPLE OF HUMANITY" IN INTERNATIONAL HUMANITARIAN LAW 72, 72–74 (Kjetil Mujezinovic Larsen, Camilla Guldahl Cooper & Gro Nystuen eds., 2013). Either way, it carries some normative force, either as a moral requirement or as a background legal principle that informs our understanding of more specific legal requirements.

24. IMMANUEL KANT, GROUNDING FOR THE METAPHYSICS OF MORALS 36 (James W. Ellington trans., 1981) (1785).

25. Michael N. Schmitt, *Military Necessity and Humanity in International Humanitarian Law: Preserving the Delicate Balance*, 50 VA. J. INT'L L. 795 (2010).

26. *Id.* at 799.

whether these principles can indeed be balanced if the principle of military necessity contains such a strong presumption in favor of the right of soldiers to kill as many enemy soldiers as possible. How though can soldiers be treated humanely if they can be killed at will? Indeed, notice that the formulation that Schmitt gives for the principle of humanity calls for the protection of combatants—not only noncombatants.

At this point, we propose that soldiers be not only afforded the right not to suffer unnecessarily but also the right not to be killed unnecessarily.[27] We should note at this stage that we regard our proposal about extending to soldiers the right not to be killed unnecessarily as a moderate proposal. Some authors have recently argued for a more expansive principle, namely, the least harmful means principle. This principle would sweep across all decisions by commanders during war, and would require that commanders only order that use of force that is the least harmful. Our proposal only calls for less than lethal force when it is not necessary to use lethal force, that is when the goals of the war can be accomplished without recourse to lethal force. In future chapters we will explore when this proposed principle might require minimal revision of current practices in warfare, and what strategic military action might look like if conducted in accordance with this new proposal. Indeed, it is possible that the trend in modern asymmetrical conflicts is moving in this direction anyway, as the United States engages in lethal targeting against the most important targets and foregoes lethal force against minor participants who pose little to no strategic threat to the United States.

As we will see, our minimalist proposal would only require modest alterations to existing practices and would not undo the entire structure of modern warfare, nor would it collapse *jus in bello* with peacetime law enforcement. Such a proposal would be unrealistic and normatively implausible. Indeed, in many combat situations, lethal force is the only reasonable means of accomplishing the legitimate objectives of the attacking force. However, in those, perhaps rare, circumstances where military objectives can be reasonably accomplished without lethal force, our principle suggests

27. Yishai Beer proposes a similar requirement to not kill enemy combatants unnecessarily, although he purports to find this obligation in the extension of military norms of professionalism into the concept of necessity. *See* Yishai Beer, *Humanity Considerations Cannot Reduce War's Hazards Alone: Revitalizing the Concept of Military Necessity*, 26 EUR. J. INT'L L. 801, 804 (2016) ("exercise of brute force by militaries, though common, derives from professional incompetency and external forces (for example, political, psychological and cultural or a combination thereof) . . . the interest of a trained military is to constrain and contain these unnecessary—indeed, unprofessional—forces").

a moral duty to deploy them. Our proposal will not affect non-lethal use of force and is hence not nearly as restrictive as the least harmful means principle. Throughout this chapter, we have attempted to defend a commonsensical way to think of humanitarian rights, namely as applying a strict necessity constraint on military actions that risk the killing of soldiers, our own or enemy. In the next chapter we consider in some detail an example from the use of force where there is a clear difference between the least-harmful-means standard and the right not to be unnecessarily killed standard.

PART C

Applying Necessity to Contemporary Conflicts

CHAPTER 8

Combatants and Civilians in Asymmetric Wars

In this third part of the book, we now apply our account of necessity to the changing nature of warfare in contemporary conflicts, many of which are asymmetric conflicts against nonstate actors and terrorist organizations. We address four interrelated controversies: disabling versus killing in war, the duty to capture prior to using lethal force, the legitimacy of prioritizing force protection over enemy civilians, and the dividing line between combatants and civilians in asymmetric wars where one side deploys force without using a traditional army with uniformed soldiers. Each of these controversies implicates the concept of necessity in diverse ways. Until this point, we have not drawn firm conclusions regarding their resolution until we first clarified, at a conceptual level, the relationship between necessity and other principles in *jus ad bellum* and *jus in bello*, both in legal and philosophical discourse. What emerged from that analysis was a portrait of necessity as a Janus-faced concept, one performing multiple roles depending on the context.

In the prior chapters we stripped away the multiple meanings, leaving us with different versions of the concept of necessity that varied as to their power to legitimate the deployment of force. In those situations where necessity is at its most constraining (human rights principles), we asked skeptical questions about whether the law had taken the constraining power of necessity too far when it was applied to armed conflict. In those situations where necessity is at its most expansive (criminal law and military necessity as an exception to legitimate rules of warfare), we supported proposals to reign in and substantially curtail (and in some cases eliminate) necessity's power to craft a state of exception to legitimate rules. Now we apply these very general considerations to concrete cases.

Most wars today are fought between a State and some kind of nonstate actor, such as an insurgent group. The insurgent groups, often called terrorist groups, do not always conform to the laws of war. How should such considerations affect the application of the *ad bellum* and *in bello* principles of necessity? Concerning *ad bellum* issues, what would count as an emergency situation requiring recourse to war by an insurgent group? Concerning *in bello* issues, should combatants on the side of the State conform to the principle of necessity when there is good reason to believe that the combatants on the insurgent side will not? Things get somewhat clearer when the insurgent forces are representing a people that is being oppressed rather than a group of insurgents that are simply engaging in terrorist tactics to jockey for a position of leadership among other terrorist groups in a region.

In this chapter we will begin by looking at some of the historical accounts of how pirates were treated during war. In the second section, we turn to Grotius, who has a lengthy discussion of how nonstate actors are obligated by the laws of war. In the third section we will consider *ad bellum* issues. And in the fourth we will consider *in bello* issues. We will end with a discussion of how civilian immunity is best understood in asymmetrical wars. Throughout we will be concerned to argue that the rules of war should not be much adjusted, especially the principle of necessity, merely because the war in question is an asymmetric one.

I. PIRATES AND INSURGENTS AT WAR

Alberico Gentili, writing at the end of the sixteenth century, provides us with a good place to begin. He argues that the laws of war do not apply to pirates since they stand outside the system of rules that governs States during times of war.

> There is another reason why such men do not come under the law of war, namely, because that law is derived from the law of nations, and malefactors do not enjoy the privileges of a law to which they are foes. How can the law, which is nothing but an agreement and a compact, extend to those who have withdrawn from the agreement and broken the treaty of the human race as Florus puts it?
>
> Pirates are the common enemies of all mankind [*hostes humani generis*].[1]

1. Alberico Gentili, De Jure Belli, (The Law of War) Bk. I, ch. 4, at 22 (John Rolfe trans., 1933) (1598).

This is representative of sixteenth and seventeenth century thinkers on the topic, but not of thinkers who wrote in earlier centuries of the Just War tradition.

The early Just War theorists were not as committed to the idea that only States can justly wage war. At least part of the explanation is that until the sixteenth century there was not such a clear divide between States and other political entities, and similarly it was not clear that nonstate actors were always illegitimate actors during war. Unincorporated nonstate actors were much more plentiful in these early eras, and it was not out of the question that they could wage just wars in self-defense. There is also an old tradition of thinking that everyone is entitled to humane treatment, even those who are our worst enemies. Indeed, as we will see there was a debate in the early modern period about whether even pirates should be treated humanely, although it should be clear that thinkers such as Gentili were on the side of the majority of theorists that denied this thesis.

Before leaving Gentili, we wish to comment a bit more on the idea of *hostes humani generis*, common enemies of humanity, a term that today is sometimes also applied to terrorists. This term, or an equivalent, was probably first used by Cicero in his *De Officiis*.[2] But although the term appears to be used in both more ancient sources as well as in seventeenth century debates, it is not at all clear that the term has always had the same meaning.[3] Indeed, it seems to us that there are several distinct meanings of *hostes humani generis* that are not necessarily related to each other.

1) One of the earliest examples of the idea behind this term relates simply to people who had rejected the rules of how States are to be formed, and lived without a centralized authority.
2) The term also seems sometimes to have been applied to those political associations, even States, which failed to follow the rules that other States had established concerning property or preservation of life.
3) The term seems to have been most often used for those bands of robbers who operated on the high seas and recognized no rules of property or preservation of life.

It is interesting to speculate why these very different examples came to be captured with the same term and what it was that made people think that each case is truly a threat to humanity, not merely to those States in the region where they operated.

2. *See* Alfred P. Rubin, The Law of Piracy 15–17 (2d ed. 1995).
3. *Id.* at 90–95.

The rationale for seeing the groups in the first category as enemies of humanity is merely that they reject the model of State formation as the way to organize political society. One can think of examples today of unincorporated groups that manage to function well and not to threaten their neighbors unduly. Not organizing as States is only the loosest of threats to humanity, and is really only a threat if one thinks that States are the best form of political organization. Indeed, one could see the proliferation of other forms of political organization as a healthy, indeed perhaps necessary, means to promote the development of humanity.

The second category is also not obviously a group that poses a threat to, and should be labeled as an enemy of, humanity. At least in part it depends on whether the rules that most States live by are better than the rules that the nonstate actors, or "rogue" groups, subscribe to. Here there are three distinct possibilities: the rules of the rogue group are worse than, better than, or no worse than those of the other States. Only in the first case is there cause for alarm, as is true today when some terrorist groups seem to have completely different rules of engagement that put civilians at much greater risk than would be true if they followed the traditional rules of engagement of States and their armies. Humanity would not be harmed if there were merely different rules that one State, or nonstate actor, followed than were followed by other States. There is often some loss in predictability or efficiency when there is no conformity of rule following, but such a situation hardly places humanity in jeopardy.

The third category is the worrisome one, since here the nonstate actor simply does not play by the rules at all, and is seemingly unrestrained in its behavior toward all with whom it comes into contact. The pirates who flew the skull and crossbones might have been signaling that anyone was at risk of death who happened to come into contact with these pirates. This category seems most clearly to be an enemy of humanity. But even here, it depends on whether the nonstate actor does in fact have much interaction with the rest of the world. If this lawless group kept to itself, such as a White supremacist group in Montana, it is not at all clear that it poses a threat to humanity merely by its existence. How these groups conduct their societies may be reprehensible, but if the members are there uncoerced, it may be that interference is unjustified nonetheless.

This third category may also include some contemporary insurgent or terrorist groups. Indeed, what makes some terrorist groups morally and legally problematic is that they do not recognize the legitimacy of the rules of war, especially the rule against targeting civilians. In this sense many insurgent or terrorist groups do not play by the rules. But unlike some pirates of old, insurgents or terrorists normally play by other rules than those rules that would be recognized by States around the world. Indeed, many insurgent or terrorist groups see themselves not as enemies of humanity but as forces fighting repressive regimes. There is a sense in which some insurgent or terrorist groups see themselves as acting much as some States see themselves acting in situations of humanitarian intervention. In this sense, some terrorist groups not only mainly play by the rules but also see themselves as the ultimate protector of those for whom the rules are not providing protection.

One could argue that the mere fact that insurgent or terrorist groups do not play by the same rules, as most States do, makes them a threat to the international rules. If there are two alternative sets of rules that one can adhere to, it may seem that no one is held to any particular rules at all, thereby undermining the continued existence of any rules at all. We are not convinced that having alternative rules weakens or jeopardizes all rules. Think of the alternative ways of computing U.S. taxes, or of doing double entry accounting. Although cumbersome, and ripe for unfairness, having alternative sets of rules between which one can choose does not necessarily undermine the rules.

The situation of pirates and their treatment in earlier times may still provide valuable lessons for how to regard some terrorists. As Alfred Rubin points out, in Roman times some pirate groups were treated as no different from small States, where some of these nonstate groups were the proper subject of war on the part of Rome, and where others were simply given no moral or legal status since they were enemies of humanity.[4] Today, one could similarly divide "terrorist" groups into those that behaved more in State-like ways than others. Some pirates were treated like brigands, and others were given quasi-State status. Today, similarly, we could think of terrorist groups such as the Bader Meinhoff group as more like criminal gangs and brigands, and groups such as Hamas, which in fact won a significant election in Palestine in 2006, as sufficiently State-like to be given a different status.

II. GROTIUS ON NONSTATE ACTORS IN WAR

Grotius generally opposed Gentili's views in early modern international legal thought. Grotius claims that pirates are beyond the moral pale in the sense that they are "banded together for wrongdoing."[5] Yet he thinks that

4. *Id.* at 13–17.
5. Hugo Grotius, De Jure Belli ac Pacis (On the Law of War and Peace) 631 (Francis W. Kelsey trans., 1925) (1625).

pirates should be treated in a humane way. According to Grotius, pirates must have their rights protected, not for their own sake, but for the sake of God or other parties. If we fail to take the rights of pirates seriously, there is a sense in which rights themselves are jeopardized since we share in common with all other humans this protection of rights.[6] There is a difference between asking whether the life of a pirate is to be condemned and asking how the rights of pirates should be treated, especially in war. We will somewhat follow Grotius here in thinking that we can see insurgents or terrorists to be like pirates, as *hostes humani generis* and yet still as having rights that need to be protected. Even as they are common enemies of humanity they are also members of humanity.

In Book III Chapter 3 of *De Jure Belli ac Pacis*, Grotius distinguishes between those persons who have sovereign power and those who "possess the sovereign power in part."[7] Those who only hold sovereign power in part "may to that extent wage a lawful war." [8] In Grotius' view, a sick State is still a State, and a "marauding nation" is "still a nation."[9] Sick States or "marauding" nations can be said to have partial sovereignty and hence can be seen as legitimate enough to have rights of self-defense. Grotius cites Augustine who says "If by accessions of desperate men this evil grows to such proportions that it holds lands, establishes fixed settlements, seizes upon states and subjugates peoples, it assumes the name of a kingdom."[10] Here we see that it is not even necessary that the acts of a people be good acts; as long as they are sufficiently coordinated the people can come to have state-like status, and may wage war as well as have some of the rights of war.

It is of course curious that Grotius would follow Augustine in thinking that a nonstate actor should be afforded rights when its bad acts accumulate sufficiently. But it is not the badness of the acts that matter the most but the fact that the nonstate actor has accumulated territory and has control of a settled population. Here Grotius and Augustine point to the fact that there can be bad as well as good States, and some nonstate actors can become States even though the States in question are bad ones. Groups of people can attain rights even as there are other reasons to think that the people should be morally criticized, even strongly so.

There are historical examples of groups of pirates that attain something like the status of States. The most obvious case is the Barbary Pirates who

6. *Id.* at 373–74.
7. *Id.* at 633.
8. *Id.*
9. *Id.* at 632.
10. *Id.* at 633, *citing* AUGUSTINE, CITY OF GOD, Bk. IV, ch. IV.

were operating from the fourteenth century, but were most powerful in the sixteenth and seventeenth centuries. The Barbary Pirates held considerable land along the North African coast, and waged wars against cities and were the object of wars waged by European States. This is no doubt one of the examples that Grotius has in mind when he discusses pirate groups that act like at least partial States.

In terms of necessity and immunity, how are we to assess pirate groups and other insurgent groups that have taken on the status of States? Our view of insurgents and terrorists is similar to Grotius's view of pirates. As we said above, it does make a difference what kind of insurgents or terrorist we are talking about for some considerations. But in general, we will maintain that we can see even those terrorists who are common enemies of humanity as nonetheless also members of humanity. As members of humanity, terrorists are owed the same human rights considerations as any other member of humanity, since human rights attach merely to membership, not to what the person otherwise deserves. And when insurgent groups become State-like in how they act, the principles of necessity and immunity will also apply. It will remain problematic though if these groups do not themselves follow the rules of war, as we will see in subsequent sections of this chapter.

III. *JUS AD BELLUM* ISSUES

The central insight, elementary though it may be, that we wish to bring to this issue is merely that some insurgent and terrorist groups are able to act in such similar ways to the way that some States do, that there is little practical reason to distinguish between such insurgent groups and States. In fact, some States are not able to act on the world stage with nearly the efficacy that some terrorist groups are able to act. The events of September 11, 2001, cited so many times recently for the wrong reasons, can here be cited just to affirm the fact of the efficacious power of some terrorist groups—no State had previously managed a successful attack on the American mainland prior to the September 11th attacks. That these attacks were not carried out by another State but by a terrorist group is truly significant. Also consider Hamas, a powerful insurgent group that managed to capture the government in certain parts of Palestine.

In our view, the most important question is whether an insurgent or terrorist group acts as an effective State-like agent—if it does so, then it can be held responsible as if it were a State. Indeed, if the insurgent or terrorist group acts, or fails to act in a way that constitutes an omission, this may trigger its responsibility, both moral and legal. Today, few people would argue that some insurgent or terrorist groups are not effective actors on the world stage. But the question will nonetheless arise about whether we should count what insurgent or terrorist groups do as "war." The U.S. administration has said that it is engaged in an ongoing armed conflict with al-Qaeda, and talks as if this is a real war, not merely a metaphor for real war such as the "war on drugs." Most recently, the United States has effectively declared war on the Islamic State operating in Syria and Iraq (not by declaring war in the constitutional sense but rather by launching a military campaign against the group). Once again, this group holds territory and controls oil production and the maintenance of certain social services in the territories it holds.

One of the questions about whether a terrorist group such as the Islamic State or al-Qaeda could wage a war at all concerns whether it sees itself as playing by the normal rules of war. If not, then it is an "outlaw" group, and as such it may be that its members also fall outside the realm of law, including international criminal law, as some pirates were once regarded. The only solution to piracy was to kill them all, or so it seemed to many sixteenth and seventeenth century thinkers. Similarly, today it seems that we non-terrorists could kill all terrorists with impunity since we need not worry about the rules of war since neither did they. If terrorist groups are not seen as even being able to wage war, whether defensively or aggressively, then there are certain things that follow from this, one of them being that insurgents or terrorists do not need to be treated according to the normal restraints we recognize even when we are dealing with people who are waging aggressive, that is unjustified war. There are worse things than waging aggressive war, and one of those things is the choice to be outside all law and rules, regardless of how efficacious and State-like a terrorist group might otherwise appear.

But we wish to suggest that one of the tests for whether to think that a group can wage war and be subject to, and demand others to restrain themselves by, the rules of war, is whether the group in question is able to act like a State or a quasi-State. Such a claim needs defense, and we will try to provide it in the remainder of this section. The first thing to note is that being able to act like a State is already a pretty high bar that must be crossed. Individuals, and even many groups of individuals, lack the coordination to be able to do anything even vaguely State-like. The idea is that States are the paradigm case of entities that can wage war, but that if there are other entities that can act like States, then it may be that they too can wage war. Waging war actually provides one with a kind of legal framework within which one operates. If one cannot be said to wage war, then one is outside this set of laws and rules.

Yet, it turns out that some insurgent or terrorist groups, and other nonstate actors, can indeed do all of the things that normally are thought to constitute waging war. A good contemporary example is al-Qaeda. Al-Qaeda sees itself as being at war with the United States and its Western allies. It has training camps throughout the world for the purpose of creating a group of people who will be the front line "soldiers" in such a war. There are "ministers" who are in charge of various aspects of the international armed conflict that al-Qaeda is waging against Western powers. There are also elaborate, although secret chains of command that link all of the far-flung members to a kind of central authority—with Osama bin Laden's successor at its head. Most significant, al-Qaeda is highly successful at its operations and has for a number of years battled the Pakistani army to a near standstill. Even though al-Qaeda does not occupy a territory or have a normal governmental structure it is able to do what, if done by a State, we would call the waging of war. In other words, it is capable of launching attacks in an organized way—so much so that it is capable of being a belligerent in an armed conflict.

The Islamic State insurgent group is also an interesting example in that it even calls itself a State, and sees one of its main missions to conquer additional lands that would form a reconstituted caliphate. What though are we to make of the fact that there are no formal declarations of war before the Islamic State attacks cities and villages that are part of other existing States in the region? Here is a group that has even more powerful armies than those of the Iraq or Syrian governments. And so denying to the Islamic State the *jus ad bellum* rights and obligations seems somewhat arbitrary.

Indeed, it is rather uncontroversial to claim that nonstate actors are capable of being parties to an armed conflict. All civil wars involve armed conflicts between a State and a nonstate entity, and almost no one questions that a civil war can constitute a bona fide war. For example, we can think of insurgent groups, such as the Tamil Tigers for instance, that similarly operate quite an effective paramilitary operation that stalemates the armed forces of a government in the State where they operate their insurgency. Most civil wars these days are truly wars in every sense indistinguishable from non-civil wars in the world. The civil war is a struggle for control of the territory of a State, not a struggle among States. But in every other respect, the sides of the struggle employ the same tactics, the same command structure, and the same efficacy of waging and winning, or likelihood of winning, battles. Civil wars are not misnamed but should truly be seen as wars. And this is one of the best reasons for thinking that nonstate actors can wage war and have rights and obligations that come with the waging of war.

The issue is whether we have a principled reason for treating States and State-like entities differently even if they can do most of the same things during armed struggles. Once we have dispensed with the legitimate authority objection, it is not clear what else can be said other than that nonstate actors cannot do those things that States can do. Yet, in the current section we have given strong reasons to doubt that this other reason is true either. Indeed, especially in a civil war, where the insurgents are nearing the end of their campaign and about to seize control of the government, the State actor seems actually weaker than the nonstate actor, that is the State actor is capable of less than the nonstate actor in terms of the waging of war. For this reason it does not appear that it will be easy to show that there is a principled reason to distinguish State actors from nonstate actors in terms of the waging of either defensive or aggressive war, and the corresponding obligations of *ad bellum* necessity. The conclusion to reach is that some insurgent or terrorist groups can be said to wage war, and if the war that is waged is an unnecessary war, then those insurgent or terrorist groups should be subject to sanction by the international community, just as is true when a State engages in an unnecessary war. In the context of civil wars, this thought is sometimes expressed as *jus ad bellum interno*—or the idea that *jus ad bellum* principles of justification can and should be applied even in an internal conflict with a nonstate actor. From there, it is a short jump to the conclusion that the very same principles should also constrain a State when engaged in an external conflict with a nonstate actor, such as an insurgent or terrorist group.

IV. *JUS IN BELLO* ISSUES

One major difference between the criminal law enforcement model and the war model is that in the war model, the assumption is that it does not matter which of the individuals are assaulted.[11] The *war model* assumes that there will be other individual combatants who will rise to replace any fallen or captured combatants. The *criminal law enforcement model* assumes that the individual perpetrators will not necessarily be replaced by others, so that the key is to capture and prosecute the right individuals, for only if the wrong ones are captured will there still be others out there who might attack again.

11. For more on the differences between the war model and the law/crime model for dealing with terrorism, see David Luban, *The War on Terrorism and the End of Human Rights*, *in* War after September 11 (Verna V. Gehring ed., 2003), *reprinted in* The Morality of War 413–21 (Larry May, Eric Rovie & Steve Viner eds., 2006).

In most war situations, no matter who is captured, there will be others ready to attack, so the only thing that matters is deterring these others by what is done to the one who has been captured. Of course, this sets the stage for thinking that even torturing the non-guilty could be justified as deterrence. In the criminal law enforcement model, there does not appear to be any incentive to capturing and punishing those who are non-guilty.

So, should insurgency and terrorism be best viewed under the criminal law enforcement model or the war model? We are inclined to think that the war model makes more sense. Insurgents and terrorists are more like regular combatants in that they are replaceable. This is especially true since there is rarely any direct personal payoff for the insurgent, as there would often be for the normal criminal. But this also means that as in war, it will indeed be hard to deter insurgents and terrorists from future attacks since they are not motivated by personal considerations of gain and probably also will not be motivated by personal considerations of loss. Nonetheless, we are inclined to think that the war model does make more sense than the criminal law enforcement model in how we initially think about insurgent fighters and terrorists.

But then what are these fighters owed from the perspective of the war model? Those who would argue that the individual insurgents or terrorists are only owed retribution now have a more difficult task than they may have thought. For unlike standard criminals, insurgents or terrorists do not do what they do out of a hope for personal gain, and someone else probably would have replaced them if they had not been able or willing to do what they did. Since insurgents or terrorists do not generally engage in violence unless others have told them to do so, they are like combatants in that they are not really proper subjects of retribution. Rather, it is their leaders, if anyone, who are subject to retribution.

So, if even on the war model individual insurgents and terrorists are not due retribution, what if anything is their due? And here we come to the crux of the matter, for unless it is claimed that insurgents and terrorists are neither criminals nor combatants, they will be owed what is normally owed to people in one or the other category. If insurgents or terrorists are combatants then they are owed the type of mutual respect that is paid to all combatants according to the Just War tradition. If we are to use the criminal law enforcement model, then insurgents or terrorists are owed the full due process considerations that apply to any criminal suspect. This is why the administration of George W. Bush tried to create an intermediate category for terrorists, because on either of the reigning categories, terrorists are owed quite a lot. For terrorists to be subject to torture and abuse, they could not fall into either standard category.

The idea that insurgents and terrorists are not criminals or combatants is an imaginative way to get out of the bind articulated above. The term "illegal combatant" is meant to signify this intermediate status. But even if we agree that this is the proper way to characterize insurgents and terrorists, it is not clear at all that this category involves fewer rights than either of the categories that it is in-between. For this intermediate category could be one that incorporated protections from both categories rather than having the protections of neither. The chief reason to disagree has to do with the idea that insurgents and terrorists have by refusing to conform to the rules of war seemingly waived or forfeited whatever protection they might otherwise have by refusing to conform to the rules of war.

Even if insurgents and terrorists are illegal combatants, this does not mean that they should be treated without restraint either from the perspective of the rule of law or the rules of war. Someone could claim that terrorists are simply outlaws and hence outside any system of rules. Such a view is like treating terrorists as pirates were once treated in the sixteenth and seventeenth centuries, where their voluntary acts were thought to have waived, or forfeited, any rights that they would otherwise be entitled to. But as with similar views about other types of criminal acts, it is not at all clear that we should endorse the view that a waiver has occurred, especially since people in question surely do not recognize what they have done as constituting such a waiver.

If a State's soldiers who violate the rules of war are not categorized as illegal combatants, why think that terrorists who do not accept the rules of war are best categorized as illegal combatants? What is typically thought is that soldiers who violate the rules of war should be tried as war criminals, and that such trials should themselves be conducted according to the rules of war. This is similar to what is thought about domestic criminals as well. We do not hang suspected criminals from trees, as was tragically done in the Ox Bow Incident, but instead treat them according to the rules that apply to anyone who is standing trial. It is normally thought that those who have broken the law, even if cavalierly done, still deserve the law's protection. Indeed, this is the hallmark of a liberal society that recognizes the rule of law, as opposed to a vigilante-based society.

In the end, we see no reason to think that insurgents and terrorists are not owed what is considered the minimum for all humans, and that this should be drawn in terms of both considerations of justice and humanity. And if one is convinced of this claim, then it is just a short step to thinking that insurgents and terrorists, like everyone else, are owed a minimum amount of compassion and mercy, as well as a minimum amount of justice, at least procedural justice as epitomized in rule of law considerations. This conclusion is largely a negative one—namely, there are no good reasons to reject this claim on behalf of insurgents or terrorists.

There are also positive reasons for thinking that it is a good thing for insurgents and terrorists to be treated humanely. Such a positive argument would turn on the idea of honor, an idea at least as old as Homer and central to the thought of the theorists such as Seneca and Grotius. Both the Just War tradition and contemporary international humanitarian law are deeply entwined with considerations of honor and conscience. A soldier's honor is deeply entwined with a conscientious sense that the soldier is doing the right thing by engaging in violence. For centuries this idea has itself been instilled by reference to a set of restraints that soldiers are bound by, most significant that they would not allow their own sense of hatred or revenge to dictate how to act toward enemy combatants.[12] One could wonder why it is that soldiers could not get their hands dirty just as is true for many other role-based professions.[13] Politicians for instance seem to have little difficulty seeing that in certain cases it is important, indeed necessary, that they act in ways that would otherwise be considered to be immoral. Why not think that soldiers could conceive of themselves this way as well when confronting insurgents and terrorists?

The problem is that soldiers assault and kill as a matter of professional training and even of professional duty, where such behavior would normally be considered immoral. So to argue that they should have dirty hands also in the way that they carry out their terrible duty toward insurgents and terrorists is truly troubling. This would mean that soldiers would lose any sense that their own actions are conscience- or honor-based. For conscience and honor only work if there is some line that should not be crossed.[14] If soldiers may treat insurgent and terrorist combatants—or anyone for that matter—inhumanely, then there is no line that cannot be crossed.[15] The soldiers then will find it difficult to see themselves as anything other than paid assaulters and killers. And it will be increasingly hard for soldiers to see what they did as soldiers as something that they can accept after war is over as they tell their tales to their children or even to themselves.

Grotius was well aware of such problems when he wrote during the first half of the seventeenth century. Indeed, Grotius links the law of nature with the sense of honor. Honor provides the motivation for following the

12. *See* SHANNON FRENCH, THE CODE OF THE WARRIOR (2003).

13. *See* the excellent collection of papers on the problem of dirty hands, CRUELTY AND DECEPTION (Paul Raynard & David Shugarman eds., 2000).

14. Shannon French has an especially good discussion of this issue in chapter 9 of her book.

15. *See* Larry May, *On Conscience*, 20 AM. PHIL. Q. 57 (1983).

laws of nature, a sense of inner restraint that is crucial for the maintenance of the various duties that are stipulated by natural law.[16] Good people, who are deserving of praise, will restrain themselves beyond what is required by justice, says Grotius.[17] And even in war, good people will not merely look to what is permissible, but also to what will give credit to them. Grotius also suggests that a sense of honor can replace a sense of fear on the battlefield, hence contributing to the success of armies. But the overriding consideration is that a sense of honor leads people to exercise greater restraint than would be required by law or even by considerations of justice.

We would here adapt an argument from David Rodin. Rodin argues that thinking of soldiers as being differently situated, based on whether they fight on the just or unjust side of a war, should not be seen as lowering the bar for what is required of soldiers on the just side, but only in raising the bar for what is required from soldiers who fight on the unjust side.[18] Similarly, we would argue that nonstate combatants have a higher bar as compared to what is required from State combatants. But there are nonetheless honor-based reasons for State combatants not to act toward insurgents or terrorists in ways that are otherwise permitted.

V. CIVIL WARS AND CIVILIANS

Civil wars have been seen as problematic wars since there are clearly not two States attacking each other. There has been significant disagreement about how if at all an insurgent group could satisfy the legitimate authority condition of the *jus ad bellum*. But others have convincingly argued that insurgents often represent the peoples on behalf of whom they fight.[19] And it has also been argued that legitimate authority is not a condition of the Just War once we move away from the statist positions of the Westphalian model.

A seemingly intractable problem with civil wars is how to assess the lives of civilians in the calculations of necessity. The source of this problem is that it is much harder than normal to identify who is a civilian in civil wars and other wars of insurgency than in wars between States. Indeed, insurgents often move back and forth between being combatants and civilians during civil war. Insurgents are not normally part of regular army units,

16. Grotius, *supra* note 5, at 716–17.
17. *Id.* at 716.
18. David Rodin, *The Moral Inequality of Soldiers: Why* Jus in Bello *Asymmetry Is Half Right*, *in* Just and Unjust Warriors 44–68 (David Rodin & Henry Shue eds., 2008).
19. *See* Cecile Fabre, Cosmopolitan War 144 (2012).

and their dress and behavior is civilian in appearance. So, it is very difficult to conform to the principle that civilians not be directly targeted if it is very hard to distinguish between civilians and combatants in the first place. Some insurgents make it especially hard to conform to the principle of distinction when they intentionally hide among civilians.

Concerning necessity, there are also problems caused by the porous border between civilians and combatants in asymmetric wars. *Jus in bello* necessity turns on a showing of immediate and imminent need to kill or otherwise assault members of the enemy. In order to make this determination, normally one must ascertain who members of the enemy forces are. When such determinations are very difficult to make, it is also hard to see whether one has satisfied the principle of necessity.

Complicity may be a factor if civilians hide insurgent combatants, or if civilians shield military targets. Civilians can themselves participate in hostilities and make themselves legitimate targets of attack. In insurgencies and civil wars, many more civilians are potentially complicit than in wars fought between States. The necessity to attack civilians will turn on the complicit status of these civilians. In addition, when insurgent fighters move back into the civilian population there are also serious questions of whether or not they can then be still targetable on necessity grounds.

If status is one of the chief markers for necessity calculations, as has been held to be true following the Lieber Code, then one can readily see why insurgencies pose such a problem. On the status-based model all enemy combatants can be killed without worries about violating the principle of necessity. But if the border between combatants and civilians is unclear, we are thrust back into a situation where individual behavior is again important and where status cannot alone tell us who it is militarily necessary to kill or assault. As we saw in our chapter on human rights law, if conduct or behavior is the marker for necessity then it is much more difficult to justify lethal force than if status is the marker.

Perhaps of even greater significance than the difficulty of satisfying the necessity condition in insurgencies and civil wars is that of satisfying the distinction or discrimination condition. Civil wars and insurgencies risk the destruction of the rule of civilian immunity. Many theorists look to this principle for the modern turn toward making wars more humane, as we saw in earlier chapters. As more and more wars do not involve two States, we will be forced to rethink how to understand the principle of distinction and its connection to the principle of necessity.

One specific question that arises with some urgency is whether the principle of distinction can be somewhat loosened when an insurgent group must employ tactics against civilians in order to have any chance of succeeding against an oppressive State in which the insurgent group resides. Here necessity would seem to be in opposition to distinction. There is something of a dilemma here in that if the rules of war are loosened in this case there may be permanent damage to these rules, and yet if the rules are not loosened then the insurgency is condemned to remain under the oppressive regime.[20]

Today many just war theorists will distinguish between the case of insurgency that has a just cause and an insurgency that does not. The dilemma is generated principally by considering only cases of the former sort. There the restriction on tactics that are necessary but that violate the principle of distinction or civilian immunity seems unjustified since then the just cause will not be realized, and Just War theory will favor the oppressor—something that theorists at least since Emer Vattel have cautioned against.

Here again complicity is an important issue. If the civilians who support the oppressive State have done enough to constitute "participation" in the oppression, then their own status has at least somewhat changed. These civilians are now quasi-combatants insofar as they actively aid the soldiers who carry out the State-ordered oppression. And because of this change in status, perhaps these "civilians" can be targeted. Yet, the worry is that we are on a slippery slope that will destroy the principle of distinction or civilian immunity, since it is often very hard to distinguish between civilians who have crossed the line and those who have not crossed the line into being complicit in their State's oppression. And things are even worse if it is the insurgency that is in the wrong and some of its civilian supporters are also complicit.

Let us here briefly take up the human shields issue that has so plagued insurgencies and terrorist group activity in many recent wars. We are especially interested in the question of whether those who minimally aid the insurgents by providing them protection from assault by intermingling with the insurgents means that these civilians are voluntary human shields who have changed status.[21] But the problem is that if civilians can change status fairly easily then the principle of civilian immunity will be nearly unworkable as a guide and unenforceable as a rule.

If people place themselves in front of military targets, then things are easier to conceptualize since they can be readily identified as having

20. *See* David Rodin, *The Ethics of Asymmetric War*, *in* The Ethics of War: Shared Problems in Different Traditions (Richard Sorabji & David Rodin eds., 2006); *see also* Cecile Fabre, *supra* note 19 (ch. 7).

21. *See* Michael Newton & Larry May, Proportionality in International Law (2014) (ch. 9).

changed status. But the case that is worrisome is where civilians shield not military hardware but other members of their group who are conducting military operations against the State. In this case there is a risk to the principle of distinction and also to the principle of necessity. The principle of necessity is jeopardized because we are forced to make determinations about the justifiability of tactics on a case-by-case basis where the actual necessity of killing is very hard to determine.

These difficult cases that are generated by the proliferation of asymmetric and civil wars are disconcerting. But the general framework we have laid out in previous chapters gives us both a sense of why these cases are difficult and also how they need to be resolved. The resolution will call for abandoning the fiction that all enemy combatants are to be treated the same. And yet in abandoning that fiction, justifying war will be increasingly difficult, at least war as we have known it. Especially in the case of necessity, asymmetric war creates problems that can be resolved only seemingly by moving from a status-based standard to a conduct-based standard. But at that point the principle of necessity and the principle of distinction will push in different directions, and the conflict between them will be hard, or perhaps impossible, to resolve.

The key point here is that status retains—and should retain—its moral significance in the regulation of warfare. However, status is not immutable; the increased role of civilians directly participating in hostilities shows that targeting on the basis of conduct will become more and more important in the asymmetric wars of the future. The key philosophical point is that status and conduct are two opposite points on a spectrum, but not different in kind. What unifies both of them is that even status is based, at some level, on deeper issues of conduct. So the uniformed soldier's "status" as a solider is ultimately based on a cluster of smaller pieces of someone's conduct: his joining the army, his wearing the uniform, his brandishing of a service rifle. It would be wrong to exaggerate the point and suggest that the distinction between status and conduct is illusory because everything is just conduct. That is not true. Rather, the difference pertains to *stickiness*. If someone is targetable based on his or her status, that status is sticky and the person remains targetable even when the conditions that gave rise to that person's dangerousness—some conduct—no longer apply in that individual moment. In contrast, targeting on the basis of conduct alone is not sticky at all—the target can move in and out of targetability simply based on the target's conduct at that moment in time. Status is sticky; conduct is not.

Ultimately, the question is how "sticky" the categories should be. Recently, the ICRC has thrown its weight behind the proposal that civilians who exercise a "continuous combat function" as part of an organized armed group (a nonstate actor) can be targeted on this basis, regardless of their conduct at the moment when they are targeted. This proposal is a hybrid between status and conduct. The status is sticky but perhaps not as sticky as the notion of membership in a traditional state army, although it comes pretty close. But it is much more sticky than the notion that a civilian can only be targeted "for such time" as that person is directly participating in hostilities.

This hybrid proposal seeks to retain the legitimacy and relevancy of both necessity and distinction as key concepts of *jus in bello*, and ensure they have a role to play in the asymmetric conflicts of today and tomorrow. It does not go the entire way toward a conduct-based standard that might better exemplify necessity as that term is understood in human rights and criminal law (based on conduct and individual threat assessments). What it does do is provide a hybrid-status-based framework that allows *jus in bello* necessity and distinction to continue to have relevance in today's armed conflict, within a workable framework that can be applied by all parties to an armed conflict.

CHAPTER 9

Disabling versus Killing in War

In the present chapter we ask whether necessity permits and requires that attacking forces always kill (as opposed to disable) the enemy. Chapter 10 will then extend the analysis to whether attacking forces should only be permitted to kill the enemy once capture is impossible or infeasible. We turn now to the first of these two questions: Why do soldiers shoot to kill? What if they could injure the enemy instead of killing them? The question is devastatingly simple and straightforward but it hides a cluster of philosophical and legal questions. The issue is not whether a soldier can kill an injured enemy who is so hurt that he cannot fight—that is clearly impermissible because the soldier is hors de combat or outside the zone of combat. The question is whether the appropriate intention of a soldier, when faced with an able-bodied enemy combatant, should be to first incapacitate the enemy with the least amount of force *necessary*, which in some situations might entail disabling versus killing in battle. Or may the soldier engage the enemy with the intention of killing him outright in the first instance? The question can only be answered relative to the prevailing account of necessity, which is precisely what is contested in this theoretical inquiry. In this chapter we first start with a legal evaluation of a putative duty to disable rather than kill in warfare, before turning to a normative analysis regarding which direction the law should take in the future. Again, this is a question of application that builds on the previous chapters examining the concept of necessity in *jus in bello*.

Legal scholars with a progressive reading of the law have mounted a multi-pronged defense of a legal requirement to use the least amount of force possible during armed conflict. Their arguments include the following propositions (1) the law of war already severely restricts the use of force in various contexts by virtue of specific prohibitions on methods of warfare, (2) the law of war already prohibits killing enemy combatants who are rendered hors de combat, and (3) the drafters of the Additional Protocols supported a "least-harmful-means" interpretation of the concept of necessity, meaning that killing is only lawful when soldiers have no other way of neutralizing the enemy (e.g., disabling or capture is not feasible).

These recent arguments exist in a long line of diplomatic and scholarly attempts to redefine the concept of necessity to give it more regulatory bite. The modern attempts begin in 1973–1974 with Jean Pictet, who argued in favor of a least-harmful-means interpretation of necessity in Geneva during the negotiations that led to the drafting of the Additional Protocols to the Geneva Conventions.[1] Nils Melzer's monograph from 2008 also seeks to buttress the least-harmful-means interpretation.[2] Finally, the International Committee of the Red Cross's *Interpretive Guidance on Direct Participation in Hostilities* also supported a least-harmful-means interpretation of necessity (and by extension a requirement to disable rather than kill if possible), though this conclusion was controversial and unsupported by many of the experts involved in the original drafting process.[3]

At the same time, philosophers and ethicists have conducted a parallel debate regarding the value of combatant lives and whether their liability to *summary* killing in battle is morally justified. For example, a recent essay by Gabriella Blum concedes that the current law codifies a permissive version of military necessity, but questions whether the law should evolve toward a narrower conception of military necessity. At the same time, Just War theorists have struggled to identify the particular element of combatancy that makes an individual subject to summary killing while protecting civilians in almost any situation except their direct participation in hostilities. As Jeff McMahan has noted, there may be moral reasons to permit the targeting of civilians who are causally responsible for an unjust war effort—a conclusion that stands in stark contrast with today's codification of the laws of war. So the concept of necessity as a baseline principle for military targeting is being questioned in both philosophical and legal domains. While legal scholars are making arguments about the state of the law today, *lex lata*, philosophers are making arguments about the way the law ought to be, *de lege ferenda*.

1. According to Goodman, Pictet did not stand alone in this attempt but was supported by other experts. *See* Ryan Goodman, *The Power to Kill or Capture Enemy Combatants*, 24 Eur. J. Int'l L. 819, 842 (2013).

2. *See* Nils Melzer, Targeted Killing in International Law (2008).

3. The final document was eventually drafted by Nils Melzer.

For reasons that we will articulate in the following sections, we believe that none of the arguments sounding in *lex lata* provide definitive support for a requirement to disable instead of killing under existing laws of war. Although generally each piece of evidence cited by the progressive lawyers is correct, we believe that the legal evidence paints a different picture as far as the conclusion is concerned. Military necessity has always permitted the summary killing of enemy military personnel, and nothing in the Geneva Conventions or the Additional Protocols changed that. However, the philosophical questions are far more complex and their analysis produces a far more nuanced result. Philosophers are generally correct that justifying the wholesale killing of enemy soldiers is difficult to do, especially when they could be disabled rather than killed. Furthermore, the difference between an enemy soldier and an enemy civilian may be nothing more than thirty days in basic training and the issuance of a service rifle that has never been fired (for a soldier conscripted into a poorly trained and equipped army).

That being said, changing the principle of necessity to a least-harmful-means test would have significant consequences that affect the philosophical calculus. Specifically, a requirement to disable instead of killing requires an analysis of an individual's level of threat that may be difficult to operationalize in practice.[4] In a sense, this problem is similar to the one encountered by revisionist Just War theorists who believe that morality suggests that soldiers should be permitted to attack civilians who are contributing to an unjust war effort. The objection to this philosophical argument has always been that soldiers would be poorly suited to making individual assessments of the culpability of particular civilians for their contributions to the war effort. Also, soldiers would have to make assessments regarding the justness of the overall war. The question here is whether the least-harmful-means version of necessity would require a similarly impractical assessment of an individual's level of danger. The one virtue of the current legal regime—which allows soldiers to shoot to kill—is that it provides bright-line rules that are easy for soldiers to apply. This is not just a side consideration; a normative assessment of a moral framework must include at least some consideration of actual compliance. That being said, it is also important not to swing too far in the opposite direction, that is, to privilege the current state of affairs and fall victim to a failure of imagination.

Section I of this chapter begins by considering the specific prohibitions of the laws of war, and concludes that these specific prohibitions do not

4. *See* Richard H. Pildes & Samuel Issacharoff, *Targeted Warfare: Individuating Enemy Responsibility*, 88 N.Y.U. L. Rev. 1521 (2013).

add up to a more general duty to refrain from using lethal force against enemy combatants. Section II then looks at the legal prohibition regarding killing soldiers who are hors de combat, and concludes that it provides no support for a requirement to use non-lethal force. In fact, despite popular misconception, wounded soldiers are only hors de combat if they are receiving medical treatment or incapable of engaging in belligerency. Section III then examines the *travaux preparatoires* for the Additional Protocols to the Geneva Conventions, and concludes that the least-harmful-means test, though by all means a subject of discussion at the Geneva conferences, was not codified into the Additional Protocols. The result was that the traditional conception of military necessity remains in force, unbroken, from Francis Lieber's time, through the St. Petersburg Declaration, and enduring in the present.[5] Finally, Section IV considers the question from the perspective of normative theory and asks whether principles of moral philosophy require a change in the law. In the end, we support a progressive development of the law in order to make warfare less lethal, though not by crafting an explicit and affirmative legal requirement to disable enemy soldiers rather than kill them. In fact, there are alternative legal mechanisms that could be used to bring the law closer to the demands of morality.

I. SPECIFIC PROHIBITIONS VERSUS GENERAL DUTIES

Progressive lawyers who argue for a legal requirement to disable soldiers are making arguments regarding *lex lata*: ambitious claims not just about what the law ought to be in the future but what the law is today. As an interpretation of *lex lata*, these arguments are highly provocative and have encouraged legal scholars to question some prior assumptions about the state of the law. However, we are unaware of a single prosecution at an international tribunal of a soldier or commander for killing enemy soldiers who had not surrendered or were incapacitated. There are not only no convictions, there are also no *indictments* of this nature at the ICTY, ICTR, ICC, STL, SCSL, ECCC, or any other international criminal tribunal. Of course, one might argue that the asserted restrictions on the use of force are not criminal prohibitions—just violations of international humanitarian law. But it is telling that the restrictions on the use of force asserted by these

5. See Preamble to the St. Petersburg Declaration ("The only legitimate object which States should endeavour to accomplish during war is to weaken the military forces of the enemy."). *See also* Janina Dill & Henry Shue, *Limiting the Killing in War: Military Necessity and the St. Petersburg Assumption*, 26 Ethics & Int'l Affairs 311, 321 (2012).

progressive lawyers are out of step not only with the actual practice of international criminal law but also with the actual practice of modern aerial warfare.

If there was a duty to use non-lethal force in the law of war, then it is hard to understand how any aerial military campaign could be legal, given that an infantry campaign could disable enemy soldiers whereas a bombing campaign would most likely kill them. Does this mean that every State that has engaged in aerial warfare since 1973 has violated the least-harmful-means test and its requirement to disable attackers? After the 1999 NATO bombing of Serbian targets, there was widespread discussion of whether NATO's 15,000-foot flight ceiling impermissibly prioritized allied force protection over enemy civilian casualties; the ICTY prosecutor declined to commence an investigation based on this controversy.[6] But few claimed that the bombing was per se illegal because it killed enemy soldiers when they could have been disabled in an infantry campaign. If there were any complaints about the lack of an infantry campaign, it was due to the aerial campaign's perceived impotence at stemming the ethnic cleansing occurring on the ground, and a question about whether the rules of engagement represented an obstacle to compliance with the principle of distinction.

One of the most interesting examples of the progressive lawyers is the recent scholarship of Ryan Goodman, who has performed an important service by unearthing the lost legislative history of the Geneva Convention's Additional Protocols. We say "lost" because, although this history is well known to those who participated in the negotiations, the recent literature on the law of armed conflict has forgotten many of the details that Goodman helpfully excavates. Goodman is surely right that many recent statements regarding the Additional Protocol negotiations are conclusory and fail to capture the nuance of the negotiations.[7]

Goodman catalogs the various prohibitions on means and methods of warfare—prohibitions that provide evidence that the right to kill enemy combatants is not unlimited.[8] Perfidy is not permitted, nor is wounding treacherously. A combatant may not declare that no quarter will be given; indeed this is a war crime once the words are uttered even before the killing begins. Reprisals are also forbidden.[9] If a unit is unable to logistically

6. *See* Final Report to the Prosecutor by the Committee Established to Review the NATO Bombing Campaign against the Federal Republic of Yugoslavia, para. 56, *available at* http://www.icty.org/x/file/About/OTP/otp_report_nato_bombing_en.pdf.

7. *See* Goodman, *supra* note 1, at 842.

8. *Id.* at 822–36.

9. One must be careful in the sense that the recent history of the laws of war has shown remarkable development regarding this norm in a very short period of time,

handle the captivity of a group of soldiers that it has taken prisoner, it cannot summarily execute them—even if the only alternative is to let them go free.[10] Finally, various types and classes of weapons are prohibited.

Perhaps this long catalog of specific prohibitions provides evidence for a general IHL principle regarding restrictions on the use of force (RUF), of which the least-harmful-means test would be the prime example. The argument here is that the law of armed conflict already engages in restrictions on the use of force.[11] Although this last statement is undoubtedly true, the question is whether this proposition provides an additional reason to believe in a wholesale principle, already codified in law, which requires that the least amount of force be used during a military engagement.

The reason that the use of force is restricted in these situations is precisely because the relevant treaties codified *specific prohibitions* against weapons and methods that produced unnecessary suffering, and specific actions, such as perfidy and treachery, that made the return to peace too difficult. One could argue that the least-restrictive-means test can also be justified because unrestrained force would make the return to peace too difficult.[12] But this argument is inapposite. It does not matter whether both could conceivably be justified by the same type of normative arguments. The important point is that the specific prohibitions and a general restriction on the use of force are operating on different levels. One cannot turn the specific prohibitions on their head; the *specific* prohibitions of *jus in bello* would become superfluous when swamped by a more general principle, such as a human rights inspired notion of necessity, that restricts the use of force. With a restrictive general principle in place, the specific prohibitions would lose much of their urgency and raison d'être.

Arguments for a progressive reading of the principle of necessity are sometimes insensitive to the historical development of the laws of war.[13]

and the exact scope of the current prohibition may be controversial. *See* CUSTOMARY INTERNATIONAL HUMANITARIAN LAW, Rule 147 at 523 (Jean-Marie Henckaerts & Louise Doswald-Beck eds., 2005) ("Because of existing contrary practice, albeit very limited, it is difficult to conclude that there has yet crystallised a customary rule specifically prohibiting reprisals against civilians during the conduct of hostilities.").

10. *See* Goodman, *supra* note 1, at 822.

11. *Id.* at 853 ("In the final analysis, this body of evidence most clearly indicates that RUF—and the LRM approach in particular—is well grounded in international law and institutional practice.").

12. *See* Ryan Goodman, *The Power to Kill or Capture Enemy Combatants*, NYU School of Law, Public Law Research Paper No. 13-02, at 18 n.81, *available at* http://ssrn.com/abstract=2213960.

13. *Id.* at 17.

We should not forget Francis Lieber's definition of military necessity codified in the Lieber Code; this definition was absolutely central to the history and development of *jus in bello*, and it represents the greatest obstacle to the least-harmful-means interpretation of military necessity.[14] Whatever Lieber meant by military necessity, the phrase clearly did not mean the least restrictive means, a definition of necessity that now reigns in human rights law. As a previous chapter explained, necessity in human rights law is not the same as necessity in *jus in bello*, and one should not be lured into thinking they are the same concepts just because they carry the same label.[15] Although the progressive IHL lawyers are not applying human rights law in their analysis, their arguments rely on a human rights interpretation of the principle of military necessity instead of its technical meaning that can be traced back to the Lieber Code and earlier.[16] Jean Pictet and other international lawyers have tried to displace that definition of military necessity, but it must be conceded that the historical definition of necessity in the Lieber Code did not mean the "least-restrictive means."

II. THE HORS DE COMBAT ARGUMENT

Restrictions on the use of lethal force might also be achieved through another doctrinal route: the prohibition against killing soldiers who are hors de combat. This would not represent the same argument as the least-harmful-means interpretation of necessity, but it would cover roughly the same conceptual ground by producing a similar result: fewer instances in which lethal force would be permitted, and an increased duty to use non-lethal force (disabling the enemy instead of killing him or her). But as the following analysis will make clear, although we are sympathetic, from the perspective of moral theory, to the argument and even share its inspiration (to make warfare more humane), it is probably an exaggeration to claim that it is already codified in existing principles of international humanitarian law. Here is why: we believe that an excessively broad legal interpretation of the hors de combat rule conflates soldiers who might be defenseless in the future with soldiers who are presently defenseless (two completely

14. Instructions for the Government of Armies of the United States in the Field, General Order No. 100, Apr. 24, 1863 [hereinafter cited as *Lieber Code*].

15. *See also* Jens David Ohlin, *The Duty to Capture*, 97 MINN. L. REV. 1268, 1270–72 (2013).

16. *Id.*

different scenarios). As a matter of existing law, the former are hors de combat whereas the latter are not. A full explanation of this point follows.

Consider Goodman's argument for a broad interpretation of the hors de combat rule. He notes that a wounded or completely defenseless soldier is hors de combat and not a legitimate target.[17] Consequently, the rules restricting force against persons hors de combat occupy much of the same conceptual space as general restrictions on the use of force embodied by a least-harmful-means interpretation of the concept of necessity. In fact, Goodman writes that "a very broad definition of *hors de combat* could even place more limits on the use of force than RUF,"[18] and the two types of restrictions "can effectuate the same result."[19] If a combatant falls hors de combat, he cannot be killed and must be "apprehended and detained."[20] These considerations are important because they recognize that restrictions on lethal force might be located in multiple doctrinal sources, and a least-harmful-means interpretation of the principle of necessity is just one of them. The prohibition against killing soldiers hors de combat is another, and it too can be interpreted narrowly and broadly. A broad reading of the hors de combat rule might effectuate the same practical result as the attempt to redefine necessity in least-harmful-means terms. But like the principle of necessity, caution is warranted when dealing with expansive definitions of *hors de combat*.

It is clear that combatants receiving medical attention, having surrendered, or been taken into custody, are all hors de combat and cannot be attacked under existing rules of *jus in bello*. However, there are seeds for a more ambitious reading of the rule in Article 41(2) of Additional Protocol I, which defines a person as hors de combat if "he has been rendered unconscious or is otherwise incapacitated by wounds or sickness, and therefore is incapable of defending himself; provided that in any of these cases he abstains from any hostile act and does not attempt to escape."[21] So one might argue that a soldier who shoots and wounds an enemy combatant is prohibited from deploying a second kill shot if the wounded soldier is truly "incapable of defending himself." This prohibition was very much at issue in the Navy Seals raid that targeted Osama bin Laden in Abbottabad, Pakistan. Critics complained that U.S. forces may have violated the rule if

17. Goodman, *supra* note 12, at 20–26.
18. *Id.* at 20.
19. *Id.*
20. *Id.*
21. *See* Protocol Additional to the Geneva Conventions of 12 August 1949, and Relating to the Protection of Victims of International Armed Conflicts, June 8, 1977, 1125 U.N.T.S. 3 (hereinafter cited as *Additional Protocol I*), art. 41(2).

they shot bin Laden after he was already incapacitated, though there might be a factual dispute regarding whether he was sufficiently incapacitated so as to prevent him from deploying a suicide explosive. However, it seems clear that absent a reasonable suspicion that he was holding such a device, his killing may have violated the hors de combat rule if he was already incapacitated by the first attack and genuinely unable to offer any resistance.

Although this conclusion arguably represents a legitimate interpretation of the current prohibitions,[22] it is hard to see its relevance. Goodman concludes that "in the final analysis, the rules defining *hors de combat* share much in common with RUF . . . RUF regulate the kind and degree of violence that can be employed against individuals who are legitimate military targets."[23] But this represents a fundamental misinterpretation of the rules regarding persons hors de combat. The hors de combat rules are specific provisions that remove specified *targets* from the category of legitimate combatants.[24] They do not, however, count as restrictions against the use of force against combatants. Why? Because a soldier hors de combat—whether a prisoner of war, a hospitalized patient, or an unconscious and incapacitated individual—is the functional equivalent of a civilian (i.e., a noncombatant) and hence is a protected person in the eyes of the law and its chivalric conception of warfare. The specified rules regarding when a soldier is hors de combat are *lex specialis* rules against the more general legal regime of *jus in bello* that allows summary killing of enemy combatants

22. Not all commentators agree with Goodman's interpretation. Henderson notes that the ICRC study on customary law suggests that defenselessness is limited to unconsciousness, shipwreck, wounds, or sickness. *See* Ian Henderson, *Comments*, EJIL Talk (Feb. 21, 2013), *available at* http://www.ejiltalk.org/the-power-to-kill-or-capture-and-the-doj-white-paper/.

23. Goodman, *supra* note 12, at 25.

24. Goodman's account of the hors de combat rules suffers from the same conceptual infirmity as his account of the specific prohibitions on methods of warfare discussed in part I of this commentary: both arguments confuse the *lex specialis* rules with the *lex generalis*. Although his description of the various rules are arguably correct readings of the existing law, it is unclear whether they do the argumentative work that he assigns to them; he uses the *lex specialis* as evidence for an imaginary *lex generalis* that does not exist. To be fair, Goodman never claims that the specific prohibitions on methods of warfare, or the rules on hors de combat, provide *direct* evidence for RUF. Rather, he only asserts that they provide *indirect* evidence. *Id.* at 20 ("The degree to which this alternate set of rules generates the same legal effects as RUF will—even more directly than the rules previously discussed—support the case for RUF."). However, even this assertion sounds like a category mistake. One cannot use the specific prohibitions as evidence for a general principle that exceeds the contours of the specific prohibitions; this argumentative move ignores and betrays the very specificity of these prohibitions, which were designed to regulate isolated activity.

who are lawful targets—as long as there is no specific legal prohibition against it.

However, there is a much more powerful argument regarding the definition of hors de combat that threatens to unravel the conceptual clarity of the prohibition. Some scholars argue that *defenseless* soldiers are hors de combat, and cite as their evidence the Additional Protocol reference to a soldier who is "incapable of defending himself." Then, in an attempt to define defenselessness, they include situations where the soldier is facing overwhelming firepower and is incapable of surviving the assault. His victory and survival are practically impossible because the attacking force has greater numbers and greater firepower. In this situation, is not the soldier, for all practical purposes, defenseless and thus hors de combat? If this is the case, then the attacking force has a duty to refrain from using lethal force, since the killing of a defenseless soldier would violate the prohibition against killing personnel who are hors de combat. The inevitable conclusion of this argument gets to the same result as a least-harmful-means interpretation of necessity, except via a different doctrinal route.

Although this argument is appealing from the perspective of moral theory, the argument is problematic as an interpretation of existing law. The Additional Protocol only prohibits the killing of defenseless soldiers whose defenselessness is caused by unconsciousness or incapacitating wounds and sickness. Defenselessness might be caused by other factors—such as overwhelming firepower or an imbalance in military strength—but this type of defenselessness is not covered by the prohibitions regarding killing soldiers hors de combat. This might seem unnecessarily harsh, though it is important to remember that soldiers in such a situation are protected by another provision, that is, the prohibition against killing soldiers who have effectively communicated their decision to surrender. To understand why the current Additional Protocol prohibition on killing soldiers hors de combat does not include soldiers who are facing overwhelming firepower, consider the next two points.

The expansive interpretation of the hors de combat argument is problematic because it infringes on the conceptual territory of the prohibition on targeting *surrendered* soldiers. If soldiers are facing overwhelming force and they feel that their resistance would be futile, then they always retain the option of laying down their arms and communicating their surrender to their adversary. The result of surrendering is that the soldier regains protected status and becomes the functional equivalent of a civilian. However, the wide version of the hors de combat rule effectively replicates this result, except it skips over the step where the soldier actually needs to surrender.

In this sense, the wide hors de combat argument infringes on the surrender rule, but without requiring the actual fulfillment of that rule, that is, the requirement that the soldier *actually* communicate his or her surrender. One might even view this as an impermissible end run around the surrender rule.

Finally, the expansive interpretation of the hors de combat rule jumps the causal chain that is anticipated by the rule. A soldier who is facing overwhelming firepower is not necessarily hors de combat in any meaningful sense. Nor is a soldier who is simply wounded. A soldier facing an overwhelming level of force may *become* hors de combat once injured, assuming that he or she survives the original onslaught and is severely injured in the attack. This outcome might seem very likely from the standpoint of probabilities, but it is by no means absolutely certain, nor has the anticipated result come to pass. Similarly, an injured soldier may become hors de combat if his injury is sufficient to render him incapacitated and unable to mount any defense at all. But the point here is that one must follow the causal chain to the required result, not preempt the causal chain and simply *assume* the result. The soldier must be *actually* defenseless, not potentially defenseless in the future by virtue of his inferior firepower or tactics at his disposal. Similarly, the wounded soldier must be *actually* incapacitated and incapable of participating in combat, as opposed to simply being wounded in a way that might lead, through the passage of time, to incapacitation. What matters is the state of the combatant at the time of the attack, and even a wounded soldier is capable of engaging in defensive actions. If the soldier retains the ability to respond at that moment, then he remains a legitimate target under the current law.

In short, it is important not to jump this causal chain and skip to the end, without letting the chain of causation run its course. It is possible for a severely injured soldier to stay within the zone of combat by continuing to represent a threat. These soldiers might fire their weapons, communicate with other combatants to coordinate counterattacks (thus taking part in hostilities), or deploy an explosive as a suicide device directed solely against the enemy. These are all actions that a severely wounded soldier might engage in. It is therefore not necessarily the case that severely wounded soldiers are automatically hors de combat. They are *likely* to fall hors de combat eventually, though this is by no means certain. The law of war only places restrictions on their targeting once they become incapacitated to the point of being unable to engage in any threatening or belligerent actions, not before.

Consider the case of Sergeant Alexander Blackman, a U.K. serviceman sentenced to life in prison for the murder of an injured Taliban soldier in

Afghanistan.[25] A helmet camera recorded the killing, thus removing much of the factual uncertainty that lingers over most battlefield killings. In this case, Blackman was recorded approaching a Taliban insurgent who was severely wounded in an Apache helicopter strike. Blackman quoted Shakespeare—"Shuffle off this mortal coil"—and uttered some derogatory profanity before shooting the insurgent at point blank range with a pistol.[26] He was court-martialed by a British court and convicted of murder. The basis for the conviction was not simply that the Taliban soldier was wounded or that he faced overwhelming firepower from his adversary. Rather, the act of killing him was criminal simply because his injuries from the helicopter attack were so severe that he was incapable of exercising any belligerent actions at all. A minor injury would not have sufficed to render the target's killing illegal. The victim's severe infirmities rendered him hors de combat, making him a "sacred person" in Lieber's memorable phrase. Killing him was no better than killing a prisoner of war. But his protected status stemmed from his incapacitation, not from a more causally attenuated claim about his "defenselessness" in the face of superior force.

III. LEAST HARMFUL MEANS TEST AT THE GENEVA NEGOTIATIONS

Disagreements regarding the appropriate scope of the principle of necessity, and the hors de combat rule, are long-standing. The issue was discussed during the Geneva conferences in 1973–1974. If the negotiators had adopted the least-harmful-means version of necessity and codified it in the Additional Protocols, then Geneva would represent a decisive turning point in the law of war—an explicit shift away from Lieber's conception of necessity and toward a more human-rights-oriented approach to necessity. This would generate an affirmative legal obligation to use non-lethal force during war. However, though the issue was hotly debated, there is no evidence that the least-harmful-means interpretation actually carried the day and made its way into the final text of the Additional Protocols. If anything, the evidence suggests that its deliberate exclusion was indicative of the failure of the adherents of the least-harmful-means interpretation to sway the majority of the conference to their view.

25. Blackman was sentenced to life in prison but was eligible for parole after ten years.

26. The quote comes from Shakespeare's Hamlet.

Recent scholarship regarding the 1973–1974 conferences has substantially improved our understanding of the Additional Protocols. For example, Goodman has enriched our understanding of the 1973 and 1974 conferences that eventually resulted in the adoption of Additional Protocol I and II. Indeed, much of the recent scholarship on the issue has failed to take a sufficiently skeptical eye toward the version of events offered by Hays Parks, one of the leading U.S. experts on the laws of war and a participant in the ICRC process that eventually produced the *Interpretive Guidance on Direct Participation in Hostilities*.[27] Parks's view has always been that the least-harmful-means interpretation of necessity was the brain child of one individual, Jean Pictet, who argued in Geneva that "if a combatant can be put out of action by taking him prisoner, he should not be injured; if he can be put out of action by injury, he should not be killed; and if he can be put out of action by light injury, grave injury should be avoided."[28] Parks concludes that Pictet's statement gained no support from other delegations or scholars, with the exception of its rehabilitation three decades later by Nils Melzer, the ICRC expert responsible for drafting the recent *Interpretive Guidance* that included the controversial Chapter IX that supported a duty to use non-lethal force, including capture instead of killing.[29] Parks's view is that Melzer dusted off Pictet's universally rejected theory and falsely presented it as representative of the Additional Protocol negotiations.[30] This difference in opinion explains Parks's forceful assault against the process and substance of the *Interpretive Guidance*.[31]

27. *See* W. Hays Parks, *Part IX of the ICRC "Direct Participation in Hostilities" Study: No Mandate, No Expertise, and Legally Incorrect*, 42 N.Y.U. J. INT'L L. & POL. 769, 786 (2010).

28. *See* ICRC, WEAPONS THAT MAY CAUSE UNNECESSARY SUFFERING OR HAVE INDISCRIMINATE EFFECTS: REPORT ON THE WORK OF EXPERTS 13, ¶ 23 (1973), *cited in* Goodman, *supra* note 12, at 33.

29. It should be noted that the *Interpretive Guidance* supports a duty to capture but only within the context of civilians directly participating in hostilities, a point that the Guidance makes by citing the Israeli *Targeted Killings* case and *U.K. v. McCann*, a European Court of Human Rights case that did not arise during armed conflict. *See McCann v. United Kingdom*, 21 E.H.R.R. 97 (1995); HCJ 769/02 *Pub. Comm. against Torture in Isr. v. Gov't of Isr.* 53(4) PD 459 [2005]. The scope of the *Interpretive Guidance* was limited to the appropriate use of force against civilians who engage in combatancy, and it said nothing about a generalized duty to capture with regard to enemy combatants per se.

30. *See* Parks, *supra* note 27, at 807.

31. *Id.* at 830 ("The decision by the ICRC to press forward with Section IX against the knowledge, experience, and advice of its experts was not only unfortunate but wrong. As the article shows, it was not a matter of reasonable people disagreeing. It is that the ICRC in Section IX began with a faulty argument for which it failed to provide any, much less credible, supporting information.").

Goodman has surveyed the *travaux preparatoires* from 1973 and 1974 and discovered that Hays Parks is almost certainly wrong.[32] It may very well be the case that Parks overstated his case when he claimed that Pictet was an outlier and that his views were decidedly rejected, or even ignored, at these conferences.[33] At the very least, Goodman has quite rightly demonstrated that there were others besides Pictet who either shared his view or espoused very similar positions.[34] Indeed, Goodman notes that the famous "Pictet" quote appeared in an expert conference report from 1973, and that therefore it is not properly attributed to Pictet personally, but rather to the group of experts as a whole—a group that included, inter alia, Hans Blix of Sweden and Frits Kalshoven.[35] Other experts made statements in support of Pictet's views, and other experts made their own pronouncements that were substantially similar to Pictet's view.[36] It is therefore incorrect to suggest, as Parks does, that Pictet was the *only* individual to discuss and support the least-harmful-means interpretation of necessity. The overemphasis to the point of obsession on Pictet—and his one quote—has no doubt distorted the scholarship of this important topic.[37] Goodman's scholarship is a valuable corrective in this regard.

But one need not claim that Pictet had little support to conclude, as we do, that Pictet was trying to change the law of war but ultimately failed to accomplish this goal at Geneva. First of all, one of these conferences was an expert meeting, and although experts and "publicists" of international law might be a secondary source of law, they are just that—secondary. And the same goes for the analysis of the leading ICRC commentaries, at least some of which were written by the same experts.[38] Of course, it is important to avoid *Commentary*-fetish. They are, by definition, secondary interpretations of existing primary texts. Although sometimes suggestive of scholarly consensus, their status as law is only as persuasive as the quality of the underlying legal analysis. Indeed, it matters little whether the views

32. Goodman, *supra* note 12, at 25.
33. *See* Parks, *supra* note 27, at 815.
34. *See* Goodman, *supra* note 12, at 33.
35. *Id.* at 33–34.
36. *Id.*
37. To be fair to Hays Parks, the quote is also correctly attributable to Pictet personally. Pictet uses the quote in his own publications, and other scholars, including proponents of the least-harmful-means theory, attribute the quote to his writings. *See* Jean Pictet, Development and Principles of International Humanitarian Law 75 (1985) (presenting the same quote), *cited in* Melzer, *supra* note 2, at 288 and *Interpretive Guidance*, *supra* note 29, at 82 n.221.
38. *See, e.g.*, Michael Bothe, Karl Partsch & Waldemar Solf, New Rules for Victims of Armed Conflicts (1982).

of Pictet or any other expert represent a majority or minority view of the field—what matters is whether their views are *correct*. That being said, it is true that the views of the experts are important insofar as they might provide an interpretive gloss on the text of a major international treaty. But in that case, the experts and commentaries are relevant not as scholarly opinion but only as evidence of legislative intent when a given treaty or protocol was being drafted by experts.

Even with this in mind, we do not read the *travaux preparatoires* of the Additional Protocols as supporting a duty to use non-lethal force. Assuming *arguendo* that Pictet had support from several colleagues at the conferences (including Hans Blix of Sweden or even the majority of his expert subgroup), this does not mean that Pictet's view on non-lethal force won the day, or even that his view was then carried over and codified in the Additional Protocol. Indeed, it was not. The *travaux preparatoires* confirm that other experts *disagreed* with Pictet.[39] The official record summarized the opposing view in the following way:

> Other experts held, in contrast, that the element of military necessity in the choice of weapons included, besides their capacity to disable enemy combatants, such other requirements as the destruction or neutralization of enemy materiel, restriction of movement, interdiction of lines of communication, weakening of resources and, last but not least, enhancement of the security of friendly forces.[40]

Strangely, Goodman takes this quote as evidence in *favor* of the least-harmful-means test, on the theory that even Pictet's opponents were using a theoretical rubric that could be encompassed by the least harmful means test. This argument is hard to countenance, though, because the quoted passage is limited to a choice-of-weapons situation—not a generalized claim about the least-harmful-means theory. In fact, the U.S. "support" for this view also makes clear that the point was limited to choice of weapons.[41]

39. Goodman, *supra* note 12, at 36–37 (noting that there were concerns raised at the conference that the least-harmful-means interpretation was not practicable for implementation on the battlefield).

40. ICRC Lucerne Conference Report 9, ¶ 25, *cited in* Goodman, *supra* note 12, at 36 n.170.

41. *See* U.S. State Department, Report of US Delegation to Lucerne Conference 5 ("There was a general agreement that the basic test of whether a weapon causes 'unnecessary suffering' requires comparing the suffering caused with the military utility of the weapon. However, there was considerable divergence as to the relative weight to be given to the military considerations as opposed to what factors should be considered as components of military utility."), *cited in* Goodman, *supra* note 12, at 36 n.170.

A more plausible reading of the passage is that it concerns the prohibition on *unnecessary suffering*, which requires a balancing analysis that considers, among other things, friendly force protection to determine whether the suffering is necessary or not.

Perhaps the Additional Protocol restriction on unnecessary suffering represents a *codification* of the least-harmful-means theory. If the two concepts are two sides of the same coin, then perhaps the least-restrictive-means interpretation of necessity *was* adopted at Geneva. However, we do not share this reading of the "unnecessary suffering" provisions in the Additional Protocols, as the following analysis will explain.

In order to demonstrate that a generalized duty to use non-lethal force was codified in Geneva in 1973–1974, one would need to conclude that Pictet's view carried the day and that it won over in a contest against his adversaries when it came time to draft a final version of the Additional Protocols.[42] But concluding that the majority of the experts who helped negotiate the instrument believed in this interpretation—even if this were true—does not demonstrate that the Additional Protocol codifies a least-harmful-means test. Negotiators of an international treaty hold many views, and only *some* of them manage to make themselves into the actual text of the treaty, or are relevant for interpreting its text. One need not be an ardent textualist to accept this proposition. Indeed, any canon of interpretation must concede that the legal understanding of the drafters is most relevant when it concerns a specific provision of the treaty that has an ambiguous meaning. Then the views of the drafters carry great weight in interpreting the provision.

So where does the least-harmful-means view emerge in the text of Additional Protocol I? One possibility might be Article 35(1), which states that "In any armed conflict, the right of the Parties to the conflict to choose methods or means of warfare is not unlimited." Similarly, Article 35(2) states that "It is prohibited to employ weapons, projectiles and material and methods of warfare of a nature to cause superfluous injury or unnecessary suffering." Goodman, for example, reads Article 35 as codifying Pictet's view: "Pictet's promotion of such a model was consistent with the positions adopted by several important legal authorities. The best reading of Additional Protocol I is that it maintained this understanding in Article 35. Indeed, a mountain of evidence strongly supports that conclusion."[43]

42. *See* Goodman, *supra* note 12, at 41 ("It must be admitted, however, that Protocol I does not expressly codify such an understanding . . . but the Protocol contemplates the LRM model").

43. Goodman, *supra* note 12, at 44.

However, this argument is only valid if the Article 35 prohibition on unnecessary suffering tells us something about a putative prohibition on unnecessary killing or the least-harmful-means theory. But the two are not the same thing, nor does the former provide evidentiary support for the latter.

Article 35 deals with unnecessary suffering, not unnecessary killing, which are two very different ideas. The former deals with cases where soldiers are injured and the extensive nature of their suffering does nothing to improve the military standing of the attacking force. As such, Article 35 and the laws of war prohibit weaponry and methods of attack that simply increase the suffering and pain of enemy soldiers but confer no military advantage for the attacking force. So Article 35 appears to do the exact opposite from what Goodman wants it to do; it gives attacking forces license to quickly and cleanly kill enemy combatants, and prohibits them from inflicting injuries that needlessly prolong those combatants' pain. Kevin Jon Heller makes the nice point that Article 35(2) quite explicitly does *not* use the terms "unnecessary killing" or "unnecessary death"—both of which would have indicated unambiguous support for a duty to capture.[44] In the absence of those terms in current IHL, unnecessary suffering simply refers to pain and suffering related to injury, not death. But we will give further normative reasons to think that some extension of current IHL may be warranted.

Moreover, it is not clear that the leading ICRC *Commentary* on the Additional Protocol supports a duty to use non-lethal force either. As Heller puts the point sharply, "the ICRC views Art. 35(2) as limited to combatants who survive an attack; dead combatants have no feelings."[45] Consider the following passage from the ICRC *Commentary*:

> [T]he rule of proportionality also applies with regard to the combatants, up to a point. The deliberate and pointless extermination of the defending enemy constitutes disproportionate damage as compared with the concrete and direct advantage that the attacker has the right to achieve. It is sufficient to render the adversary "hors de combat." The prohibition of refusing quarter therefore complements the principle expressed in Article 35 "(Basic rules)," paragraph 2, which prohibits methods of warfare of a nature to cause superfluous injury or unnecessary suffering.[46]

44. *See* Kevin Jon Heller, *The Capture-or-Kill Debate #8: Kevin Heller Joins the Conversation*, LAWFARE (Mar. 4, 2013), *available at* http://www.lawfareblog.com/2013/03/the-capture-or-kill-debate-8-kevin-heller-joins-the-conversation/.

45. *Id.*

46. *See, e.g.*, INTERNATIONAL COMMITTEE OF THE RED CROSS, COMMENTARY ON THE ADDITIONAL PROTOCOLS OF 8 JUNE 1977 TO THE GENEVA CONVENTIONS OF 12

First, it is unclear if the *Commentary* has sufficient evidence for applying the *jus in bello* concept of proportionality to combatant deaths—a controversial proposition since *jus in bello* proportionality calculations are traditionally reserved for civilian collateral deaths.[47] Assuming, *arguendo*, that the *Commentary's* interpretation of proportionality is legitimate, it ties the concept of pointless *extermination* that it claims underlies the principle of proportionality with the concept of pointless *suffering* that underlies the Article 35 prohibition of unnecessary suffering caused by injuries. The unifying element of this passage is pointlessness, not death.

Some have argued that the introduction of the technical term *maux superflus* was designed to shift the meaning of unnecessary suffering to a broader conception that includes unnecessary killing as well. Under this argument, the shift to the French legal term was a meaningful—not accidental—attempt to get around the folk conception of unnecessary suffering, which would seem to have little room to encompass painless killings as a form of unnecessary suffering. But with a new French term, or so the argument goes, a broader conception was introduced into the language of the Additional Protocols.

Although it is plausible to think that the introduction of the *maux superflus* term was designed to incorporate a broader conception of unnecessary suffering, there is little support to conclude that it was designed to incorporate unnecessary but painless killings within its ambit.[48] For example, Ingrid Detter Delupis notes that the shift to *maux superflus* was designed to preserve a broader mental element than its English correlate—a change that has nothing to do with unnecessary killings.[49] Under this account, the English phrase "calculated to cause" suggests that the principle is only designed to prohibit situations where the attacking force *intends* to cause unnecessary suffering (by virtue of its choice of weapon). The move toward the French phrase *maux superflus* represented a shift away from

August 1949 (Sandoz et al. eds., 1987), at 477 para. 1598, *cited in* Goodman, *supra* note 12, at 43.

47. It should be noted that a *jus ad bellum* proportionality calculation may be relevant to such situations, although that analysis falls under a different legal domain.

48. For a discussion of the evolution of the rule, see HPCR Manual on International Law Applicable to Air and Missile Warfare, at 63–64 (not mentioning unnecessary killing). *See also* Frits Kalshoven, *The Diplomatic Conference in Armed Conflicts, Geneva, 1974–77*, *in* Reflections on the Law of War: Collected Essays 252 (2007) ("Perhaps not surprisingly, the Conference records contribute precious little to a clear understanding of this phrase."); Su Wei, *Application of Rules Protecting Combatants and Civilians*, *in* 1 Implementation of International Humanitarian Law: Research Papers 382–83 (1989) (Hague conference proceedings "do not show what precisely this principle means").

49. *See* Ingrid Detter Delupis, The Law of War 165 (2000).

this heightened mental state requirement, such that weapons that cause unnecessary suffering, objectively considered, would violate the principle regardless of the intent of the attacking force. This issue has nothing to do with the issue of unnecessary suffering versus unnecessary killings. Other accounts suggest that the switch to the French version was designed to include both physical and psychological suffering, whereas the English version only prohibited the former.[50]

Finally, Article 35(1) does little, by itself, to support the Pictet view, since it merely points to the other more specific prohibitions regulating the use of force, which are then codified in the rest of Article 35. In the end, the fact that the least-harmful-means test was not explicitly included in the Additional Protocol indicates either that there was insufficient support to include it, or *at best*, that a fundamental disagreement was left unresolved in the final text. But the actual result in Additional Protocol I does *not* confirm that the least-harmful-means view was codified in treaty law. In fact, it reads like the exact opposite: Pictet's views, although interesting and even garnering support from other experts and delegations, did not find their way into the Additional Protocol. If they *had*, Article 35 would have been drafted quite differently.[51]

In the end, it is clear that the prohibition against unnecessary suffering made its way into the Additional Protocol, but some scholars read this result backward. The prohibition applies to weapons that cause suffering to their victims, but as to weapons that kill quickly the rule is silent—and this result is telling. Although it may be true that one diplomat referred to this as "false humanitarianism,"[52] it is the only humanitarianism that the Additional Protocol has left us with.

IV. SHOULD *JUS IN BELLO* REQUIRE DISABLING BEFORE KILLING?

Although we believe that the law of war does not currently include a general duty to use non-lethal measures in all circumstances, we are nonetheless sympathetic to the inspiration behind these arguments. As a matter

50. *See* EITAN BARAK, DEADLY METAL RAIN: THE LEGALITY OF FLECHETTE WEAPONS IN INTERNATIONAL LAW 135 (2011).

51. The United States is not a party to Additional Protocol I, and one cannot simply assume that each and every norm of API represents custom or *jus cogens*; some are certainly not. So the Additional Protocol does not necessarily represent the totality of the international law analysis on the duty to capture, though it does represent an appropriate starting point for the analysis, which is the spirit in which Goodman's intervention is presented.

52. *See* Goodman, *supra* note 12, at 34.

of moral theory, combatants have a right to kill in warfare in order to accomplish the justified aim of war: to defeat the enemy as quickly as possible. In situations where killing the enemy does not advance that goal, and disabling the enemy would suffice, then there is seemingly a strong moral argument against the unrestricted killing of enemy combatants.

One can express this point as a balancing between the principles of necessity and humanity—as we have argued in Chapter 7. Although killing is required in order to engage in warfare, the principle of humanity requires that we do it as little as possible, and as painlessly as possible, in order to make warfare as humane as possible. Although this sounds like a contradiction in terms, the entire history of ethical and legal constraints on warfare is based on the idea that this result is possible. War can be tamed and made civilized. That being said, it is also possible that war can be overregulated. If stretched past the breaking point, constrained warfare might be prolonged to such a point that war lingers and produces more suffering. This was Lieber's point when he said that "sharp wars are brief."

The question is where to locate the equilibrium point. It is not entirely clear that the current state of the law gets it absolutely correct. As it stands now, the law is geared toward summary killing of enemy combatants—a state of affairs that may open up a gap between codified law and the demands of morality, which suggest that soldiers should sometimes refrain from killing the enemy when non-lethal measures will suffice. The real question is how to close the gap.

The most obvious strategy for closing the gap between law and morality here is to codify a strict prohibition against killing enemy soldiers when disabling them would be possible. However, conforming to such a standard is difficult since soldiers are notoriously ill-suited to this task. Compliance with the law of war increases when it codifies easy-to-apply, clear, and bright-line rules. International humanitarian law, unlike other areas of the law, requires rules that are easy to apply, both for the soldiers as well as third parties who should be able to view the situation quickly and ascertain whether violations have occurred. In contrast, domestic fields of law with strong ex post fact-finding in domestic courts of law can afford to adopt rules that require great subtlety to their application. But in international humanitarian law, simplicity is a virtue.

Ironically, then, closing the gap between law and morality by codifying a duty to use non-lethal force in war may actually make matters worse, not better. Does this suggest that the law has already gone as far as it can? Not necessarily. It is possible that the gap might be eliminated, or perhaps shortened, by proactively adopting other legal rules that might reduce the number of unnecessarily lethal attacks during battle. This possibility might sound odd, because usually the law acts as a mirror to morality, codifying ethical restrictions in the form of legally binding prohibitions that mirror the content of the underlying moral prohibition. But there is nothing required about this mirroring process, and sometimes the law operationalizes moral considerations in indirect or subtle ways. In fact, we suggest that there are two areas where the law might be strengthened, and that doing so will help close the gap between law and morality without directly codifying a duty to use non-lethal force and disable enemy soldiers instead of killing them.

First, the law could strengthen the prohibition against causing disproportionate damages in the case of civilian collateral damage. The standard rule is that civilian deaths are only permissible if they are incidental to an attack against a legitimate military target, and the civilian deaths are not disproportionate to the anticipated value of the military advantage. In recent years, the U.S. military has significantly increased its arsenal of precision-guided munitions with low-yield explosives. These weapons allow the United States and allies to strike targets with increasingly diminished loss of civilian lives. By strengthening the legal prohibition against causing disproportionate collateral damage, one obvious result is that the number of deaths will diminish in war—not just for civilians but for combatants as well. If attacking forces drop a bomb with a low-yield warhead on a building, as opposed to simply carpet-bombing the entire area, then the number of killings of both civilians and soldiers will be diminished. Some soldiers will be incapacitated instead of simply being incinerated.

The law is already evolving toward stricter standards regarding disproportionate attacks, but that process is not yet complete. The Additional Protocol requires that States take "all feasible" precautions to reduce collateral damage, but some States are not parties to the Additional Protocol. Furthermore, there is a real question over what it means to take "feasible" precautions. Clearly this means that a military commander in the field should use the most discriminating weapons at his disposal. But does the military in general have a duty to deploy better and higher quality weapons to the battlefield as part of the "feasibility" calculation? Many experts on the laws of war writing today think not. Regardless of the state of the law today, we believe that this ought to be the law, and that strengthening the obligation to use more precise weaponry might result in fewer *combatant* deaths in wartime as well.

Second, the law could increase the number of weapons that are specifically prohibited during warfare. In general, international humanitarian law takes a dim view of nuclear weapons that are almost always (though perhaps not necessarily so in some hypothetical situations) indiscriminate in nature. Chemical weapons are also indiscriminate, and a special treaty now prohibits their use, as the recent intervention in Syria brought to the forefront. Almost every State recognizes the ban on land mines, though the United States has so far refused to sign the treaty banning them. There are other prohibited weapons as well, but the point is that the list is very small.

So another way to close the gap between law and morality might be to further restrict the type of weapons that can be used in battle. One good example is cluster munitions, which can cause indiscriminate damage, though some of the world's major powers are not signatories to the convention that restricts them. If the law were to increase the number and type of weapons prohibited during battle, this could decrease the number of killings during battle, and might increase the percentage of soldiers who survive battle.

All of this suggests that the law can be structured to reduce killing in warfare without directly codifying a general requirement to use non-lethal force. Indeed, these indirect methods might accomplish the task more successfully. Part of the reason that the indirect method might work better is because for many years the law of war has worried more about soldiers suffering a lingering death from weapons that hurt them without killing them. These weapons required regulation because they increased suffering without increasing the lethality of the weapon. They produced suffering simply to strike fear in the hearts of enemy soldiers and give them an incentive to desert the army. Given this underlying concern about *painful* killings, law-mindful militaries have worked to produce weapons that cause death instantly. Now, if the law wants to require an attacking force to injure but not kill the enemy, the law needs to go about that effort in an intelligent way. And the best method may be indirectly achieving those results by increasing the strength of other prohibitions in the *jus in bello*.

If one were to codify the restriction internally within *jus in bello*, one way of doing so might be to prohibit unnecessary killings and mandate that attacking forces capture or disable enemy forces (instead of killing them) when they can do so without any additional risk to the enemy force. In recent publications the ICRC has explored this view. For example, the ICRC wrote in one expert meeting report:

> Under the law enforcement paradigm, the presumption is that State agents must arrest persons and not kill them on sight (i.e. "capture rather than kill"). It is only if the arrest is at risk, and if the person poses an imminent threat to life, that the use of lethal force is authorised as a last resort. Under the conduct of hostilities paradigm, the presumption is the reverse. In the ICRC's view, a legitimate target may be killed at any time, unless it is clear that he/she may

> be captured or otherwise rendered hors de combat without additional risk to the operating forces. This is so because "it would defy basic notions of humanity to kill an adversary or to refrain from giving him or her an opportunity to surrender where there manifestly is no necessity for the use of lethal force. This fundamental difference indicates that the determination of the applicable paradigm is crucial."[53]

The key idea here is that the duty to refrain from using lethal force is *conditional*. And moreover, the condition is rather substantial because it pegs the higher duty to refrain from using force to the attacking force's ability to comply with the duty without any further risk to themselves. If fulfillment of the duty (refraining from lethal force) involves burdening the attacking force with additional risk, then the duty disappears. Lethal force becomes lawful again, according to this view.

We are skeptical of this conditional duty in both law and morality—but ironically for opposite reasons. As stated above, we do not believe that customary law or the Additional Protocols currently require attacking forces engaged in an armed conflict to refrain from using lethal force, even if they can do so without additional risk to themselves. Historically and presently, the concept of military necessity permits lethal force against lawful targets, even when non-lethal force might be sufficient as a first resort.

As a matter of morality and an expression of how the law should develop, we are much more sympathetic to the proposal, although in this case we believe the conditional duty is far too weak. That is because the duty is conditional on the attacking force not bearing *any* additional risk when exercising non-lethal force. In almost every practical situation, the deployment of non-lethal force will involve *some* additional risk to the attacking forces, even if it is de minimis, as compared to the risk involved in summary killing. An attacking soldier will always be risking something by using non-lethal force because she will be unsure whether the targets might successfully resist after they survive the attack. Lethal force prevents that resistance and therefore is always less risky. It therefore seems that the conditional duty applies to a null set of cases. It is a hypothetical duty with no real world application. The only situation where non-lethal force is truly riskless is when the target is surrendering, but that situation is already

53. International Committee of the Red Cross, The Use of Force in Armed Conflicts: Interplay between the Conduct of Hostilities and Law Enforcement Paradigms 17 (2013), *citing* ICRC, Interpretive Guidance on the Notion of Direct Participation in Hostilities 82 (2009).

governed by the prohibition against killing soldiers hors de combat who have successfully communicated their surrender.

Our moral inquiry into the nature of necessity suggests that the requirement of "no additional risk" is far too categorical. In order to understand what military necessity permits and demands, we first need to understand how much force protection is legitimate and how much risk it is appropriate for attacking soldiers to bear. Only that inquiry will properly balance the demands of military necessity with the broader principle of humanity. Indeed, it is already the case that the law imposes all sorts of risks on attacking soldiers that are generated by the requirements of following specific prohibitions in *jus in bello*, and the law bases this calculation on the moral conclusion that attacking forces should legitimately bear some risk. Consequently, we conclude that the moral duty to use non-lethal force should apply when the attacking force can fulfill the duty without incurring an *unreasonable* risk to itself. What counts as a reasonable risk? This requires extensive discussion, so we defend a full account of reasonable and unreasonable risks in force protection in Chapter 11. But before we engage in that effort, we must first examine how the lethal versus non-lethal debate plays out in the context of capturing (as opposed to killing) enemy forces. That involves a parallel evaluation of this chapter's investigation into disabling versus killing.

V. NECESSITY AND KILLING FLEEING SOLDIERS

Now consider an example from the first Iraq War. On February 26–27, 1991, Iraqi soldiers mingled with a column of panicked civilians who were trying to leave Mutlai, Kuwait, and escape to Basra, Iraq. Responding to Iraqi small-arms fire, a five-mile-long column of retreating Hammurabi Division forces was attacked. U.S. airpower disabled vehicles at the front and rear of the convoy, thereby creating a seven-mile-long traffic jam. Many Iraqi soldiers and civilians died in the seven hours of subsequent strafing along what became known as "the Highway of Death."[54] General McCaffrey's official report concluded that 34 tanks were destroyed along with 224 trucks, 41 armored personnel carriers, 43 artillery pieces, and

54. *See* Carl Connetta, *The Wages of War: Iraqi Combatant and Noncombatant Fatalities in the 2003 Conflict*, Project on Defense Alternatives Research Monograph # 8, Appendix 2, Oct. 2003, *available at* http//www.comw.org/pda/0310rm8ap2.html#5.TheHighway(s)of.

319 anti-tank guns, and an estimated 400 Iraqi soldiers were killed with no loss of American life.[55]

It seems that it would be hard to defend such killings on the grounds of the self-defense rights of the coalition forces that killed these 400 Iraqi soldiers. Indeed, that there were no coalition casualties is partial support for this proposition. In addition, fleeing soldiers at the time they are fleeing do not pose a threat to anyone. And unlike the soldier taking a bath, fleeing soldiers are unlikely to reverse course in the immediate future. The question is whether or not these soldiers retain some status that allows them to be attacked in this situation.

At approximately 450 B.C., the author of the Apastamba, one of the Dharmasutra law codes of Ancient India, condemned "the killing of those who are fleeing during war."[56] Nonetheless one of the traditional defenses of actions such as the one that occurred on the Highway of Death is that even fleeing soldiers could easily regroup at another place and launch an attack on one's own soldiers. Killing as many enemy soldiers as one can conforms to the traditional view, associated with the Lieber Code, that it is justified to do what is necessary to shorten the war and hence shorten the amount of time where there will be the killing of soldiers. In most cases, the overall saving of life is best accomplished by granting to each combatant the right to kill as many enemy soldiers as possible in the shortest period of time. And in some respects, the Iraq War was probably shortened by the slaughter that took place on the Highway of Death. But notice that many commentators used the term "slaughter," just as we just did, not calling it a normal exercise of pursuing a needed military objective.

Fleeing soldiers, and even soldiers taking a bath or playing games, are especially vulnerable. But it is true that they could pick up their weapons and put on their uniforms and become active threats again. In the case of the naked soldier, our moral intuitions would counsel that it would be in some sense wrong to kill the unarmed and naked "soldier."[57] Although intuitions can sometimes be unreliable guides to what should be done, especially in an all-things-considered context, most people who have been faced with such a case have thought that it was wrong to kill.[58]

Military necessity is best understood normatively when it is qualified by temporal, spatial, and causal restrictions. The ideas of "imminence" and

55. For more on this example, see also MICHAEL NEWTON & LARRY MAY, PROPORTIONALITY IN INTERNATIONAL LAW (2014) (ch. 4).

56. DHARMASUTRA PARALLELS 210 (Patrick Olivelle trans., 2005).

57. *See* LARRY MAY, WAR CRIMES AND JUST WAR (2007) (ch. 5).

58. *See* MICHAEL WALZER, JUST AND UNJUST WARS (2007).

"immediacy" are crucial for a plausible understanding of the principle of military necessity. From a Grotian standpoint, for an action to conform to a plausible view of military necessity there must be no other non-lethal action that would accomplish what the lethal action can accomplish, and where the objective must be a needed military objective at this point in time and in the current circumstances, or temporal and spatial conditions that are very close to the actual ones at the moment. From this perspective, killing fleeing soldiers can not be seen as meeting the necessity requirement.

It is simply too easy to be allowed to say that sometime in the undetermined future this war, like all wars, will be for the best if it is ended more quickly than not. In some cases it may indeed be that a war is likely to be ended quite quickly if lethal means are used when they are not practically necessary at the moment. But, a principle that allowed for whatever is necessary to shorten a war would not be accepted by Just War theorists, or international legal theorists either. It is possible simply to drop an atomic bomb on a region, or poison the water supply of a region, and obliterate all of the enemy soldiers therein. Yet, the use of atomic bombs or poisons are generally seen as illegal or immoral regardless of the fact that they would bring a war to a conclusion very quickly indeed.

On the other hand, we certainly do not want a principle of military necessity that is so strong that it makes it impossible to fight justified wars of any sort. Even many pacifists today (who call themselves contingent pacifists, Just War pacifists, or conditional pacifists) would not argue for ruling out in advance the possibility of justifiably fighting in any war. There seem to be at least some conceivable worlds where it would be justified to kill enemy soldiers for a needed military objective.

The strategy that we will pursue is to try to find a reasonable principle of military necessity that neither permits every action in war, nor rules out every action in war. And we have opted for a normative understanding of necessity, which conforms to most intuitions about what necessity means, and also seems to fit best with philosophical understandings. Of course, there are many points along the spectrum between these two extreme positions of the supporter of *Kriegsraison* and absolute pacifism. We will say more about this point in subsequent sections, but we remain open to precisely where to draw the line along this spectrum. What seems to be clear though is that the line needs to be drawn somewhere in the middle rather than at or near either end of this spectrum.

One other thing to say about the question of how a commander is to ascertain whether it is necessary to kill an enemy soldier, is that the commander need only consider possible worlds that are close to the actual here-and-now world the commander currently occupies. In this respect, we are adapting David Lewis's idea of counterpart analysis.[59] To ascertain if something is possible or necessary in a practical sense, we need only consider possible worlds that resemble our world "closely enough."[60]

In a sense, to talk of what it is possible or necessary to do is to talk of what are vicarious experiences for a given agent here and now. To say that it is possible that Jones regain her fluency in Ancient Greek is to say that it is vicariously so in some world that is close enough to the actual world that she occupies here and now. To say that it is necessary that Smith employ a certain tactic in an armed conflict is to say that it is vicariously so in all worlds that are close enough to the world that he occupies here and now. In the second case, the commander need not think beyond what is conceivable, understood in this way as close enough to the commander's actual world here and now.

This is to say that possible worlds are counterparts to this world insofar as they are vicarious worlds for me as a commander. And to say something practically relevant about what is possible or necessary for me is to say what is vicariously experienced in worlds that are close enough to my actual world here and now. This analysis has not yet said where on the spectrum to locate decisions about what is possible or necessary but it does locate the point along the spectrum as those points that are "close enough" to one's actual world here and now. The "here and now" is a way to make a bit more conceptual sense of the Grotian dictum that what counts as militarily necessary is what satisfies imminence and immediacy.

The tricky questions of course are what "close enough" means and who is to make that decision. Our answer to both questions is to restrict the domain to the commander on the ground and only to stipulate that although it is the commander who is to determine how to understand "close enough," he or she is to do so bound by considerations of what a reasonable commander in this commander's shoes would agree to. The reasonableness constraint is aimed at ruling out utterly arbitrary characterizations of the realm of possible worlds in the assessment of military necessity. Appeal to a reasonableness standard is also supposed not to allow the determination of military necessity to be based completely on the commander's subjective considerations. Reasonableness is at least a partially objective standard. How such a standard will be enforced is not part of the purview of this chapter, but we envision commanders continuing to be under the purview of international criminal standards that would hold open the possibility of sanctions against those commanders who acted in disregard of the principle of military necessity.

59. David K. Lewis, Counterfactuals 39–43 (1973). We adapt Lewis's counterpart analysis so as to make it relevant for practical decision-making, as here we are concerned with practical necessity, not logical or metaphysical necessity.

60. *Id.* at 39. We thank Jeffrey Tlumak for suggesting this line of argument.

CHAPTER 10

The Duty to Capture

The recent growth of the U.S. targeted killing program has prompted no shortage of reaction, but the most trenchant criticism is that the targets should have been captured and prosecuted rather than targeted and killed. These are assassinations, the critics claim. However, finding a duty to attempt capture prior to resorting to lethal force is in some tension with the laws of war, which generally allows the summary killing of enemy combatants.[1] The laws of war protect enemy civilians from attack (under the principle of distinction), but enemy combatants are subject to the summary killing and reciprocal risk implicit in the core principles of *jus in bello*.

Critics have focused on the two most well-known strikes: the Navy Seal raid against bin Laden's compound in Abbottabad,[2] Pakistan, and the drone strike in Yemen that killed the leader of al-Qaeda in the Arabian Peninsula (AQAP), Anwar al-Awlaki.[3] In particular, political critics questioned the Obama administration's decision to use lethal force. Why were the targets not arrested and placed on trial, either before a military commission or a federal district court? Their deaths were ordered by executive branch officials and then personally confirmed by the president. To some, this smacked of an imperial presidency, unencumbered by judicial restraint.[4]

1. *See* Jens David Ohlin, *The Duty to Capture*, 97 MINN. L. REV. 1268 (2013).
2. *See How U.S. Forces Killed Osama Bin Laden*, CNN (May 3, 2011), *available at* http://edition.cnn.com/2011/WORLD/asiapcf/05/02/bin.laden.raid/index.html.
3. *See Al Qaeda's Anwar al-Awlaki Killed in Yemen*, CBS NEWS (Sept. 30, 2011), *available at* http://www.cbsnews.com/2100-202_162-20113732.html.
4. *See, e.g.*, Tom Junod, *The Lethal Presidency of Barack Obama*, ESQUIRE MAG., Aug. 2012, at 100.

Although death by jury—capital punishment—is still the law of the land in the United States, death by executive fiat is presumably unconstitutional under domestic law and illegal under international law.[5] When transposed in legal terms, the criticism implied that the United States had a duty to capture bin Laden and al-Awlaki, or at the very least had a duty to *attempt* capture before resorting to lethal force. Although this "duty to capture" argument is essential to resolving the legality of targeted killings, the legal contours of this duty are often poorly understood, in part because the duty to capture depends entirely on which body of law—and which version of the principle of necessity—applies to the situation at hand.

For example, the U.S. constitutional norms that attach to domestic criminal law situations clearly entail a duty to attempt capture.[6] In cases of individual self-defense, a citizen may only kill his or her attacker if a non-lethal means—say escape, retreat, or capture—is unavailable, impossible, or impracticable.[7] Generally speaking, killings are justified as lawful self-defense only if the action is, in a sense, unavoidable.[8] In practical terms, though, the capture requirement will rarely affect the analysis if the attacker is armed with a weapon. In such situations, it is usually assumed that a private citizen could not capture the attacker without unduly risking his own life. If there is a trade-off to be made between protecting the life of the culpable aggressor and the innocent defender, the law comes down on the side of protecting the life of the defender.[9] Consequently, the duty to capture is paramount in law enforcement situations. Police officers have a duty to attempt capture and are only permitted to use lethal force against a fleeing felon if the police have probable cause to believe that the felon constitutes a danger to the public.[10] In a recent case, for example, the Supreme Court concluded that a fleeing motorist was driving so recklessly that the police were constitutionally entitled to believe that his reckless driving constituted a danger to the public.[11]

The situation is markedly different in international humanitarian law (IHL) and its version of necessity, where there simply is no *codified* duty to

5. *Id.* at 104.
6. *See* Tennessee v. Garner, 471 U.S. 1, 11–12 (1985).
7. *See* People v. Goetz, 497 N.E.2d 41, 47 (N.Y. 1986).
8. *Id.* at 41.
9. For a discussion of the curious relevance of the wrongfulness of the attacker, see generally George P. Fletcher, *Proportionality and the Psychotic Aggressor: A Vignette in Comparative Criminal Theory*, 8 Isr. L. Rev. 367 (1973) (comparing Western jurisdictional approaches to basing a right to self-defense on the reasonableness or proportionality of the response to the provocation).
10. *See Garner*, 471 U.S. at 11 (applying the Fourth Amendment).
11. *See* Scott v. Harris, 550 U.S. 372, 384 (2007).

attempt the capture of enemy combatants, as we argued in the previous chapter.[12] Combatants open themselves up to the reciprocal risk of killing, and the lawfulness of killing combatants is based entirely on their status as combatants.[13] Indeed, to suggest that combatants could only be killed if capture was unfeasible would seem to make the modern practice of aerial bombardment illegal. But despite how it seems, there will be cases where it is either too hard to tell if capture is feasible, or where the risk of capture is too great. We hold the moral view that only limited additional risk is required of commanders and soldiers. They are not morally required to take more than limited risk in order to capture instead of kill enemy combatants. The right not to be unnecessarily killed does not sweep so far, as a moral principle, to render practices such as aerial bombardment unjustified. But there will be cases nonetheless where morally speaking some risk should be taken in capturing so as not to kill the enemy.[14]

The duty to capture certainly applies in the absence of armed conflict when human rights law and civilian policing principles apply. As demonstrated in Chapter 5, the principle of necessity in human rights law requires that the government achieve its objectives with the least harmful means, that is, the minimalist deprivation to the injured party. In some cases that might entail killing, as when a police officer or security agent kills a suspect when there is no other means to neutralize a deadly and imminent threat. However, in most situations capture is at least prima facie available as an option and therefore required by human rights necessity. So almost everything turns on whether the laws of armed conflict or human rights law governs the situation.

Some legal scholars have tried to defend a duty to capture even during armed conflict, concluding that attacking soldiers have a duty to attempt capture and can only use lethal force if capture is not feasible.[15] However, this argument is far more ambitious than a human-rights-oriented argument because it purports to find the duty to capture in the laws of war *simpliciter*, without importing any norms from international human rights

12. *See* Beth Van Schaack, *The Killing of Osama Bin Laden and Anwar Al-Aulaqi: Uncharted Legal Territory*, 14 Y.B. INT'L HUMANITARIAN L. 255, 292 (2012) ("As a matter of established IHL doctrine, there is no express duty to capture privileged combatants in IACs in lieu of killing them in the absence of an unambiguous offer of unconditional surrender.").

13. *Id.* at 292.

14. For a historical analysis of aerial bombardment, see Charles S. Maier, *Targeting the City: Debates and Silences about the Aerial Bombing of World War II*, 87 INT'L REV. RED CROSS 429, 433 (2005).

15. *See* Ryan Goodman, *The Power to Kill or Capture Enemy Combatants*, 24 EURO. J. INT'L L. 819 (2013).

law.[16] This is a strong claim since many commentators writing today assume that the laws of war simply do not impose a duty to capture. Nonetheless, progressive international lawyers have argued that the standard view is wrong. For example, when the International Committee on the Red Cross (ICRC) commissioned an expert report on the notion of civilian "direct participation in hostilities," the final report included a controversial section that referred to the duty to capture under the laws of war.[17] The report generated a scholarly shouting match among the experts that spilled over to the pages of numerous law reviews.[18]

The duty to capture under IHL raises a host of complex philosophical issues, which will be addressed in Sections I and II. For example, IHL does include a duty to respect *surrender*. Both the Geneva Conventions and the underlying chivalric customs of warfare require that an intention to surrender, effectively and unambiguously communicated, ought to be respected by opposing combatants.[19] The rationale for this rule is that surrendered combatants are hors de combat, one step removed from prisoner-of-war (POW) status only because they have not yet been received into custody.[20]

16. *See* Ryan Goodman, *A Surreply to the Second Critique by Corn, Blank, Jenks, and Jensen*, LAWFARE (Mar. 4, 2013), *available at* http://www.lawfareblog.com/2013/03/the-capture-or-kill-debate-7-goodman-responds/ (emphasizing that his argument does not rely on human rights analysis).

17. *See* INTERNATIONAL COMMITTEE OF THE RED CROSS, INTERPRETIVE GUIDANCE ON THE NOTION OF DIRECT PARTICIPATION IN HOSTILITIES UNDER INTERNATIONAL HUMANITARIAN LAW (2009) [hereafter cited as *ICRC Interpretive Guidance*].

18. *Compare* W. Hays Parks, *Part IX of the ICRC "Direct Participation in Hostilities" Study: No Mandate, No Expertise, and Legally Incorrect*, N.Y.U. J. INT'L L. & POL. 769, 805 (2010), *with* Nils Melzer, *Keeping the Balance between Military Necessity and Humanity: A Response to Four Critiques of the ICRC's Interpretive Guidance on the Notion of Direct Participation in Hostilities*, 42 N.Y.U. J. INT'L L. & POL. 831 (2010).

19. *See* Rome Statute of the International Criminal Court art. 8(2)(b)(xii), July 17, 1998, 2187 U.N.T.S. 90 [hereinafter Rome Statute] (giving jurisdiction of war crimes to the International Criminal Court, including the refusal to give quarter); Protocol Additional to the Geneva Conventions of 12 August 1949, and Relating to the Protection of Victims of International Armed Conflicts art. 41, June 8, 1977, 1125 U.N.T.S. 3 [hereinafter Additional Protocol I] (protecting those who express an intention to surrender or are incapacitated from attack); Geneva Convention Relative to the Treatment of Prisoners of War art. 3, Aug. 12, 1949, 6 U.S.T. 3316, 75 U.N.T.S. 135 [hereinafter Geneva Conventions] (regulating treatment of "[p]ersons taking no active part in the hostilities, including members of armed forces who have laid down their arms . . . ."); Francis Lieber, Instructions for the Government of Armies of the United States in the Field, General Order No. 100, art. 60 (Apr. 24, 1863) [hereinafter Lieber Code] ("No body of troops has the right to declare that it will not give, and therefore will not expect, quarter . . . .").

20. *See, e.g.*, Geneva Conventions, *supra* note 19, art. 3, 75 U.N.T.S. at 136–38 (regulating the treatment of all combatants hors de combat [outside the fight], whether due to sickness or surrender).

But the duty to respect surrender should not be confused with an alleged duty to offer the enemy the *opportunity* to surrender, nor is there a duty to attempt a capture prior to attempting killing. The requirement to announce one's presence and demand surrender—as the police do—is a creature of the domestic law-enforcement paradigm, not the laws of war as they currently read.

Section III will consider the possibility of a constitutional overlay to the analysis. The source of the overlay might attach to the conduct because the Constitution follows the flag, so to speak,[21] or more likely, constitutional rights attach because the target is an American citizen such as al-Awlaki. But the overlay is arguably inconsistent with historical practice, since citizen combatants during World War II—fighting for the Nazi Army—were not granted a special right to be captured, and were targeted in a similar manner to their German comrades.[22] Moreover, confederate soldiers during the Civil War, all American citizens, were not owed a duty to capture either.[23] Consequently, predicating the *constitutional* duty to capture on the American citizenship of the target requires the marshaling of an additional argument.

In such a case, either the Fourth or Fifth Amendments might require the U.S. government to afford the target with a chance to contest the executive branch's determination of his status before a neutral decision-maker. Unfortunately, the best Supreme Court precedents to establish this constitutional overlay all take place either within the domestic law-enforcement context or, if they are wartime cases, within the detention context, not targeting.[24] Deep problems emerge when one analogizes from one context to the other, particularly because the U.S. Supreme Court cases on detention all refer back to IHL in order to establish the parameters of the constitutional protection regarding detention.[25]

This chapter suggests that the analysis inevitably swings back full circle to the original issue: whether domestic or wartime principles of

21. *See* Kal Raustiala, Does the Constitution Follow the Flag?: The Evolution of Territoriality in American Law 241–47 (2009) (analyzing the way geography and territoriality affect the scope of the American legal system).

22. *See* Michael A. Newton, *Exceptional Engagement: Protocol I and a World United against Terrorism*, 45 Tex. Int'l L.J. 323, 338 (2009).

23. *See* Andrew Kent, *Federal Courts, Practice and Procedure: The Constitution and the Laws of War during the Civil War*, 85 Notre Dame L. Rev. 1839, 1868 (2010).

24. *Compare* Tennessee v. Garner, 471 U.S. 1, 1 (1985) (discussing the constitutionality of a Tennessee statute granting officers the right to use deadly force), *with* Hamdi v. Rumsfeld, 542 U.S. 507, 539–40 (2004) (granting U.S. citizen enemy combatants the right of habeas corpus to challenge their detention).

25. *See, e.g.*, *Hamdi*, 542 U.S. at 507 (citing the Geneva Conventions).

necessity apply. The answer lies in determining whether the U.S. government, when targeting its own citizen, is acting as a sovereign or acting as a belligerent. If the former, then the normative constraints of human rights law certainly apply; if the latter, then the regulations of IHL apply. Does the citizen-belligerent stop being a citizen-subject when he or she takes up arms against his own government? This was certainly the case when the United States fought the Civil War against Confederate soldiers. Presumably, though, there is something deeply distressing about concluding that the U.S. government might consider a citizen-belligerent targetable wherever that person is located, perhaps even within the continental United States. The limiting principle that prevents this universal extension of citizen-belligerency is whether the sovereign has complete control over the territory in question. In such instances, the sovereign is indeed acting as a sovereign with regard to its subject and is constrained by the IHRL principle of necessity. In areas where the sovereign is not in complete territorial control—is not *sovereign* in a sense—then the sovereign meets even the citizen (and the armed group to which he belongs) on the battlefield as a coequal belligerent, and their interactions are governed by IHL's version of necessity.

The chapter concludes, in Section IV, with our examination of how the law should develop in the future. We conclude that critics rightly criticize targeted killing operations when they fall outside the scope of an armed conflict. The criticisms might also be valid when an armed conflict exists but the United States was unjustified in its decision to wage the armed conflict. In that case, however, the complaint is really about *jus ad bellum* necessity, not *jus in bello* necessity. Finally, we ask whether the law could adopt a rule against unnecessary killing that would require a duty to attempt capture in war, and we inquire under what conditions and contexts that rule could be applied.

I. IS CAPTURE REQUIRED BY *JUS IN BELLO* NECESSITY?

Generally speaking, the IHL principle of military necessity does not require a duty to capture. Military necessity, by itself, never meant what it means in the human rights context: the only available option. Rather, as far back as Francis Lieber, the principle of military necessity required that the attack confer a bona fide military advantage, and necessity considerations were to be balanced against the competing principle of humanity. But the basic idea is that military necessity provided minimal constraints within the IHL universe, as opposed to say human rights law where the principle of necessity has traditionally provided a very substantial constraint on government action.

When the ICRC issued its *Interpretive Guidance on the Notion of Direct Participation in Hostilities*, it recognized a qualitative duty to capture in Chapter IX of its report, though it purported to do so solely on the basis of IHL.[26] A central element of its argument stemmed from the nature of IHL's withdrawal of protection from attack for civilians directly participating in hostilities.[27] Suggesting that this withdrawal of protection did not make such civilians always targetable, the report was a bit vague as to whether this placed civilians directly participating in hostilities in a liminal category between combatants and protected civilians, or whether the asserted restrictions regarding attacks against civilians directly participating in hostilities were applicable to attacks against combatants as well.[28]

The basis for the view that civilians directly participating in hostilities could not be targeted without restriction stemmed from its understanding of the principle of military necessity—one of the key building blocks of IHL.[29] The report correctly identified the principle as permitting "only that degree and kind of force, not otherwise prohibited by the law of armed conflict, that is required in order to achieve the legitimate purpose of the conflict, namely the complete or partial submission of the enemy at the earliest possible moment with the minimum expenditure of life and resources."[30] The question is how one moves from this general principle to the conclusion that a duty to capture is required.[31] The only way to answer this question is to provide an account of what the phrase "military necessity"

26. *See* NILS MELZER, INT'L COMM. OF THE RED CROSS, INTERPRETIVE GUIDANCE ON THE NOTION OF DIRECT PARTICIPATION IN HOSTILITIES UNDER INTERNATIONAL HUMANITARIAN LAW 82 (2009) [hereinafter ICRC INTERPRETIVE GUIDANCE] ("In such situations, the principles of military necessity and of humanity play an important role in determining the kind and degree of permissible force against legitimate military targets.").

27. *Id.* at 70.

28. *Id.*

29. *Id.* at 78; *see also* William Gerald Downey, Jr., *The Law of War and Military Necessity*, 47 AM. J. INT'L L. 251, 252 (1953) ("One of the most important concepts in the law of war is that of military necessity, but there is no concept more elusive.").

30. ICRC INTERPRETIVE GUIDANCE, *supra* note 26, at 79 (quoting UNITED KINGDOM: MINISTRY OF DEFENCE, THE MANUAL OF THE LAW OF ARMED CONFLICT § 2.2 (2004)).

31. *Compare* Robert Chesney, *Who May Be Killed? Anwar al-Awlaki as a Case Study in the International Legal Regulation of Lethal Force*, 13 Y.B. INT'L HUMANITARIAN L. 3, 46 (2010) (correctly concluding that the ICRC's position, and Melzer's argument, rests almost exclusively on the ICRC's interpretation of the principle of necessity and its logical culmination in the principle of humanity), *with* MELZER, *supra* note 26, at 290–91 (referring to the concept of *maux superflus* as a preexisting principle that supports his interpretation of the principle of necessity).

means in its *concrete application,* and what the principle permits and demands from attacking forces.

To answer this question, two issues need to be addressed. The first is whether civilians directly participating in hostilities represent a special case that requires a duty to capture. The second is whether IHL's core distinction between combatants and civilians is a crude and obsolete proxy that ought to be abandoned. If the distinction is morally incoherent, then the IHL rule that permits summary killing of enemy combatants (without requiring an attempt to capture first) is morally incoherent as well.

Perhaps the calculation required by military necessity is different when dealing with civilians who are subject to attack because they are directly participating in hostilities. Under this argument, the duty to attempt capture would not apply to regular soldiers, but would apply to civilians subject to attack. This would lead to three categories for purposes of targeting: (1) regular soldiers who can be attacked at any time; (2) innocent civilians who can never be directly attacked, but may suffer collateral consequences just as long as they are not disproportionate to the military objective; and, in between these two categories, (3) civilians directly participating in hostilities who may be captured and only killed if capture is impossible.

Under IHL, the warrant for recognizing this third, liminal category is Additional Protocol I (API). Article 57(2) of API requires the taking of "all feasible precautions in the choice of means and methods of attack with a view to avoiding, and in any event to minimizing, incidental loss of civilian life, injury to civilians and damage to civilian objects."[32] Furthermore, Article 57(3) requires that "[w]hen a choice is possible between several military objectives for obtaining a similar military advantage, the objective to be selected shall be that the attack on which may be expected to cause the least danger to civilian lives and to civilian objects."[33] Finally, Article 52 provides that civilian objects shall not be the object of attack, and that "military objectives are limited to those objects which by their nature, location, purpose or use make an effective contribution to military action and whose total or partial destruction, capture or neutralization, in the circumstances ruling at the time, offers a definite military advantage."[34]

32. Additional Protocol I, *supra* note 19, art. 57(2), 1125 U.N.T.S. at 29.

33. *Id.* art. 57(3), 1125 U.N.T.S. at 29.

34. *Id.* art. 52, 1125 U.N.T.S. at 27. Melzer concludes that Article 52 embodies Pictet's "use of force continuum," which requires that modest levels of force be contemplated before resorting to lethal force. *See* MELZER, *supra* note 26, at 289 ("If we can put a soldier out of action by capturing him, we should not wound him; if we can obtain the same result by wounding him, we must not kill him. If there are two means to achieve the same military advantage, we must choose the one which causes the lesser evil." (quoting

When combined together, these provisions might be interpreted to require attacking forces to take greater precautions to prevent harm to civilians directly participating in hostilities, killing them only if capture is impossible.

This view is problematic for several reasons.[35] It misconstrues API, which is designed to generally limit the suffering of innocent civilians, and specifically to augment the pre-Additional Protocol prohibition against causing disproportionate damage, with the added requirement to take all feasible precautions to reduce civilian damage, even below the threshold of mere proportionality. To reread these protections so as to require the capture of civilians directly participating in hostilities has perverse consequences. It would essentially discourage individuals from complying with the laws of war, because individuals who want to fight but refuse to don a uniform or carry arms openly would gain protections that far outstrip the protections that regular combatants are afforded. They would be entitled to be treated as civilians for purposes of API calculations with regard to "feasible precautions," whereas regular combatants complying with the laws of war would still be subject to wholesale attack. That cannot be the purpose of API.

The correct view is to think of civilians directly participating in hostilities as functionally equivalent to regular combatants for purposes of targeting; they are subject to the same reciprocal risk of killing by virtue of their self-insertion into the armed conflict. No special duty to capture applies to them, because in a sense they are civilians in name only; they become

JEAN PICTET, DEVELOPMENT AND PRINCIPLES OF INTERNATIONAL HUMANITARIAN LAW 75–76 (1985)). The same Pictet quote is also cited in the ICRC INTERPRETIVE GUIDANCE, *supra* note 26, at 82 n.221, for the ICRC's conclusion that "the principles of military necessity and of humanity play an important role in determining the kind and degree of permissible force against legitimate military targets." *Id.* at 84. Hays Parks mocks the ICRC's description of the Pictet quote as "famous," and concludes that it is neither famous nor correct, but mere *lex ferenda*, and contrary to both state practice and *opinio juris*. *See* Parks, *supra* note 18, at 786 n.59, 815 n.125. Parks also argues that Article 52 of API deals with civilian "objects," not civilian personnel or civilians proper. *See id.* at 796; *see also* Gabriella Blum, *The Dispensable Lives of Soldiers*, 2 J. LEGAL ANALYSIS 69, 127–30 (2010) (noting difference standards for civilian personnel and civilian objects); *but see* Ryan Goodman, *The Power to Kill or Capture Enemy Combatants*, 24 EURO. J. INT'L L. 819, 842 (2013) (concluding that Pictet's views were supported at the relevant meetings by several scholars including Hans Blix). However, Goodman points to no specific provision of the Additional Protocol that codified this view other than the Article 35 prohibition against "superfluous injury or unnecessary suffering," a phrase that makes no reference to killing per se. *See* Kevin Jon Heller, *A Response to Goodman about the (Supposed) Duty to Capture*, OPINIO JURIS (Mar. 13, 2013), *available at* http://opiniojuris.org/2013/03/13/a-response-to-goodman-about-the-supposed-duty-to-capture/.

35. *See, e.g.*, Marko Milanović, *Norm Conflicts, International Humanitarian Law, and Human Rights Law*, *in* INTERNATIONAL HUMANITARIAN LAW AND INTERNATIONAL HUMAN RIGHTS LAW 121 n.108 (Orna Ben-Naftali ed., 2011) (calling this view "unconvincing").

functional combatants. The only difference between civilians directly participating in hostilities and regular combatants is that the former category includes a transitory and temporal element, whereas the latter does not. Regular combatants are *always* subject to killing, whereas civilians directly participating in hostilities are only targetable "during such time" as they participate in hostilities; but this fact alone does not entail that their targeting status demands that they be treated like innocent civilians.[36]

II. ARE DIFFERENT RULES FOR CIVILIANS AND COMBATANTS MORALLY LEGITIMATE?

The current IHL rules, and in particular the interplay between the principles of distinction and necessity, are subject to criticism for being both under- and overinclusive.[37] The concept of distinction requires that civilians be protected whereas the concept of military necessity allows all combatants to be targeted and killed.[38] On a moral level, this scheme assumes that the categories of civilian and combatant track the morally relevant distinctions, such as threat level and dangerousness, such that combatants are dangerous and civilians are not. But these legal categories are crude proxies at best—usually matching the underlying moral reality but at the margins departing from them substantially. In that vein, it is possible to consider a combatant who is neither threatening nor dangerous, either because he is asleep or because he works at a noncombat function such as cooking or cleaning (because he is a private and also behind the front lines). As a corollary, consider the well-known example of the civilian working in the munitions factory.[39] The first is arguably not a threat but still targetable anyway; the second is making a significant contribution to the war effort

36. The one exception is civilians who exercise a continuous combat function in a nonstate armed group, who are targetable at any time in analogous fashion to regular combatants. *See* ICRC Interpretive Guidance, *supra* note 26, at 33–34.

37. Criticisms in this vein are found in a number of materials. *See* Larry May, War Crimes and Just War 112–17 (2007) (critiquing value of social categories to guide decision-making during war); Blum, *supra* note 34, at 138–39 (summarizing the status-based distinction criticism).

38. *See* Blum, *supra* note 34, at 127–30 (summarizing the effect of distinction on civilians and combatants).

39. *See id.* at 139; *cf.* Int'l Comm. of the Red Cross, Presentation: The Law of Armed Conflict: Conduct of Operations 6-3 (2002), *available at* http://www.icrc.org/eng/assets/files/other/law3_final.pdf (concluding that civilians "run a risk" by working in a munitions factory, though apparently concluding that the munitions are directly targetable whereas the civilian employees are collateral damage subject to the rule of proportionality).

but not targetable (depending on one's definition of "participating" in hostilities). Do these counterexamples suggest that the key legal categories of IHL—civilians and combatants—are antiquated or obsolete?[40]

Proxies are everywhere in the law, and the mere existence of a proxy is not by itself a sufficient argument for its elimination. Proxies provide clarity and systematicity, and promote publicity—all essential qualities for a field such as IHL that must be self-administered and self-enforced by the parties of an armed conflict. The question is whether the benefits of the proxy in this case outweigh its lack of precision at the margins; in other words, whether the IHL distinction between combatants and civilians is a crude proxy or a successful one. There are several points to be made here. First, the alleged under-inclusiveness of the rule is contestable, since there is a colorable argument that the munitions worker and the bomb maker (of say al-Qaeda) are directly participating in hostilities by virtue of their craftsmanship in the tools of warfare.[41] This leaves the problem of overinclusiveness stemming from the sleeping soldier or the proverbial army cook. In both situations, the argument for their lack of dangerousness stems entirely from a temporal dimension; the individuals may be dangerous in past or future (with different assignments) but they are not dangerous *right now*, and thus their targeting is morally problematic.

The key to the objection is really status-based targeting itself, as opposed to conduct-based targeting, which will more closely track the temporal element of dangerousness. So the central question is thought to be: Is the combatant doing anything at this moment in time that makes him dangerous enough to be targeted?

Once the real basis of this objection is revealed, it is clear why it must be rejected. The very notion of status-based targeting is carefully woven into the very fabric of existing IHL because armed conflict is a collective enterprise. Conduct-based targeting is entirely appropriate for the law of *individual* self-defense, where both private citizens and police exercising lawful force must demonstrate that the target posed an immediate risk based on his or her conduct.[42] But armed conflict is a collective endeavor between groups, whether nation-states or nonstate actors. During wartime,

40. For this reason, Van Schaack views these arguments as revisionist and not sounding in *lex lata*. Van Schaack, *supra* note 12, at 292–93.

41. For a discussion of the targetability of bomb-makers, see Amos Guiora, *The Importance of Criteria-Based Reasoning in Targeted Killing Decisions*, *in* TARGETED KILLINGS: LAW & MORALITY IN AN ASYMMETRICAL WORLD 303, 322–24 (Claire Finkelstein, Jens David Ohlin & Andrew Altman eds., 2012).

42. Both the legal system and moral philosophy require the same question in this scenario.

individuals are placed at war simply by virtue of their citizenship or membership in one of the warring parties, making each of them responsible for the actions of the whole.[43] This is the essence of Lieber's phrase that "men live in political, continuous societies, forming organized units, called states or nations, whose constituents bear, enjoy, suffer, advance and retrograde together, in peace and in war."[44] To transform IHL targeting to an entirely conduct-based system is to cling to the fiction that we can pursue war as atomic individuals.

For moral individualists, this fiction would be a virtue.[45] Moral individualists deny that collectives are relevant during wartime; they claim that the same rules of self-defense ought to apply in war as they do in peacetime.[46] One aspect of moral individualism is that killing an enemy soldier depends on whether the enemy is pursuing a just war or not.[47] Under this theory, killing a Nazi soldier would have been morally permissible because the Nazi Army was engaged in genocide and aggression, whereas killing an American soldier would have been morally wrong because the Americans were engaged in a just cause in fighting the Nazis. This philosophical view yields completely different answers from the law of war and its canonical separation of *jus ad bellum* and *jus in bello*.[48] For the most ambitious moral individualists, this disconnect is reason enough to completely re-engineer the law of war and transform its cardinal principles, unless instrumental reasons prevent it.[49]

A full-blown response on moral individualism is beyond the scope of this chapter.[50] The modest point here is simply to connect the proposal to

43. For a discussion of this issue, see Eyal Benvenisti, *Human Dignity in Combat: The Duty to Spare Enemy Civilians*, 39 ISR. L. REV. 81, 86–88 (2006).

44. Lieber Code, *supra* note 19, art. 20.

45. *See generally* Jeff McMahan, *Collectivist Defenses of the Moral Equality of Combatants*, 6 J. MILITARY ETHICS 50 (2007) (espousing a more individualist perspective and arguing that the collectivist understanding of war fails).

46. *See, e.g.*, JEFF MCMAHAN, KILLING IN WAR 84, 156 (2009).

47. *See, e.g., id.* at 36–37.

48. Incidentally, though the legal separation of *in bello* and *ad bellum* is canonical, scholars have recently asserted that the terms are of modern vintage. *See* Marko Milanović & Vidan Hadzi-Vidanovic, *A Taxonomy of Armed Conflict*, in RESEARCH HANDBOOK ON INTERNATIONAL CONFLICT AND SECURITY LAW 256 (Nigel White & Christian Henderson eds., 2013); Robert Kolb, *Origin of the Twin Terms* Jus ad Bellum/Jus in Bello, 79 INT'L REV. RED CROSS 553, 553–55 (1997).

49. *See* MCMAHAN, *supra* note 46, at 2–7.

50. For a defense of moral collectivism, see GEORGE P. FLETCHER & JENS DAVID OHLIN, DEFENDING HUMANITY 177–214 (2008); George P. Fletcher, *The Storrs Lectures: Liberals and Romantics at War: The Problem of Collective Guilt*, 111 YALE L.J. 1499, 1513–26 (2002); *cf.* Christopher Kutz, *The Difference Uniforms Make: Collective Violence in Criminal Law and War*, 33 PHIL. & PUB. AFF. 148, 153–80 (2005) (examining the themes of "collective inculpation and collective exculpation" and their impact in

move IHL toward conduct-based targeting with the philosophical position of moral individualism. The argument behind conduct-based revisionism in targeting is that it produces more *accurate* results regarding targeting (as opposed to overinclusive results). Accuracy, however, is pegged to the dangerousness of the *individual*, a standard that reigns in individual self-defense cases in domestic criminal law. This assumes that targeting is inappropriate because an individual belongs to an organized group (whether a state or a nonstate group) that collectively threatens another state that must respond with collective force of its own.[51]

One might object that collectivism of this sort entails total wars fought against civilian populations just as much as against combatants, since civilians are members of the nation that ought to "advance and retrograde" together, as Lieber says.[52] If this disreputable result is the direct consequence of collectivism, then collectivism must be wrong. But the objection proves too much. Theorists have long recognized that civilians are not morally innocent, and ought to share in the burdens of the war effort—especially unjust ones—leading to suggestions for war reparations and other strategies to make civilian populations less likely to support or tolerate domestic governments controlled by warmongers.[53] Furthermore, IHL long ago developed conventions to limit the relevant membership for purposes of targeting, so that membership in the nation is insufficient, but membership in the armed forces is sufficient to make an individual a lawful target.[54] This convention recognizes the inherent collectivism of armed conflict—that combatants represent a threat by virtue of their participation in a collective effort—by crafting a rule for targeting that all sides in the conflict can and will abide by.

There might be additional arguments that could be deployed in favor of a normative position that the law of war ought to recognize a duty to capture enemy soldiers.[55] Many of these normative arguments stem from

the treatment of irregular, non-uniformed combatants); Seth Lazar, *Necessity in Self-Defense and War*, 40 PHIL. & PUB. AFF. 3, 23–29 (2012).

51. Another alternative that by design attempts to split the difference between collectivism and individualism on such issues looks to the "group-based" character of individual actions as of great importance. In this view, collectives just are individuals in relations, but the relations themselves cannot be reduced to features of individuals. *See* LARRY MAY, THE MORALITY OF GROUPS (1987) (ch. 1).

52. Lieber Code, *supra* note 19, art 20.

53. *See, e.g.*, MCMAHAN, *supra* note 46, at 203–35; Jeff McMahan, *The Just Distribution of Harm between Combatants and Noncombatants*, 38 PHIL. & PUB. AFF. 342, 345 n.3 (2010).

54. *See* Christopher Greenwood, *Historical Development and Legal Basis*, *in* THE HANDBOOK OF INTERNATIONAL HUMANITARIAN LAW 1, 19-21 (Dieter Fleck ed., 2008).

55. *See* Blum, *supra* note 34, at 160–63.

philosophical arguments regarding the moral value of human lives even in the case of combatants. Perhaps it is wrong for the law of war to be so cavalier regarding the lives of combatants, especially in states that continue to use a draft system and so the line between "civilian" and "combatant" is only a few months in basic training. Such arguments might represent the future trajectory of the philosophy of warfare, and we will consider them in greater detail in the final section of this chapter. Suffice it to say here that the law of war has generally been conservative in its embrace of vanguard moral theories that require revision of the laws of war. Although change has come in some areas—outlawing reprisals is a classic example—the law of war only adopts them if there is a reasonable chance that states will actually follow these new prescriptions. Although human rights law has the luxury of codifying aspirational norms couched in universalistic terms, the law of war is in danger of collapsing if the content of the law runs too far ahead of the actual practice of belligerents. Therefore, the space between *lex lata* and *lex ferenda* is zealously guarded in IHL in a way that it is not in IHRL.

III. CAPTURE AS A REQUIREMENT OF CONSTITUTIONAL NECESSITY

We now turn to the final *legal* avenue that might ground a duty to capture in cases of targeted killings. In situations where the target is an American citizen, such as Anwar al-Awlaki, there is at least a colorable legal argument that the U.S. Constitution imposes additional requirements that surpass the applicable standards in cases where noncitizens are targeted.[56] Although the U.S. Constitution does not include a codified right to life—as the European Convention and many European domestic constitutions

56. Before the Obama administration launched its fatal drone strike against al-Awlaki, the Justice Department's Office of Legal Counsel reportedly drafted memoranda to the attorney general concluding that such a strike would be lawful. The memoranda have not been publicly released but a summary document was leaked in February 2012. *See* Dep't of Justice, Lawfulness of a Lethal Operation Directed Against a U.S. Citizen Who Is a Senior Operational Leaders of Al-Qa'ida or an Associated Force (2011), *available at* http://www.fas.org/irp/eprint/doj-lethal.pdf [hereinafter DOJ White Paper]. The analysis in the white paper suggests that the U.S. Constitution imposes additional constraints on the government's actions, but that the strike was permissible if capture was deemed unfeasible. *See also* Peter Finn, *In Secret Memo, Justice Department Sanctioned Strike,* Wash. Post, Oct. 1, 2011, at A9; Charlie Savage, *Secret U.S. Memo Made Legal Case to Kill a Citizen*, N.Y. Times, Oct. 9, 2011, at A1; *see also* First Amendment Coal. v. U.S. Dep't of Justice, 2012 WL 3027460, at *3–*4 (N.D. Cal. July 24, 2012) (litigation seeking release of memorandum).

do—it does include the right to due process.[57] The due-process rights afforded to U.S. citizens might provide a constitutional overlay that requires something more than summary killing—say an opportunity to contest one's status as a targeted individual or, at the very least, the opportunity to be captured and arrested and subject to the judicial process prior to the executive branch's last resort of summary killing by drone warfare.[58]

However, the precedents underlying a *constitutional* duty to capture provide less guidance than one might hope, because they set the standard for the use of lethal force by law enforcement personnel in domestic police operations. *Tennessee v. Garner* announced the modern Fourth Amendment standard that allows the police to use lethal force, instead of arrest, only when the police reasonably believe that such force is necessary to stop the fleeing felon whose conduct poses an immediate threat to the officer or others.[59] *Garner* rightly rejected—as a crude and ineffective proxy—the old common-law rule that prohibited deadly force against fleeing misdemeanants but allowed it for all felons, regardless of the level of danger they posed to the officer or the public.[60] Major Supreme Court cases applying *Garner* to different facts, such as *Scott v. Harris*,[61] all take place within the domestic context; none of them involve operations conducted by the U.S. military or the CIA, or implicate the relationship between the domestic constitutional norms and the requirements of IHL.[62]

57. U.S. CONST. amend. V.

58. *See* Al-Aulaqi v. Obama, 727 F. Supp. 2d 1, 35 (D.D.C. 2010) (suit alleging deprivation of Fifth Amendment right not to be deprived of law without due process of law dismissed because father lacked standing). In a controversial holding, the court concluded that the father lacked standing because al-Aulaqi "can access the U.S. judicial system by presenting himself in a peaceful manner . . . the same choice presented to all U.S. citizens." *Id.* at 18. In essence, the court placed the duty on the target to surrender if he wanted to trigger the judicial process, rather than place the duty on the government.

59. *See* 471 U.S. 1, 2 (1985); *see also* DOJ White Paper, *supra* note 56, at 9 (concluding that the Fourth Amendment requires balancing individual and governmental interests).

60. *See* Tennessee v. Garner, 471 U.S. 1, 11–12 (1985).

61. *See* Scott v. Harris, 550 U.S. 372, 383–84 (2007) (applying the *Garner* formulation to car chases); *see also* DOJ White Paper, *supra* note 56, at 9 (noting that Fourth Amendment test is "situation-dependent").

62. In fact, the Justice Department white paper concludes that "there exists no appropriate judicial forum to evaluate these constitutional considerations." *See* DOJ White Paper, *supra* note 56, at 10. Although the white paper appears to concede that these constitutional considerations are applicable extraterritorially, it is possible that the analysis was designed as an alternative argument designed to win the day assuming *arguendo* that the Fourth of Fifth Amendments applied. *Id.* at 5 ("The Department assumes that the rights afforded by the Fifth Amendment's Due Process Clause, as well as the Fourth Amendment, attach to a U.S. citizen even while he is abroad.").

Nor do the other standard precedents on extraterritorial application of the Constitution shed any light on the issue or represent facts even remotely similar to targeting situations. *Reid v. Covert*,[63] a standard citation for the proposition that the Constitution follows the flag,[64] involved a murder committed on a U.S. military installation overseas—an environment where the federal government was already exercising control.[65] The holding simply asserted that no treaty or executive agreement could allow the federal government to circumvent the Bill of Rights.[66] The *Insular Cases* involved even *more* control than was exercised in *Reid v. Covert*, since the federal government governed the territories in question though they were not incorporated as states.[67] *Boumediene v. Bush* applied the Constitution extraterritorially, but only in a very weak sense since the Court concluded that the federal government had de facto control over Guantanamo Bay.[68] In cases where the United States had little or no territorial control, the decisions go in the opposite direction.[69] One might rely on Justice Harlan's famous concurring dictum in *Reid v. Covert* that the Fifth Amendment did not always apply to Americans overseas when it would be anomalous and impracticable, which some commentators might seize upon as a hinge to suggest that constitutionally protected targeting decisions during war would be analogous and impracticable.[70] But one need not rely on or appeal to such pragmatics. The simpler answer is that all of the precedents applying the Constitution extraterritorially have taken place outside of armed conflict, or in situations in which the United States exercised control

63. 354 U.S. 1 (1957).

64. *See* Raustiala, *supra* note 21, at 150 (noting one theory out of *Reid* was "that the Constitution applied to the United States government wherever and whenever it acted").

65. *Reid*, 354 U.S. at 3.

66. *Id.* at 6 ("When the Government reaches out to punish a citizen who is abroad, the shield which the Bill of Rights and other parts of the Constitution provide to protect his life and liberty should not be stripped away just because he happens to be in another land."); *see* Raustiala, *supra* note 21, at 141–50.

67. The *Insular Cases* are a series of Supreme Court decisions that addressed the legal status of newly acquired U.S. overseas territories. *Id.* at 80. They include Balzac v. Porto Rico, 258 U.S. 298 (1922); Dorr v. United States, 195 U.S. 138 (1904); Hawaii v. Mankichi, 190 U.S. 197 (1903); Downes v. Bidwell, 182 U.S. 244 (1901).

68. 553 U.S. 723, 755 (2008); *see* Anthony J. Colangelo, *"De Facto Sovereignty":* Boumediene *and Beyond*, 77 Geo. Wash. L. Rev. 623, 625 (2009); *see also* United States v. Tiede, 86 F.R.D. 227, 244 (U.S. Ct. Berlin 1979) (extending the right to a jury trial to civilians charged with nonmilitary offenses in U.S.-occupied Berlin); Stephen Breyer, The Court and the World (2015) (ch. 4).

69. *See, e.g.*, United States v. Verdugo-Urquidez, 494 U.S. 259, 261 (1990) (denying extraterritorial application of the Fourth Amendment).

70. *Reid*, 354 U.S. at 74 (Harlan, J., concurring).

verging on jurisdiction, or in scenarios involving detention but not targeting (detention necessarily implying some level of territorial control).

However, an entire line of cases analyzing the due process rights of Americans during armed conflict might prove more promising. In *Hamdi v. Rumsfeld*, the Court concluded that under the due process clause a citizen-belligerent detained on the battlefield was entitled to contest his detention before a neutral decision-maker;[71] the Bush administration responded by creating the Combatant Status Review Tribunals (CSRTs) to satisfy this requirement.[72] Might the same reasoning apply in targeting cases? In other words, if the due process clause requires the opportunity to contest one's detention before a neutral decision-maker, then surely being targeted for summary killing—a far worse fate—must trigger, at a minimum, the same level of due process, or perhaps an even greater level of scrutiny.[73] It would produce a system of perverse incentives if one could short-circuit the requirements of the due process clause by killing, rather than simply detaining, the citizen-belligerent.[74] Such an argument turns upside down the liberty interest at stake in these cases.[75]

The problem with this legal argument is that the *Hamdi* case looked to the *international* (i.e., IHL) rules of detention to generate a gloss on the scope of Congress's use-of-force authorization to the executive branch.[76] As far as detention goes, the relevant proscription in Geneva is the requirement articulated in Article 5 of the Third Geneva Convention, which provides:

> Should any doubt arise as to whether persons, having committed a belligerent act and having fallen into the hands of the enemy, belong to any of the categories enumerated in Article 4 [entitling them to POW status], such persons shall enjoy the protection of the present Convention until such time as their status has been determined by a competent tribunal.[77]

71. 542 U.S. 507, 533 (2004).
72. *Boumediene*, 553 U.S. at 734.
73. *See, e.g.*, Richard Murphy & Afsheen John Radsan, *Due Process and Targeted Killing of Terrorists*, 31 CARDOZO L. REV. 405, 409–10 (2009) (arguing that, under *Boumediene*, the executive branch has the due process obligation to develop fair and rational procedures for reviewing targeted killings, wherever they take place).
74. *See* Ido Rosenzweig & Yuval Shany, *Supreme Court Rejects Tort Claim following Targeted Killing Operation*, 37 TERRORISM & DEMOCRACY, Jan. 2012, *available at* http://en.idi.org.il/analysis/terrorism-and-democracy/issueno-37/supreme-court-rejects-tort-claim-following-targeted-killing-operation/.
75. *See* Murphy & Radsan, *supra* note 73, at 437 ("[T]he executive branch has an obligation to use fair and reasonable procedures to control how it goes about depriving people of life, liberty, or property anywhere in the world.").
76. *Hamdi*, 542 U.S. at 520–21.
77. Geneva Convention Relative to the Treatment of Prisoners of War, Aug. 12, 1949, art. 5, 6 U.S.T. 3316, 75 U.N.T.S. 135, 140–42 [hereinafter Geneva Convention III].

So, in a sense, the foundation for the Constitution's requirement that Hamdi and other citizen belligerents were entitled to contest their determination turned out to be a function of preexisting IHL requirements.[78]

None of this suggests that *Hamdi* cannot serve as a precedent for a duty to capture in targeting cases.[79] But rather, two things are apparent about *Hamdi*. First, it does not do much to establish a domestic constitutional overlay that would change or alter the analysis in any way, since much of the *content* of the analysis in *Hamdi* curls back around and relies on the relevant rules of IHL. So when transposed to the realm of targeting, one cannot use *Hamdi* as an anchor for an argument that the Constitution requires something in *addition* to what IHL already requires. Rather, *Hamdi* arguably stands for the proposition that the Constitution requires what IHL requires.[80] Although this might be thought to render the due process clause superfluous in these cases, it does limit the degree to which the executive and legislative branches can depart from the international requirements.

Second, *Hamdi* cannot stand for the proposition that the Fifth Amendment requires an extra level of process for American citizens. Although that was nominally what *Hamdi* stated, this was simply because *Hamdi* himself was an American citizen and the Court was not confronted with the question of how the due process clause applied with regard to the

78. Ostensibly, O'Connor's plurality opinion in *Hamdi* applied the "balancing of interests" due process analysis first articulated in *Mathews v. Eldridge*, 424 U.S. 319, 335 (1976). *Hamdi*, 542 U.S. at 529. However, *Hamdi*'s analysis of the scope of Congress's authorization to the executive (including detention) was "based on longstanding law-of-war principles." *Id.* at 521.

79. *See* Murphy & Radsan, *supra* note 73, at 440 (arguing that the *Hamdi/Boumediene* model proposes subjecting targeted killings to a form of judicial review in civil actions initiated by private parties, such as a *Bivens*-style action); *see also* DOJ White Paper, *supra* note 56, at 6 (concluding that a due process balancing test would find that the government need not provide "further process" to a citizen belligerent if capture is infeasible and the "targeted individual poses an imminent threat of violent attack").

80. *But see* Jenny S. Martinez, *International Decision: Availability of U.S. Courts to Review Decision to Hold U.S. Citizens as Enemy Combatant—Executive Power in War on Terror*, 98 AM. J. INT'L L. 782, 785 (2004) (arguing that *Hamdi* evidences an uncertain relationship between U.S. law and IHL); David Weissbrodt & Nathaniel H. Nesbitt, *The Role of the United States Supreme Court in Interpreting and Developing Humanitarian Law*, 95 MINN. L. REV. 1339, 1395 (2011) ("The complexities of humanitarian law are at the center of the plurality opinion's lack of clarity."). One possible interpretation of *Hamdi* is that IHL law influenced the Court's analysis of Congress's grant of power to the executive branch, as a matter of statutory interpretation of the Authorization for Use of Military Force (AUMF), but that the same IHL norms played no rule in the constitutional analysis of due process under the *Mathews* framework. *See* Murphy & Radsan, *supra* note 73, at 424–25 (discussing how Justice O'Connor's plurality opinion "straddled the civil liberties and executive supremacy camps").

detention of noncitizens. When it came time to explain the reasons for its holding in *Hamdi*, none of the Court's reasons applied solely to citizens; rather, in relying on basic principles of detention regulation under IHL, the Court was providing reasons that apply to both citizens and noncitizens. So although citizenship mattered for the formal holding of *Hamdi*,[81] citizenship did *not* matter for the *reasons* relied upon in the *Hamdi* opinion.

When it came time to determine the rights of noncitizen detainees at Guantanamo Bay in *Boumediene v. Bush*, the Court reaffirmed the detainees' constitutional right to habeas corpus and the full effect of the suspension clause at Guantanamo (which had not been satisfied).[82] Since the habeas corpus rights vindicated in *Boumediene* were greater than those asserted in *Hamdi*, it is clear that even the Court itself recognized that the due process clause analysis in *Hamdi* had little basis in citizenship.[83] In a sense, the outcome in *Boumediene* was written on the wall once *Hamdi* was decided and its decidedly noncitizen reasons for decision articulated.

So even under the *Hamdi* and *Boumediene* framework, much of the constitutional analysis is arguably structured by the question of whether IHL is triggered and what IHL provides.[84] In Chapter 5, we critically examined the possibility of co-applying IHRL and IHL together—a legal strategy fraught with difficulty given the competing normative frameworks of the two fields. That said, we offered no positive argument for which paradigm applied and whether IHL or IHRL should govern such attacks. Furthermore, given the conclusions of *Hamdi* and *Boumediene*, it is unlikely that a target's status as an American citizen will alter whether IHL or IHRL should apply.

However, the public's commonsense intuitions about the killing of American citizens, even if they play no formal role in the analysis, are

81. Hamdi v. Rumsfeld, 542 U.S. 507, 523–24 (2004) (making clear that the Court's holding was tied to the facts of the case, i.e., the detention of an American citizen captured on a foreign battlefield); *see also* DOJ White Paper, *supra* note 56, at 6 (discussing "realities of combat" and the government's compelling interest).

82. Boumediene v. Bush, 553 U.S. 723, 743 (2008) (concluding that "[b]ecause the Constitution's separation-of-powers structure, like the substantive guarantees of the Fifth and Fourteenth Amendments, protects persons as well as citizens, foreign nationals who have the privilege of litigating in our courts can seek to enforce separation-of-powers principles" (citations omitted)).

83. *Id.* at 804 (Roberts, C.J., dissenting) (criticizing the majority opinion because "surely the Due Process Clause does not afford *non*-citizens in such circumstances greater protection than citizens are due").

84. Although *Hamdi* did not critically examine the question of whether IHL was triggered by the conflict with al-Qaeda, the question was squarely addressed in *Hamdan v. Rumsfeld*, 548 U.S. 557, 630–31 (2006) (concluding that an armed conflict "not of an international character" exists between the United States and al-Qaeda, triggering the applicability of Common Article 3 of the Geneva Conventions).

highly relevant for examining what is so troubling about the al-Awlaki incident. Does the government have the power to order the summary killing of one of its citizens? In a speech at Northwestern Law School, Attorney General Eric Holder argued that the requirements of the due process clause were satisfied by the internal deliberative process that the executive branch—involving personal decisions by President Obama himself—undergoes before deciding to place an individual on the target list (which in effect is a kill list).[85] Furthermore, Holder noted that an extra level of due process analysis is triggered when the target is an American citizen.[86] The process involves no check on executive-branch discretion, however, which is precisely what many consider to be at the core of due process protections, though there are other examples of constitutional "process" that do not involve judicial-branch determinations.[87] Even so, this sovereign

85. Eric Holder, Att'y Gen., Address at Northwestern Law School (Mar. 15, 2012), *available at* http://www.justice.gov/iso/opa/ag/speeches/2012/ag-speech-1203051.html (explaining the due process analysis conducted by the executive branch prior to using lethal force against a target).

86. *See id.* (concluding that "the government must take into account all relevant constitutional considerations with respect to United States citizens—even those who are leading efforts to kill innocent Americans. Of these, the most relevant is the Fifth Amendment's Due Process Clause, which says that the government may not deprive a citizen of his or her life without due process of law."). Holder also noted that the United States only targets citizens after determining that capture is not feasible, though he was vague as to whether the administration views this as a legal or prudential constraint: "Let me be clear: an operation using lethal force in a foreign country, targeted against a U.S. citizen who is a senior operational leader of al Qaeda or associated forces, and who is actively engaged in planning to kill Americans, would be lawful *at least* in the following circumstances: First, the U.S. government has determined, after a thorough and careful review, that the individual poses an imminent threat of violent attack against the United States; second, capture is not feasible; and third, the operation would be conducted in a manner consistent with applicable law of war principles." *Id.* (emphasis added).

87. However, most of these examples involve neutral decision-makers, such as administrative law judges, situated within the executive branch. *See generally Mission, Constitution and Bylaws*, FED. ADMIN. L. JUDGES CONF., *available at* http://www.faljc.org/mission-constitution-bylaws/ (describing the role of Administrative Law Judges in upholding the right to due process) (amended as of Nov. 2012). Indeed, the *Hamdi*-inspired CSRTs are precisely a case in point: judicial-like proceedings performed within an Article II setting. *See* Memorandum from the Deputy Sec'y of Def. to the Sec'ys of the Military Dep'ts Enclosure 1 (July 14, 2006), *available at* http://www.defense.gov/news/Aug2006/d20060809CSRTProcedures.pdf. In contrast, the executive determinations described by Holder in his Northwestern speech, *supra* note 85, are purely extrajudicial. These create the very asymmetry that provokes anxiety among the citizenry: the administration provides greater due process protection for detainees, in the form of CSRTs and constitutionally guaranteed habeas corpus proceedings in district courts, as compared with targeted killings, which are subject only to internal executive branch deliberations without judicial involvement. The DOJ White Paper speaks of an "informed, high-level official" of the executive branch who makes the determination regarding the target's threat. *See* DOJ White Paper, *supra* note 56, at 6.

entitlement—the killing of a citizen without judicial review—smacks of royal prerogative and represents precisely the kind of unchecked power that both human rights law and the domestic due process clause were designed to constrain.[88] This intuition is legitimate and ought to be the basis for further analysis. It contains the seeds of a strong argument.

At issue in this intuition is the relationship between the citizen and his government—a relationship that is trampled or infringed when the government orders his summary killing. Indeed, there is something problematic going on when a citizen is killed by his own government. Although there are other examples—capital punishment being the most obvious—these other examples usually involve prior judicial review. Although killing a terrorist as part of the armed conflict with al-Qaeda will always generate controversy, the killing of a terrorist by his own government inevitably raises eyebrows. Indeed, the sovereignty of the government—its capacity to act—ought to be at its lowest ebb when it engages in the killing of one of its own subjects.

IV. THE MORAL ARGUMENTS FOR A DUTY TO CAPTURE

The duty to capture rests at the fault line between IHRL and IHL on their different conceptions of necessity. The core protection of IHRL is the right to life; the core privilege of IHL is combatancy, the right to kill with impunity. Although this formulation throws the normative tension of the two bodies of law into sharp relief, the gulf is inevitable and inescapable. The duty to capture applies in the former body of law but not the latter. Straddling these bodies of law is the ever-present concept of necessity. But the preceding analysis has argued that a unified notion of necessity that extends across domains is overambitious and inevitably risks covertly importing the norms of one body of law across the divide into the other body of law. Necessity in human rights means that the government, when acting as sovereign with regards to its subjects, must pursue the least restrictive means of securing its interests when doing so involves a deprivation of the rights of its subjects. In such situations, the duty to attempt capture, if feasible, applies. In contrast, necessity in IHL means that the government meets its enemies as a coequal belligerent and destroys "life and limb" in order to secure the aims of the war (victory) with the fewest possible

88. *See* Murphy & Radsan, *supra* note 73, at 408 (describing how human rights law limits a state's law enforcement operations).

casualties to its troops. In such situations, the duty to capture fades away, replaced by the privilege of belligerency and the core principles that find their purest expression in the concept of military necessity.

However, this does not end the matter. There are two potential *moral* arguments for finding a duty to capture that should be expanded in the law. As we discussed in Chapter 5, the triggering of an armed conflict is only permissible if it is the last resort to vindicate the nation's rights. In the context of counterterrorism operations, then, a state might rightly be criticized for resorting to armed conflict too quickly when other non-forcible measures—including regular policing—might resolve the threat. This would entail that the State's resort to war is ethically problematic because it is not truly necessary. But in such a situation, the correct way to conceptualize the complaint is *not* that the State has violated *jus in bello* necessity (it has not), but rather that the State has violated *jus ad bellum* necessity by creating a state of armed conflict when measures short of war might have satisfied its legitimate counterterrorism needs. Critics of the overly aggressive U.S. approach to counterterrorism sometimes err when in discussing targeted killings they focus on *jus in bello* necessity to the exclusion of *jus ad bellum* necessity. In many situations the real nature of the objection is that the United States is engaged in armed conflicts that are not truly necessary.

Second, the law could evolve and codify a prohibition against unnecessary killing, as already discussed in Chapter 9. If the law included a prohibition against unnecessary killing during war, then one consequence of this legal requirement is that the government would be required to attempt capture before killing a terrorism suspect. If the government simply killed the suspect without even attempting or considering capture, the killing would not be truly necessary, and would therefore violate the proposed prohibition on unnecessary killings.

As we discussed in previous chapters, a legal prohibition against unnecessary killings would have to be carefully circumscribed. It would be difficult to make it a universal rule that applied in all situations. One example where it could be applied is the case of retreating soldiers. In that situation, perhaps an attacking force should disable or capture the soldiers instead of killing them remotely without giving them the opportunity to surrender. However, could this rule be applied to every situation where soldiers are retreating? This might have perverse and dangerous consequences. It would allow military units to select for themselves the conditions under which the enemy could engage them with lethal force. In other words, they would be allowed to attack with lethal force and then turn and run; by retreating they would trigger the enemy's obligation to capture rather than kill. This would create an unfair system of surprise attacks that would advantage a force that commits surprise attacks in the same manner as an insurgency or guerrilla unit, and protects its military assets to launch new attacks on another day. The enemy may not be able to destroy the military targets tomorrow, but they can destroy them today while they are retreating. Furthermore, it might not always be the case that the weaker military is the one protected by the rule. One could imagine a strong military with overwhelming firepower launching attacks and, despite their overwhelming firepower, retreating so as to immunize themselves from lethal force. This would not produce the right kind of rule.

The task is to identify the precise *type* of situations when the use of lethal force against retreating soldiers would constitute an unnecessary killing. The classic scenario would be one where the retreating force is very near to losing the armed conflict, and the outcome of the armed conflict is almost certain. At that point, the attacking force is simply engaged in superfluous killing by bombing the retreating soldiers instead of giving them an opportunity to surrender and then capturing them. In this scenario, the retreating soldiers are part of an enemy force that is nearing defeat, and their killing does little to advance the interests of the attacking force. The correct moral outcome is for the attacking force to refrain from using lethal force and to capture the combatants instead.

The important point here is to understand that the deep structure of this prohibition would not be a *jus in bello* prohibition. Rather, its structure flows from *jus ad bellum* or *jus ex bello*.[89] The principles in *jus ad bellum* not only govern when a State can resort to military force at the beginning of an armed conflict, but it also governs how long a State can continue to wage the war. At a certain point in time, the necessity that gave rise to the resort to force has evaporated, and continued prosecution of the war effort is immoral because war is no longer necessary to vindicate the interests of the State. Some Just War theorists argue that a State may be required to stop launching military attacks before the enemy has unconditionally surrendered, because the continued use of force is unnecessary. This is a *jus ex bello* condition—a moral requirement governing when a State must end an armed conflict.[90]

These moral requirements of *jus ad bellum* or *jus ex bello* might underlay the prohibition against unnecessary killing. In some situations, the killing of enemy soldiers, whether because they are retreating or for other reasons, might be unnecessary because their deaths will do nothing to vindicate the

89. Darrel Mollendorf, *Jus Ex Bello*, 16 J. POLITICAL PHIL. 131 (2008).
90. *Id.*

interests of the attacking State. In that sense, their deaths really are superfluous. If the interests of the State could just as easily be accomplished by capturing them instead of killing them, then the State is morally bound to refrain from using lethal force. But the situation where this is most likely to occur is when the soldiers belong to a fighting force that is already on the verge of defeat.

CHAPTER 11

Force Protection

The desire to protect one's own troops is universal and has been discussed since there have been writings about war. The ancient Chinese theorist and tactician, Sun Tzu, strongly advised generals not to send troops into hopeless causes, to treat those troops well, and to send them into battle only when all other avenues have been exhausted. The Roman historian, Livy, also often cautions that commanders must do all they can to protect their troops from unnecessary harm. The idea that one's own soldiers are to be treated well has a long pedigree. In this chapter we ask how necessity should be understood, *ad bellum* and *in bello*, in light of the strong sentiments expressed over the millennia in favor of protecting one's own troops.

Force protection is the idea that commanders can legitimately design strategy and make decisions that protect their own troops, even if this means that other important goals such as protecting civilians is given less weight. This issue has recently come to a head in Israel where a debate has raged about what is called the Hannibal procedure, whereby making sure Israeli troops are not captured is given paramount weight. Here issues of necessity intersect with issues of proportionality, but the literature has focused exclusively on proportionality. We will address how necessity affects this issue.

In this chapter, the first section will examine several historical examples of theorists who supported force protection, and also attempt to define force protection. In the second section, we will discuss how force protection is influenced by and also influences *jus ad bellum* necessity. In the third section we will examine how *jus in bello* necessity is influenced by and influences force protection. In the fourth section we will examine Israel's controversial Hannibal procedure. And in the final section we attempt to differentiate reasonable from unreasonable approaches to force protection in light of the associative duties that commanders and their superiors have for their soldiers.

I. UNDERSTANDING FORCE PROTECTION

At approximately 450 B.C., the Chinese theorist Sun Tzu wrote one of the greatest treatises on war, *The Art of War*.[1] In this small tome he argues first and foremost against unnecessary killing. Indeed, Sun Tzu argues that it is always better to capture the enemy's army than to destroy it.[2] He also argues against protracted wars and wars fought against cities because of the futility of sacrificing so many troops for little likelihood of gain.[3] Indeed, Sun Tzu thought that even enemy soldiers' lives had great value, and that it is a mistake to abuse or slaughter the enemy.[4] These ancient Chinese strategies carry a heavy moral burden for the commander. As a result, the generals are to be "just and righteous" nearly above all else.[5]

In 399 B.C., the Greek general and historian, Xenophon, wrote movingly about the 3,000-mile trek chronicled in *The March Up Country (Anabasis)*.[6] In extremely clear language, Xenophon argues for protection of his own troops against all odds and over all other values. After assuming the leadership of the Greek armies operating deep in India, he says:

> But now it is high time for me to finish; perhaps the enemy will be here soon. Then let those who think I am right support me at once, that my proposals may be carried out. Or if anyone has anything better, let him speak up boldly and say so, even if he is a private soldier, for our common safety is our common need.[7]

And often Xenophon argued for the disregard of civilian lives so that the common safety of his troops could be preserved.

From 23 B.C. to 17 A.D., approximately, the Roman historian Livy wrote his multivolume work, *History of Rome*.[8] Like Sun Tzu and Xenophon,

1. Sun Tzu, The Art of War (Samuel Griffith trans., 1963).
2. *Id.* at 77.
3. *Id.* at 78, 134
4. *Id.*, at 63, 76.
5. *Id.* at 64.
6. Xenophon, The March up Country (Anabasis) (W.H.D. Rouse trans., 1947).
7. *Id.* at 70.
8. Livy, History of Rome (B.O. Foster trans., 1922).

Livy also spends much time discussing the importance of treating one's own troops well, especially concerning unnecessary suffering and death. He says:

> It is not a wall or rampart that blocks your path, but armed men like yourselves. In courage you are their equals; in necessity, which is the last and chiefest weapon, you are the better men.[9]

Livy also is one of the very first to criticize the commanders who violated the rights of humanity by ordering unnecessary killing and slaughter.[10]

The prohibition on unnecessary suffering and killing of soldiers continues into the medieval period. But in the early modern period, two of the most significant treatises on military affairs, by Balthazar Ayala[11] and Pierino Belli,[12] treat soldiers only as those who are obligated to do what they are commanded to do, unless the war is clearly unjust. The lives of civilians are given priority over the lives of soldiers. Soldiers are said to have certain privileges but not rights. Yet, the idea that soldiers' lives should matter to a certain extent, in strategic terms if not in moral terms, is never doubted. Indeed, even in the classic nineteenth century text by Clausewitz,[13] that is normally cited as defending the view that anything in war is just, there are strong claims made against the unnecessary killing of soldiers. In Book 7, Chapter 6, Clausewitz cautions against "pointless battles."[14]

Force protection generally concerns giving priority to preserving the lives of one's own troops, although giving priority to the lives of enemy troops is also a related idea. The quandary posed by the idea of force protection, which seems so commonsensical, is that over the centuries the laws of war have been formulated to favor civilian lives over the lives of soldiers, so that even the lives of enemy civilians should be spared before the lives of one's own soldiers. Yet, although this is a nearly unbroken modern tradition of respecting civilian immunity, there is also a strong historical tradition that allows for favoring the lives of one's own troops, and cautions

9. *Id.*, Vol. II, Bk. IV, ch. xxviii, at 349 (Loeb edition).

10. *Id.*, Vol. III, Bk. V, ch. XXXVI, at 127 (Loeb edition).

11. *See* Balthazar Ayala, Three Books on the Law of War and on the Duties Connected with War and on Military Discipline (De Jure et Officiis Bellicis et Disciplina Militari Libri III) (John Pawley Bate trans., 1912).

12. Pierino Belli, A Treatise on Military Matters and Warfare (De Re Militari et Bello Tractatus) (Herbert C. Nutting trans., 1936).

13. Carl Von Clausewitz, On War (Michael Howard & Peter Paret trans., 1976).

14. *Id.* at 529.

against the unnecessary killing of one's own troops or allowing one's troops to be killed.

In one sense force protection is utterly uncontroversial. Today, nearly all treatments of the morality of war urge that soldiers not be made to suffer unnecessarily. At least since the Lieber Code and the St. Petersburg Declaration, weapons that cause superfluous suffering have been considered to be illegal or immoral. And prisoners who surrender are thought to have a right to be treated well, going beyond the prohibition that soldiers not to be made to suffer. But the death of soldiers has not been treated in the same way as the suffering of soldiers, as we saw in previous chapters. Indeed, in some sense war is about the killing of soldiers, whether this occurs quickly or not.

Although force protection can concern the protection from unnecessary suffering of soldiers, force protection is most commonly associated with protecting soldiers from unnecessary death. There is a good question, of course, whether the very institution of war can be sustained if force protection is the main, or one of the main, values. We will not here address the connection between force protection and pacifism, except to note that normally the best way to protect soldiers is not to ask them to go into combat at all. This strategy would, in most cases, best protect the lives of soldiers, although not in all cases, as we will see next.

II. *JUS AD BELLUM* NECESSITY AND FORCE PROTECTION

It is commonly recognized that to wage war or initiate armed conflict, the last resort or *ad bellum* necessity condition must be satisfied. One question to pose is how to figure out if waging war to protect one's own troops is the kind of thing that could be justified, and then how necessity or just cause is to be understood in such a context. There are many historical examples of wars waged at least initially to protect one's own troops from being overrun. The major question that has been posed is the cost of protecting one's troops. This is a question concerning proportionality. But there are also several *ad bellum* necessity questions that arise as well. For example, if the worry is about protecting each and every soldier, does necessity actually function to rule out certain wars altogether because of the extremely low likelihood that this could be accomplished? Another question is whether doing what is necessary to protect just one soldier can be seen as justified.

The *ad bellum* necessity condition must normally be paired with the just cause condition since in order to figure out if waging war or armed conflict is necessary, one needs to also figure out whether the objective for which war is to be waged is itself a justified objective or aim. And here the question concerning force protection is whether it is a just cause to initiate war or armed conflict so as to save the lives of one's troops. Is it sufficient that the only act of aggression is against one's own troops with no other goal in mind? Of course this is a hypothetical question in that nearly every attack on troops is aimed at something further such as conquering a people or territory.

But if we leave aside the question of other just causes that depend on troop protection and just focus on waging war to protect one's own troops, there are still two questions that are difficult to answer. First, is there a lower limit to how small a unit of one's troops that needs to be protected can constitute a just cause to wage war? It may be necessary to kill many enemy troops to make sure that any particular one of our troops is not killed. Can the necessity of taking such an extreme action for force protection be plausibly defended? Does troop protection have the same value regardless of how many troops we are talking about? Second, is there an upper limit in terms of what it will cost to protect those troops? Assume that the group of our troops that need to be protected is relatively large. How many enemy troops can be killed to protect our own troops before the cost is deemed too high? Could it be justified to kill a thousand enemy troops to save a hundred of our troops?

If we think of armed conflict, such as could exist in a situation where two groups of troops are camped near each other, it is not merely a hypothetical question of whether an attack on our troops can count as a just cause to engage in armed conflict. So in such a situation there will not only be just cause that is implicated but also necessity. It will have to be shown that there is no other non-lethal way to protect our own troops from this assault other than initiating armed conflict.

Necessity should not be understood absolutely here, for in many cases we can protect our troops from assault by having them surrender. Yet it seems intuitively clear that satisfying necessity in such a situation does not require a consideration of surrender, except in the case where our troops are doomed if they try to fight back. But what if it were possible for our troops to retreat and be saved? If there is this possibility can it still be said that it was necessary to kill enemy troops to protect our own troops? Our view is that in this case as in the case of surrender, satisfying necessity does not require exploring all other options, but only those that are reasonable. In most cases surrender or retreat are not reasonable options for protecting our own troops. But in the cases where these options are reasonable then they should be pursued. One case that seems clear is when our troops have strayed into the territory of another State. When confronted by troops from that State, force protection does not countenance initiating armed conflict when it is clearly more reasonable to retreat back across our border.

But there are hard cases that occur today and that do not have such an intuitively clear answer. Consider the one where the assault against our own troops is coming from a heavily populated area, as is common today in armed conflict waged within cities and other densely populated regions in asymmetric wars. Is force protection here, where there will clearly be many civilian casualties, justified on necessity grounds? This question begins to blur the line between *ad bellum* and *in bello* necessity. These are just a few of the questions that force protection raises in considering *jus ad bellum* necessity.

Ad bellum necessity is the requirement that all reasonable non-lethal alternative steps be pursued before lethal force is used. Force protection calls for an examination of what are limits of what is reasonable in ways that a consideration of other cases does not raise. Surrender and retreat are issues that generally do not arise in contexts outside of force protection. And as we will see, there are also issues concerning *in bello* necessity that will cause us to expand the domain in which we examine necessity. Force protection can concern the justifiability of initiating war or armed conflict and also the justifiability of particular strategies and tactics that are employed during war that can affect the lives of soldiers.

III. *JUS IN BELLO* NECESSITY AND FORCE PROTECTION

Force protection can also concern *in bello* armed conflict situations where there is already an ongoing war, and where a particular military mission risks the lives of soldiers. The traditional doctrine is that if the choice is between risking the lives of civilians, of either side, or risking the lives of soldiers, then soldiers' lives should always be risked first. This is the doctrine that those who defend force protection will argue against.

Michael Walzer has discussed one case involving risk to the lives of soldiers in the kind of detail and moral nuance that he is famous for. Here is an incident from Frank Richards' memoir of the first World War, one of the few accounts by a man from the ranks:

> When bombing dug-outs or cellars, it was always wise to throw the bombs into them first and have a look around them after. But we had to be very careful in this village as there were civilians in some of the cellars. We shouted down to them to make sure. Another man and I shouted down one cellar twice and receiving no reply were about to pull the pins out of our bombs when we heard

> a woman's voice and a young lady came up the cellar steps . . . She and the members of her family . . . If the young lady had not cried out when she did, we would have innocently murdered them all.[15]

Walzer endorses Richards's decision and says that it is not enough that soldiers intend that they not attack civilians, but that the soldiers display this intention more actively, such as in the case of Frank Richards.

Claiming to be stating the doctrine of *in bello* proportionality in both morality and law, Walzer says that "The limits of risk are fixed, then, roughly at the point where any further risk-taking would almost certainly doom the military venture or make it so costly that it could not be repeated."[16] Putting the point even more clearly and pithily, Walzer says that commanders "must risk soldiers before they kill civilians."[17] Walzer's reference to the "doom of the military venture" is a reference to military necessity. And the type of military necessity here is *jus in bello* necessity that can trump normal proportionality calculations.

In choosing strategies and tactics, one's own military forces are not to be protected if that means that civilians will be killed. Richards understood this point, and that is why he took the risk of announcing that he was about to throw a grenade into a cellar, so as to minimize the likelihood that he would be killing civilians who were in the cellar. And Richards made this decision even though he knew he was putting his own life in greater risk than if he had not announced himself. Walzer thus gives us a good defense of the traditional doctrine against force protection.

David Luban has recently given another striking defense of the traditional doctrine by, in part, stressing the fact that soldiers have changed the status quo by putting the lives of civilians at risk, and so they now owe civilians protection of their lives even when it risks the soldiers' own lives.[18] We cite Luban's position here to underscore his point about why the risk to soldiers should be given less value than the risk to civilians. It is an old principle of both law and morality that if a person puts another in harm's way, that person has different duties to that person than might exist otherwise.

It is also worth noting though that soldiers do not always put civilians' lives in danger. The issue of force protection is complicated by the

15. Michael Walzer, Just and Unjust Wars 152 (1977).
16. *Id.* at 157.
17. *Id.*
18. David Luban, *Military Necessity and the Cultures of Military Law*, 26 Leiden J. Int'l L. 315–49 (2013). *See also* David Luban & Gabriella Blum, *Unsatisfying Wars: Degrees of Risk and the* Jus ex Bello, 125 Ethics 751–80 (2015).

additional fact that soldiers normally are involved in protecting the lives of their civilians by the use of their weapons. It is true that soldiers do not act to protect the lives of enemy civilians. And so in the case of a comparison of risks to soldiers' lives versus enemy civilians' lives, Luban's point rings true. But since this is not true of the soldiers' fellow civilians, there is an odd result. Soldiers should only risk their own lives when enemy civilians' lives are at risk, but not when their own civilians' lives are at risk. And this is so counterintuitive to make us wonder whether there is much weight that should be given to the fact that soldiers can put the lives of civilians at risk.

The main question of *in bello* necessity that affects force protection is where to draw the limit: where is it necessary to protect one's own troops even though doing so risks civilian lives. And the answer is when the military mission would be "doomed" if the force was not protected. Military necessity can override civilian immunity in some force protection cases, but by no means in all such cases. The *ad bellum* limit is when not waging armed conflict dooms one's army. The *in bello* limit is reached when a squadron or group of troops would be doomed if the strategy or tactic were not employed. We will take up this particular issue, of what reasonable force protection amounts to, in the final section of this chapter. Let us complicate the issue by examining an Israeli policy that takes force protection quite a bit further: when even just one of their soldiers' lives is jeopardized, then civilian lives can be risked, as long as the war in question is an asymmetric one where the enemy does not recognize the rules of war.

IV. THE HANNIBAL PROCEDURE

In 1986, a secret order was apparently drawn up by top Israeli officers that put the highest premium on forcing the release of captured Israeli soldiers. According to an article in the Israeli newspaper, *Haaretz*, here is what the secret order called for:

> During an abduction, the major mission is to rescue our soldiers from the abductors even at the price of harming or wounding our soldiers. Light-arms fire is to be used in order to bring the abductors to the ground or to stop them. If the vehicle or the abductors do not stop, single-shot (sniper) fire should be aimed at them, deliberately, in order to hit the abductors, even if this means hitting our soldiers. In any event, everything will be done to stop the vehicle and not allow it to escape.[19]

19. Sara Leibovich-Dar, *The Hannibal Procedure*, HAARETZ (May 21, 2003), *available at* http://www.haaretz.com/the-hannibal-procedure-1.9412.

It has been suggested that the Hannibal Procedure has also licensed Israeli troops directly to kill enemy civilians and in some cases even to risk the lives of Israeli civilians in order to accomplish the goal of preventing the capture, or obtaining the release, of an Israeli soldier.

Recently the *Jerusalem Post* challenged the use of the Hannibal Procedure in the case of the capture and then the attempt to obtain the release of Lt. Hadar Golden of the Israeli Defense Forces (IDF):

> The IDF . . . twice said that "all military means were kosher to thwart Golden's capture," and "even if I destroyed structures or harmed Palestinians, it was with faith in the justness of our cause . . . as we have been educated in the IDF." . . . From the IDF perspective, it would be best if "any means necessary" was solely meant to refer to even those actions that could lead to Golden's death, and that the "structures" and "Palestinians" mentioned meant only Hamas and its military posts.[20]

Here is where force protection and the Hannibal Procedure come together in ways that are highly problematic.

In the *Golden* case, the IDF launched an armed conflict against the West Bank community of Palestinians, where thousands of civilians were killed, in order to attempt to obtain the release of Lt. Golden. Such a procedure could not satisfy proportionality; indeed soldiers' lives are not normally put into the proportionality calculation at all. Soldiers were traditionally thought to be merely the extension of their States—and dispensable for this reason. But as wars and armed conflicts have emerged to the point where it is now normal that one of the parties to an armed conflict is not a State, the traditional doctrine is called into question in various ways.

One consideration is that we cannot count on nonstate actors to train their troops in the laws of war so that these troops will exercise restraint, especially when confronting civilians. This is important because if the laws of war are not upheld by one side then it is not clear why the other side should do so given that their own civilians will be put at great risk. Some have argued that it is not for them but for ourselves that we must show restraint. Yet, it is hard to motivate such restraint when it is not reciprocated.

Another important point stressed by Asa Kasher and General Amos Yadlin is that in Israel most especially, soldiers are citizens who deserve to have their lives protected just as any other citizen of Israel. Kasher and Yadlin revised the Israeli code of ethics for the IDF, and sought to place force protection at the center of that code. It is of course true that Israel is

20. Jerusalem Post (Dec. 20, 2014).

encircled by States and nonstate actors who are or have been its enemy. And in such a precarious position, force protection may have a special appeal.

A related point, implicit in Kasher and Yadlin's position, is that Israeli troops that are successfully taken hostage pose a great risk to the State of Israel because they will be held for political advantage. So, the defense of force protection here is tied to the political problem of having one's own soldiers used as pawns in an elaborate chess game to undermine Israeli morale. Indeed, as soldiers take on a political function, force protection is less about the soldier and more about the politics of the situation.

In general, the position on force protection defended by Kasher and Yadlin is similar to the Hannibal Procedure. Here is how Kasher defends the view that it is justified to use tactics such as long range bombing that risk civilian casualties but also protect Israeli troops:

> It is important to emphasize that the state must come up with a compelling justification for endangering the lives of its soldiers . . . in the dilemma at hand the state should favor the lives of its own soldiers over the lives of the neighbors or a terrorist when it is operating in the territory that it does not effectively control.[21]

This claim in support of favoring its own soldiers can be seen as underpinning the Hannibal Procedure.

It is controversial, though, that force protection should be taken so far as to allow for the protection of any number of one's own soldiers, even one, at the expense of civilian lives, even many. Such a calculation is not likely to satisfy *in bello* proportionality no matter how that is understood. So the question is whether necessity can be brought in to turn the tide. One argument that could be adapted from Kasher and Yadlin is meant to turn the necessity argument around. Only when the State can show that killing its own soldiers is necessary for the security of the State, is the State permitted to choose tactics that would not protect its soldiers' lives. In that case, necessity trumps proportionality.

We need to distinguish what the members of a State decide in terms of how much to sacrifice for their own troops versus how much another State should have to sacrifice for foreign force protection. The first is relatively easy. If a society decides, as apparently Israel has, to treat the life of each soldier as something that needs to be protected come what may,

21. Asa Kasher, *Operation Cast Lead and Just War Theory*, 37 Azure: Ideas for the Jewish Nation 66 (2009).

then it is hard to argue against the Israelis, as long as the costs are borne by Israeli civilians. But of course Israel, or any other State, cannot demand that other States or peoples sacrifice for the protection of Israel's own soldiers. Risking the lives of enemy civilians so as to protect one's own troops is much harder to justify than the situation where it is one's own civilians who are risked to protect one's own troops.

Here is yet another place where proportionality considerations intervene in this area of dispute. Israel can choose to diminish the value of its own civilians' lives versus its soldiers' lives. But this is to say what a State is *permitted* to do concerning its own citizens. States may still be *required*, as we think they are, to protect foreign civilians and ask their own soldiers to take risks so as to protect those civilians' lives. Just because the civilians are foreign, or enemy, should not make a difference here. In any event, it seems to us that proportionality should in many cases take into account the lives of soldiers, not merely the lives of civilians. And in valuing the lives of soldiers in this way there are benefits and costs. The benefits are that force protection can be justified. The costs are that many missions will not be justifiable since the value of the lives of soldiers is not outweighed by what is accomplished by the mission.

There are many things to like about the position that Kasher and Yadlin have defended. We would single out the idea, especially in a State with compulsory conscription for the vast majority of the population, that soldiers are fellow citizens, and it is expected that they will spend only a short time in their lives being soldiers. It is also true that there are very strong intuitions against the idea that our soldiers' lives should count less than enemy civilians' lives, especially when we are talking of an asymmetric war. We would caution though that merely because a war is asymmetric does not mean that one side is best characterized as terrorists—since terrorism is often in the eye of the beholder. In general we appreciate the point that Kasher and Yadlin make about how necessity has two sides: it can be used to limit what soldiers can do, but also to expand the range of behavior that would otherwise be prohibited.

We need to think about the difference between *ad bellum* and *in bello* contexts. *Ad bellum* necessity concerns the threat to the entire nation, and in some contexts that could be synonymous with a threat to the entire army. But in *jus in bello* contexts, it is rare that a single mission is needed in order to prevent the entire nation from succumbing. *In bello* necessity is not normally linked to the fate of the nation. Soldiers' lives cannot be sacrificed just because the mission in question will fail unless the lives of soldiers are sacrificed.

As some have pointed out, we again come up against the "worry" that support for force protection of the sort epitomized in the Hannibal Procedure could lead to support for pacifism. If the *in bello* necessity standard is that soldiers' lives can only be sacrificed not for a particular mission but for the fate of the nation, then it will not be very often that such sacrifice can be justified. Hence a strong defense of pacifism runs together with a strong support for force protection. In the next section we assess whether and to what extent this strong view of force protection can indeed be justified.

V. REASONABLE FORCE PROTECTION

In this final section we examine several ways that force protection can be seen as a reasonable doctrine, especially where it is paired with a fairly stringent necessity condition. David Luban has suggested that the lives of soldiers and of "enemy civilians" should count the same in a proportionality calculation. Kasher and General Yadlin have argued that it is perfectly acceptable for Israeli commanders to count their own soldiers' lives as more valuable than the lives of enemy civilians, especially if the enemy is a terrorist group. Here the claim is that the rules have changed in this particular kind of asymmetric war. We will begin with a discussion of necessity, and then proceed to examine the issue of proportionality in force protection cases.

What has seemed reasonable over the centuries is that generals and commanders not send their soldiers into hopeless or needless wars. So, let us start with this first point—we should give enough weight to the lives of our soldiers so that the soldiers are not sent into hopeless wars. To deny this point would be to say that the lives of soldiers are virtually worthless, since these lives can be wiped out even when there is no clear point to the war, or where it is clear that the war cannot be won. And we think it is indefensible to return to the position of thinking of soldiers as cannon fodder or as disposable.

A second point is that the lives of soldiers should be weighed as having value commensurate with the dignity of the humans who occupy the role of soldier. To be reasonable this value should be weighed against the potentially offsetting value of being what Walzer called "dangerous men" who risk injury or death to others by their occupation. In this view, soldiers' lives have more value than in the first point, but not the same value as those humans who do not pose a threat to others because of their occupations. In some cases soldiers forfeit some of their rights because they are a threat to the self-preservation of other soldiers and civilians.

But there is then in addition the consideration that at least in some contexts the occupation of soldiers makes the lives of others more rather than less safe. So, the context must be examined to see which of these risk factors are most reasonable, and so whether the value of soldiers' lives should indeed be offset by the soldiers' dangerousness. The dangerousness of soldiers does not mean that in all cases they forfeit their rights, even if only temporarily. The dangerousness of soldiers is also in some contexts precisely why soldiers are so valuable—as a counterforce to aggression for instance. So, the mere fact that soldiers have been made into dangerous men (and women) does not necessarily affect their status.

A third point is that the lives of soldiers should not be permanently disvalued lest we risk treating those humans who occupy the role of soldier as not fully human, or as not fully citizens of a particular State or national group. Whatever disvaluing of the lives of soldiers that occurs, if any, should be seen as temporary so that once the person occupying the role of soldier ceases to be a soldier, he or she regains status commensurate with full dignity of human beings. The temporary disvaluing of soldiers' lives, if there is to be any disvaluing, means that nothing should be allowed to be done to soldiers that affects their lives permanently that would not be something that could be done to non-soldiers. Yet, such a consideration will raise the possibility that certain wars will be difficult to justify.

This third point raises the question of whether soldiers' lives should ever be risked. The problem is that putting a soldier's life at risk certainly risks a permanent loss, not merely a temporary one. And here is where certain versions of pacifism need to be taken seriously. If we think that our own soldiers' lives should be protected come what may, then keeping our soldiers out of harm's way should have very high priority. And it is reasonable to wonder whether and how often soldiers' lives should be risked without challenging the way we think about wars and armed conflict.

Various authors warn that putting too much stress on force protection will lead to an unwanted form of pacifism. We would comment that not all forms of pacifism are unwanted. Contingent pacifism for instance cautions against exposing soldiers to unnecessary risks, something that is not a terribly controversial doctrine, at least stated in this way.[22] What some have worried about is that protecting soldiers can have the unwanted consequence of making all wars morally and legally problematic. And we would agree that this is a worry—war should not be ruled out simply as a matter of definition. Rather it is important to examine each case to see if waging war, or using certain tactics, does indeed advance the rights of the parties in question.

22. *See* Larry May, Contingent Pacifism: Revisiting the Just War (2015).

And despite the three reasonable points defended above that can be cited in support of some sort of force protection, the question still remains how strong we should weigh force protection *ad bellum* and *in bello*. It seems to us that some fairly strong weight needs to be attached to the lives of the soldiers that we ask to serve in dangerous situations. But it also seems to us that the lives of soldiers should not count more than the lives of civilians—indeed unarmed civilians' lives should generally count more than the lives of heavily armed soldiers. Beyond this, in our view, fairly reasonable position, we are not sure what else can be concluded.

David Luban argues that it should not matter whether the lives of civilians who are put at risk are the civilians of one's own or one's enemy. But the issue does not end there. The question is, as Luban puts it, "how much risk soldiers are required to take," not how much they are permitted to take. We agree that soldiers should not take fewer risks for themselves at the cost of greater risk for civilians on either side, in most cases. But when something very important will be lost if soldiers do not risk civilians' lives then such a risk may be permitted.

What of Israel's Hannibal Procedure? As we said, we find some of the reasoning by Kasher and Yadlin to be persuasive. Soldiers are also citizens as well as fellow human beings. It is important for the States that send their young men and women into harm's way to protect them as much as they can, while still putting them into harm's way when it is necessary for protecting the society. Here the reasonable position is to regard *jus ad bellum* necessity rather strictly. If there are other non-lethal avenues for protecting the State's population other than putting young men and women on the battlefield, those avenues must be pursued first. Troops do not normally have to surrender rather than fight—but otherwise other options need to be pursued before war or armed conflict.

A consideration of force protection has led us to several insights into how to understand necessity. We have had to confront how strict necessity should be understood if it is to justify putting young citizens into harm's way. Employing necessity to justify such harm does not require that every option, including surrender, be employed first. But we believe that successfully employing necessity means that nearly every other reasonable non-lethal option be pursued short of armed conflict. This result has come home to us after thinking about force protection. States can decide how much suffering their own civilians should bear so as to protect their soldiers, but except in the most extreme cases, States cannot decide how much suffering foreign, or enemy, civilians must bear.

Conclusion

In this book we have tried to offer more than just a descriptive survey of the various ways that the concept of necessity is used in international law. We have offered a normative account that suggests how and when necessity should be deployed as a powerful concept to justify and excuse State action in various domains. However, that normative task could only be accomplished once a coherent descriptive mapping was performed. We considered the different and unique elements of necessity in international law with the hope of elucidating a deeper structure for the concept. We identified at least three different senses of necessity: as a state of exception to generally applicable laws, as a constraint on government action, and as a license to engage in conduct that is otherwise consistent with generally applicable laws. Using these conceptual distinctions, we analyzed and ultimately criticized how necessity functions in diverse areas of international law. Although the same term is used in *jus ad bellum, jus in bello*, human rights, and criminal law, the concept operates in diverse and unique ways in each field. The only way to generate a trans-field conception of necessity is to describe it at such a level of abstraction that it loses almost all of its conceptual content. Furthermore, our normative prescriptions regarding how to apply necessity in each domain of international law are different in important respects. Necessity is not a one-size-fits-all concept.

To recap that effort, Part A charted the debates regarding necessity in *jus ad bellum* in both the philosophical and legal domains. Chapter 1 looked at necessity and the principle of last resort in Just War theory. Our investigation revealed that the concept of necessity operated as a meaningful and substantial constraint on the use of force for as long as philosophers have been discussing the justice of war. In Chapter 2, we then applied this analysis to the current *jus ad bellum* framework in public international law. The constraint embodied in the Just War theory principle of last resort is carried over into the necessity constraint for the use of force. In both domains, necessity and proportionality provide twin constraints on the use of armed force. However, we also noted that the dangerous version of necessity as an exception to generally applicable rules also shows up in the necessity defense under international law, used both in the investor-state context but also the debate over humanitarian intervention. We also discussed the "unwilling or unable" test for the use of defensive force against a nonstate actor located in a third state. Properly understood, the test represents a constraint on defensive force because the force is not necessary if the host state is willing or able to resolve the threat on its own.

Part B focused on *jus in bello*. Chapter 3 traced the historical debates regarding the principle of discrimination and concluded by offering a nuanced philosophical treatment of necessity that places it on the same level with the principle of humanity. Ultimately, Chapter 3 concluded that combatants should be forced to break off lethal military attacks that have literally no possibility of succeeding, but that combatants may use lethal force in situations that reasonably raise their likelihood of success. This represents a mild amendment to currently codified legal doctrine.

Chapter 4 focused on the foundations of necessity in IHL, with a particular focus on the historical development of the concept. Inevitably this discussion centered on the Lieber Code. Chapter 5 focused on the relationship between necessity in human rights law and necessity in IHL. We concluded that the very restrictive notion of necessity that reigns in contemporary human rights law has some intellectual debt to the Just War theorists who understood necessity as offering a powerful constraint on action. In contrast, the permissive notion of necessity (as a license as long as it is consistent with generally applicable rules) that reigns in today's IHL draws its inspiration from Francis Lieber. Ultimately, there is a world of difference between these notions of necessity, and attempts to combine these legal frameworks are fraught with great difficulty. In Chapter 6 we noted how the dangerous version of necessity (as an exception) also applies in both national and international criminal law. What emerged was a portrait of necessity simultaneously providing meaningful constraints while also threatening to carve out exceptions so large that they swallowed the rules. We supported normative proposals to limit the power of the defense of necessity to grant such exceptions.

Then, in Chapter 7 we made a normative argument for striking a balance between humanity and necessity. Specifically, we concluded that soldiers do not automatically check all of their rights to humane treatment as soon as they don the uniform. They remain human beings and legitimate subjects of moral concern. There is room for human rights principles and humanity-based moral arguments in *jus in bello*, and this is perfectly consistent with our legal conclusion that human rights law should not swallow IHL, and that IHL should remain a distinct framework for legal regulation of armed conflict. Indeed, IHL is best understood as a particular body of law where human rights are protected in a distinct way, consistent with the unique context of armed conflict.

Finally, Part C of the book applied these normative assessments to contemporary asymmetric conflicts. The question posed is whether necessity remains a vital and central concept for tomorrow's conflict. The answer is undoubtedly yes—perhaps not surprising given the elastic nature of the concept. It has been stretched and pulled in many directions before, so it is no surprise that it is adaptable to the wars of tomorrow. But in what way? We pointed the way forward, first in Chapter 8 with a defense of the armed conflict paradigm for asymmetric conflicts against nonstate actors. Nonstate actors, though not States, are capable of exercising the trappings of belligerency, which can and should make them subject to regulation under *jus in bello*. But this also means that States engaged in military operations against nonstate actors are similarly constrained, and so we rejected the idea that only a peacetime model of criminal law enforcement was appropriate for regulating antiterrorism operations, as long as the terrorist or insurgent group is sufficiently organized and capable that it becomes the functional equivalent of a State or a belligerent.

In Chapter 9, our analysis of the law as it stands today confirmed that military necessity permits rather widespread summary killing of combatants. We pushed back against progressive attempts to interpret today's law as being more restrictive than it actually is. On the other hand, we pushed forward and suggested that the law could be made more restrictive in the future. In particular we noted that the avenues for such progressive development of the law might also be found outside the context of *jus in bello* in the domains of *jus ad bellum* and *jus ex bello*—constraints that might force States to stop lethal operations that are no longer necessary for vindicating essential state interests.

Chapter 10 made similar arguments regarding the duty to capture. Although IHL does not currently demand the attempt to capture before launching a lethal operation, there are some moral reasons to require States, at least in asymmetric conflicts, to exhaust some non-lethal possibilities, including capture, before resorting to lethal operations. However, any changes to the existing legal framework must be consistent with the demands of force protection—a legitimate goal that we explored in Chapter 11.

Specifically, in Chapter 11 we concluded that attacking forces should be permitted to prioritize the protection of their own forces when calculating how to conduct their military operations. That being said, we rejected the idea that force protection could be unlimited; instead, we developed and defended a standard of reasonable force protection that could be violated if an attacking force burdens enemy civilians with overwhelming damage, where the attacking force feels justified because it overvalues its own forces. Expressed differently, we defended the view that the soldiers of an attacking force are required to bear a reasonable risk in order to protect the rights and interests of enemy civilians and enemy combatants.

This makes it all the more important to test the current state of IHL, and its relatively permissive notion of necessity, with deeper principles of moral theory, as informed by the teachings of the Just War theorists. We have defended the moral legitimacy of the armed conflict paradigm, but also suggested that its specific details are not beyond revision. The law today is subject to normative question; failure to recognize this fact is to fall victim to the naturalistic fallacy (where what is becomes grounds for what should be). Nonetheless, our proposals for reform are modest indeed: that the law of war be recalibrated so that the moral duty of States to exhaust non-lethal measures first should be codified somewhere in the law, either in revised rules of IHL or perhaps also in a more robust understanding of the necessity constraint in *jus ad bellum* or *jus ex bello*. Either way, the idea is that the destructive power of war should only be unleashed when it is truly necessary. However, once that normative hurdle is met, we understand that war can and should be conducted as a war. Any proposal to over-restrict the rules of warfare and turn all status-based targeting into the conduct-based targeting of criminal law enforcement would effectively deny that war is a morally relevant event at all. Our analysis does not support this intuition. War involves a forced contest of violence between the belligerents. We have suggested that it could be rendered more humane, for soldiers and civilians alike, simply by codifying a slightly more restrictive understanding of the principle of necessity. In this book we have not considered the question of whether war should be conducted at all. Rather we have argued that if a resort to war can be justified, then the principle of necessity should be understood to limit such wars so they are humane.

INDEX

2503270438